D0455481

THE OUTSOURCING REVOLUTION

WHY IT MAKES SENSE AND HOW TO DO IT RIGHT

MICHAEL F. CORBETT

Dearborn™
Trade Publishing
A Kaplan Professional Company

Vice President and Publisher: Cynthia A. Zigmund
Acquisitions Editor: Jonathan Malysiak
Senior Managing Editor: Jack Kiburz
Interior Design: Lucy Jenkins
Cover Design: Design Solutions
Typesetting: the dotted i

Published by Dearborn Trade Publishing
A Kaplan Professional Company

Printed in the United States of America

04 05 06 10 9 8 7 6 5 4 3 2

Library of Congress Cataloging-in-Publication Data

Corbett, Michael F.
The outsourcing revolution : why it makes sense and how to do it right / by Michael F. Corbett.
p. cm.
Includes bibliographical references and index.
ISBN 0-7931-9214-5 (6x9 hardcover)
1. Contracting out—Management—Handbooks, manuals, etc. 2. Reengineering (Management)—Handbooks, manuals, etc. 3. Contract system (Labor)—Case studies. I. Title.
HD2365.C67 2004
658.4¢058—dc22

2004012318

Dearborn Trade books are available at special quantity discounts to use for sales promotions, employee premiums, or educational purposes. Please call our Special Sales Department to order or for more information at 800-621-9621 ext. 4444, e-mail trade@dearborn.com, or write to Dearborn Trade Publishing, 30 South Wacker Drive, Suite 2500, Chicago, IL 60606-7481.

Praise for *The Outsourcing Revolution*

"In a revolution, all the ground rules change. Michael Corbett's clear and compelling roadmap leads the reader through the systemic reinvention of work."

John Sculley, Former CEO, Apple Computer

"Michael Corbett has written the definitive work on outsourcing. It's clear, precise, and thorough. If you want to really understand the whys and hows, this is the book for you."

Oren Harari, PhD, Professor, University of San Francisco, and
Author of *The Leadership Principles of Colin Powell*

"Mike Corbett saw the power and value of outsourcing years before its acceptance. *The Outsourcing Revolution* is an incisive guide for any organization willing to transform and improve the bottom line."

Howard Putnam, Former CEO, Southwest Airlines, and
Author of *The Winds of Turbulence*

"A current, penetrating, and highly readable analysis of outsourcing's true payoffs and critical issues by one of the field's most knowledgeable pioneers. Michael Corbett integrates a rich array of strategic and managerial examples from his unique database of company experiences."

James Brian Quinn, Buchanan Professor of Management Emeritus,
Amos Tuck School, Dartmouth College

"Michael Corbett has long been one of the most innovative thinkers on outsourcing and is *the man* at the center of the network of best practices and new ideas. This book puts all of that into your hands."

Dr. Adrian Moore, Vice President, Reason Foundation

"*The Outsourcing Revolution* is recommended reading for anyone in search of innovative ideas about how to create effective and sustainable outsourcing relationships."

Fred L. Brown, MBA, FACHE, Founding President and CEO,
BJC Healthcare, and Past Chairman, American Hospital Association

"Michael Corbett takes his years of experience at the cutting edge of global outsourcing to clearly identify the benefits to corporations and their employees from doing it right. *The Outsourcing Revolution* is a necessary addition to anyone's bookshelf who is interested in how to improve enterprise value."

Robert E. Zahler, Partner, Shaw Pittman LLP

"There is no one more qualified than Michael Corbett as an expert on outsourcing. If you have any questions about outsourcing, this is a definite read. You can't afford to miss out on Corbett's wisdom, experience, and expertise."

Glenn Davenport, CEO and President, Morrison Management Specialists

To Debi, the love of my life, and our girls—Amanda, Dana, and Chelsea

Contents

Acknowledgments

In 1987, I was asked to take on an assignment at IBM to be the new head of software services offerings for the company's national services division. Little did I know that the assignment would set the course of my career for the next 15 years and essentially change my life. The assignment gave me the chance to become part of a revolution that has continued ever since—that revolution is outsourcing.

It also gave me the chance to work closely with some of the finest businesspeople it has been my pleasure to know, as we put together the basis for what is today the largest services organization in the world.

When I left the company in 1988, my professional network grew exponentially. Since then, I have worked with thousands of individuals in companies large and small, in the public sector as well as the private sector, here in the United States and all around the globe.

If I figure I've learned just one thing every day from someone over these years, then the acknowledgments list for this book could easily be 3,000 names long. You know who you are, and I thank each and every one of you for helping to shape my understanding of this amazing field.

Introduction

The idea of outsourcing is certainly not new. Hiring outside groups to do work that an organization either cannot do or chooses not to do for itself dates back as far as one cares to look. Explorers, traders, and mercenaries are all early examples of the concept of outsourcing. Even the term *outsourcing* is not particularly new. It was first used in the 1970s by manufacturing executives and has been gradually adopted since then by executives in just about every other business function.

As the contemporary use of the term *outsourcing* has grown, so has the actual amount of outsourcing taking place. Consider the following: The typical manufacturing company now outsources 70 to 80 percent of the content of its finished product. The entire professional services industry of accountants, lawyers, advertisers, consultants, and the like is based on the concept of outsourcing. Facilities executives routinely outsource cleaning, food services, and mailrooms. CIOs in large companies often outsource more than half of their company's information technology budget. Call center outsourcing is commonplace as well. Most recently, organizations have started outsourcing entire back offices, performing work as diverse as customer order processing, payroll, accounts receivables, and accounts payables through outside specialists. In fact, it would be difficult to find any organization that is not outsourcing, to some extent, in just about every part of its operation.

So, since neither the idea of outsourcing nor the term itself is particularly new, why take the time to read about, let alone write and publish a book on, outsourcing today?

There are a number of very important reasons. The first is that even though about one-third of the typical executive's budget is already outsourced, we are really just at the dawn of outsourcing. It is very likely that over the next decade or so, this one-third will climb to 70 or 80 percent—as it already has for manufacturing. This means that before too long most organizations are going to be far more outsourced than they are "in-sourced."

This is a fundamental restructuring of organizations that carries enormous implications for all of us—executives, managers, employees, customers, and investors alike. For executives and managers, it means that the skill sets they need to do their jobs will change dramatically. No longer is it sufficient to know how to manage internal resources; managing outside relationships with outsourcing service providers is just as, if not more, important. For employees, greater outsourcing means specialist jobs are likely to continue to migrate from current employers toward the companies that provide outsourcing services. For customers, it means the companies they are buying from are increasingly leveraging skills and resources from around the world to design, produce, and deliver their products and services. This will continue to expand customer choice while driving down costs. For investors, outsourcing is spurring the formation of thousands of new businesses seeking capital to build and grow. It also becomes increasingly important for investors in established firms to look at a company's entire external network of relationships when evaluating its current operations and future prospects. Outsourcing makes companies more productive and competitive; it also makes them more interdependent. For all these reasons and more, outsourcing's impact on organizations and on the overall economy is just at its beginning.

The second reason this book is important and timely is that while outsourcing's impact is expanding rapidly, outsourcing itself is changing in very basic and important ways. The way organizations approach outsourcing is evolving from a traditional hierarchical model to more of a cross-functional, process-centric approach—what's called business process outsourcing, or BPO. Outsourcing is also becoming an integral part of and enabler of many other organizational improvement initiatives, such as shared services and supply chain consolidation. Outsourcing is moving from a purely cost-based decision to one that is increasingly linked to a company's go-to-market strategy. At the same time, new suppliers are entering the market daily and are changing the landscape of solutions available to companies. Outsourcing is being used to commercialize existing assets and intellectual properties, changing the very nature of these outside relationships as well as their scope and impact. It is also going global, further elevating both the opportunities and the risks. All of these changes mean that new techniques, approaches, and tools for the successful and responsible use of outsourcing need to be identified, developed, and refined.

Although outsourcing continues to be driven by the relentless need to improve productivity and cut costs, it will have an even more profound effect on companies in the future. Outsourcing will be used to improve the most essential and complex business processes of companies: revenue management at hospitals, ticketing and payments at airlines and airports, employee development in manufacturing plants, and research and development at pharmaceutical companies. Outsourcing will be used to not only drive down costs, but also to increase the speed, flexibility, and level of innovation taking place within organizations of all kinds. Through outsourcing, scarce dollars will be freed for investment in improvements to current products and services and for research and development for the next generation. Outsourcing is no longer just about improving what is; it is essential to building the future. In many ways, outsourcing may well prove to be the key enabler of the 21st-century global economy.

So, outsourcing is itself at an inflection point. For it to continue to be the powerful tool it has been, leaders and their organizations need to better understand what is happening, what is likely to happen in the future and why, and how to take advantage of the opportunities created. This book is a guide for all the professionals leading that charge.

The final reason for writing this book at this time is that even though outsourcing is already widely used and is going global, it has received, until recently, very little attention outside the circle of professionals directly involved in it. Of course, there's always been coverage in the business press of the industry's "big deals" and occasional failures. But, there has been very little discussion of outsourcing in the general business press, let alone in the popular press. That all changed as the number of companies "outsourcing" white-collar jobs offshore caught the media's attention. Overnight, outsourcing entered the popular lexicon and became the center of a very public debate. The specter of massive job and skill loss in developed countries like the United States is eliciting enormous passion and real fear. With job growth lagging, offshore outsourcing is viewed by many as a big part of that problem.

This largely negative press coverage, though, does a disservice to an industry employing millions of people and providing returns to tens of millions of shareholders of the Western companies that are today the leaders in the field, companies such as American Express, AT&T, Avaya, Caterpillar, Delphi, EDS, GE, Hewlett-Packard, IBM, IKON, Johnson Controls, Lockheed Martin, McKesson, SBC Communications, Solectron, Unisys, UPS, and other Fortune 500 companies. These companies are creating and enhancing jobs for their employees, increasing returns for their shareholders, and fueling growth for the American economy. The same can be said for thousands of other large and small U.S. companies. It can also be said for a similar group of firms in Europe, Canada, Australia, and other developed countries around the world.

This newfound attention has actually raised interest in outsourcing. As a result, there is now an even greater need for the facts about outsourcing—in businesses of all types and sizes, in government, in colleges and universities, in the press, and even among the general public. Decision makers and policy makers need this information to help them set the right course for their organizations and constituents. Managers just joining the business world need to understand how outsourcing will shape the future of the organizations they work for and will someday lead. Employees need to understand how outsourcing will shape their jobs and their companies. And consumers need to understand how outsourcing is changing the corporations they buy from.

Anyone who carefully reads this book will come to recognize outsourcing not as the cause of the problems in the world around us, but as one of the most powerful tools available for fixing those problems. Outsourcing helps build better businesses, stronger economies, and a more prosperous way of life. This is true not only for the developing countries like India that are the recipients of work being outsourced offshore, but also for Western countries that are doing the outsourcing.

There is a real need for a comprehensive book on outsourcing and business process outsourcing at this moment in time. It's needed to raise the awareness and general understanding of outsourcing. It's needed to better prepare everyone involved in business for the emerging outsourced economy. It's needed to advance the management practice of outsourcing itself. If this book is successful, even in a small way, in achieving any of these goals, then the time spent writing and reading it will be well worth the investment.

How to Read *The Outsourcing Revolution*

The Outsourcing Revolution explains how executives can gain a 10- to 100-fold increase in their organizations' productivity and competitiveness by globally outsourcing critical, yet noncore business processes and by bringing in partners that can actually add to their competitive strength in the core areas of their businesses. It is written for individuals seeking both an understanding of the opportunities presented by outsourcing and a plan for implementing and sustaining these improvements. Much more than a simple how-to book, it provides a comprehensive framework for decision making and action based on the real-life experiences of executives heading up successful initiatives for their companies today.

Very few business tools have the power to fundamentally transform an organization—outsourcing is one of them. It allows companies to simultaneously reengineer their existing operations, create a more flexible and adaptable organizational structure, and tap the best minds in the world to create an innovation explosion.

This book takes the reader through the process of first understanding, then applying, and, finally, sustaining improvements in productivity and competitiveness through outsourcing. It bridges theory and practice, providing a comprehensive framework as well as a set of principles for success. Most important, it provides a quantitative formula for forecasting the potential benefits, prioritizing the opportunities, and then systematically managing for results.

This is the essential guidebook to outsourcing, combining more than a decade's experience on outsourcing, business process outsourcing, and globalization into a single, executable management system. Each chapter covers a critical aspect of outsourcing and introduces and explains essential management principles for success. These are reinforced and illustrated in practical terms through one or more mini case studies. Figures are used throughout the book to highlight, illustrate, and expand on key points. Full case studies, providing an end-to-end coverage of how specific companies planned, implemented, and continue to manage outsourcing, are presented as the book's final chapter. Research from surveys of more than 1,500 companies is used throughout the book to provide real data on what organizations around the world are doing and why, and what does and doesn't work.

Section One, "Outsourcing and the Global Economy," offers everyone who cares about what's happing in business today an essential primer on not only outsourcing's past, but more important, its present and near-term future. It covers why organizations started outsourcing decades ago and what they've learned about its impact. It expands from that base to discuss the key drivers of contemporary outsourcing—process-centric thinking and offshoring. In so doing, the opportunities and challenges of contemporary outsourcing are presented for everyone's full consideration. The final chapter of Section One proposes a set of new management principles that can be used to harness the power of outsourcing for today's organizations. It's of particular value to executives directing their organization's overall efforts.

Section Two, "The Disciplines of Outsourcing," is intended primarily for practitioners. It is not a step-by-step guide to outsourcing, but a framework on which individual executives, managers, or team members can build their own program for success. Each chapter shares the latest thinking and experiences of companies in making outsourcing an integral part of their strategic planning, implementation, and management. It is comprehensive in scope and directs the reader down a solid path for dealing with each aspect of the process.

Finally, Section Three, "The Outsourced Enterprise," looks to the future of outsourcing. It asks the question: What's next? In so doing, it looks at such topics as future sourcing, the outsourced enterprise, and tomorrow's outsourced economy. The section ends with full-length case studies illustrating all of the principles discussed throughout the book.

Section One

OUTSOURCING AND THE GLOBAL ECONOMY

Chapter

1

A BRIEF HISTORY OF OUTSOURCING

Few people realize just how extensively outsourcing is used today. Organizations of all kinds use outsourcing every day to improve the products and services they provide customers. They use outsourcing to free capital and brainpower for investment in research and development, leading to new products and new services. In fact, more than 90 percent of companies say that outsourcing is an important part of their overall business strategy.[1]

Outsourcing is critical to the growth and success of the United States and other Western economies. *Harvard Business Review* lists it as one of the most important new management ideas and practices of the 20th century.[2] Noted scholar and business visionary, James Brian Quinn of Dartmouth College, has called outsourcing "one of the greatest organizational and industry structure shifts of the century."[3] Many of America's largest and most successful companies are also the world's top providers of outsourcing services. Companies like ARAMARK, Delphi, EDS, General Electric, IBM, IKON, Unisys, UPS, Xerox, and many others have millions of employees in their outsourcing businesses. As management expert Peter Drucker says, "If you ask me what is the fastest growing industry in America—it's outsourcing."[4]

Far from being bad for businesses or their workers, outsourcing is one of the most important and powerful forces available for building successful companies, creating economic growth, and generating and enhancing jobs.

Outsourcing first came to prominence in the early 1990s at a time when the U.S. economy faced a severe recession and the very competitiveness of its businesses was in question. Companies used outsourcing then to help streamline their operations and to regain their competitive strength. The result was an unprecedented period of economic growth during the latter half of the 1990s. As we enter the mid-2000s, today's challenges may be even more pressing than those of a decade ago.

Sell the Mailroom

We live in a world that can best be described as hyper-competitive. Globalization is inextricably linking the world's major economies. Today's standard of excellence is not just best-in-class; it's best-in-world. In this global economy every company must compete against customer choices coming from everywhere and anywhere. Barriers to the marketplace are dropping quickly, with new competitors just a mouse-click away from any customer. (See Figure 1.1.)

FIGURE 1.1 OUTSOURCING: AT THE CENTER OF A FUNDAMENTAL RESTRUCTURING OF BUSINESS

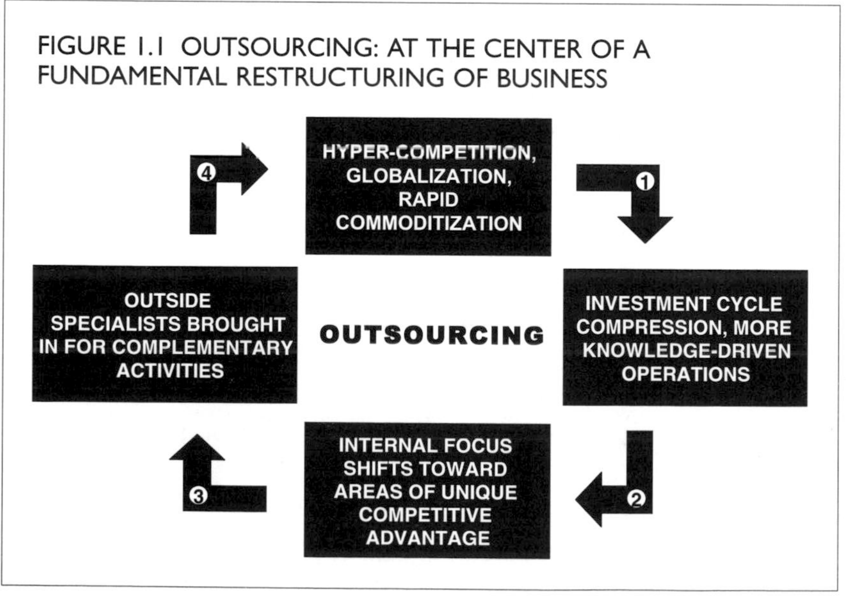

At the same time, entire industries are converging, causing companies once in completely separate fields to become direct competitors. Who could have envisioned Apple Computer getting into the music industry with iPOD, or General Motors entering the personal services industry with OnStar? Not that long ago, telecommunications carriers saw the Internet as a great new business opportunity. Today, those same telecommunications companies are fighting for their very survival as voice-over IP creates a new class of competitors.

The single most visible result of this hyper-competitive environment is rapid commoditization. Power is essentially shifting from the producers of goods and services to the consumers. A company's ability to command a higher price for the unique value it offers lasts only for a fleeting moment.

At the same time, the pressure on businesses for improved performance is unrelenting. Growth and profitability are expected. Increased shareholder value is demanded. Disappointments on any of these fronts are severely punished in the capital markets, making funding future operations even more difficult.

It is against this backdrop of hyper-competition and increasing pressure for performance that the very structural integrity of organizations is beginning to break down. The classical view was that organizations should be, by design, vertically integrated and self-sufficient: vertically integrated through a hierarchical, command-and-control structure; self-sufficient in terms of setting out to own, manage, and control as many of the factors of production as possible.

This classic approach may no longer be possible, practical, or even desirable in today's world. There are two key reasons for this: The first is that the accelerating pace of change dramatically compresses investment cycles. The competitive advantage from an organization's internal investments lasts for a shorter and shorter period of time. This unavoidably leads to an upwardly spiraling demand for new investment across the entire organization—a demand that few, if any, organizations can meet.

The second reason the vertically integrated, self-sufficient structure is breaking down is that all the operational activities across an organization are becoming increasingly specialized and knowledge-driven. Rapid advancement in every field makes it a practical impossibility for every organization to develop and sustain best-in-world expertise in every facet of its operation. Yet, whenever even a single part of the business is operating below that standard of excellence, the result is diminished capacity, reduced performance, higher costs, and competitive disadvantage.

Organizations are moving away—even being forced away—from this classical structure toward a structure based on some very powerful new principles. Doing the right thing is becoming more important than doing everything. Expertise is rivaling size as a competitive differentiator. Producing results is becoming more important, in most cases, than is the ownership of resources.

To respond to this hyper-competitive, performance-driven environment, organizations are becoming better focused and more specialized. They are evaluating each activity to determine if and how it provides a unique competitive advantage. Those areas that provide an advantage are likely to receive increased internal investment. Those that do not are likely to be either eliminated entirely or put in competition with an ever-expanding marketplace of external service providers. That is, they are considered for outsourcing.

Outsourcing, then, is in direct response to these realities of the modern world. It is organizations going through a natural "make versus buy" decision relative to how best to source those activities that need to be performed but which the organization gains little unique competitive advantage by doing itself.

Because outsourcing is essentially a market-driven process, a number of inherent factors work together to shift the balance of the value equation toward the "buy" side more and more every day. The first is the continuous increase in the number and capabilities of outsourcing service providers. Providers now exist for literally every facet of a business's operations. And, if a provider doesn't exist, one can be expected to quickly enter the market in response to a customer expressing interest in a particular service.

As service providers enter the market, build their capabilities, and successfully deliver, they then take these proof points, along with their increased capabilities, and market the solution to other prospective customers. With each new customer, the case that the activity can be successfully outsourced gets stronger and stronger. With each new customer, the service providers' knowledge and capabilities grow. Eventually the market reaches the point where the service providers are superior to just about any internal customer operation against which they might be compared.

The second driving factor toward the buy side is technology. Technology makes much of the work of the modern organization placeless. Geography is history. Most information-based activities can be done as easily half a world away as they can be across the street. Traditionally, one would think of the business as existing in a building or on a campus with its various departments operating in close proximity to each other. This is simply no longer necessary. Once these physical barriers are removed, it becomes easier to consider removing the organizational barriers as well. If the work can be done anywhere, why can't it be done by anyone?

Technology is also the primary driver of the compression of the investment cycles already discussed. When the technology cycle was five to ten years and technology investments could be depreciated over three to five years, then internal investments in technology made sense. In today's world, the technology cycles have been shortened to one to three years, but the depreciation cycle hasn't really changed. The result is that internal investments in technology are likely to be obsolete before they are depreciated, assuming that the organization implemented the right technology decision early enough in the cycle. If it made the wrong technology choice or made the choice toward the end of the cycle, then the investment may be obsolete before it's even put into service. Internal technology investments get increasingly risky all the time, making buying services, as opposed to the technology itself, the lower-risk path.

The final factor that constantly drives organizations toward the buy side is the competitive pressure placed on them. The hyper-competitive environment already discussed also means that for an organization to continue to perform an activity internally, it must be better at it than its direct competitors *and* the best outsourcing providers its competitors can hire. The standard of performance has been raised exponentially. Outsourcing is not only a result of the hyper-competitive environment organizations face, but also a contributor to it.

Peter Drucker was among the first to focus the attention of business executives on the power of outsourcing. He did so as far back as 1989 when in an op-ed piece in *The Wall Street Journal* titled "Sell the Mailroom," he made the then bold prediction that "more and more people working for organizations will actually be on the payroll of an independent outside contractor."[5]

The inefficiencies of many internal clerical, maintenance, and support operations, he argued, pose one of the biggest problems for the productivity and competitiveness of most organizations. The problem cannot really be fixed as long as these activities are performed by internal departments operating as de facto monopolies. Through outsourcing, a company places its existing internal operations into competition with the marketplace of external service providers. Although some may not like the idea of elements of a business competing in this way, competition brings out the best in people and organizations. Competition improves performance and quickly strips away unnecessary costs. Whichever way the competition comes out, the organization is better off for it. If the operation is kept inside the company, the competitive pressure leads to the much-needed improvements. If the operation is outsourced, then needed improvements are brought in from the outside.

Uncovering the Core

While outsourcing improves the performance of areas of the business that do not provide a unique competitive differentiation, it also frees needed capital and resources for investment in those areas that do. It reduces both direct costs and opportunity costs.

The areas of the business's operation that provide its unique competitive differentiation—the areas where none of its competitors nor the external marketplace of providers can deliver superior results—are its core competencies.

The term *core competencies* was first introduced to a wide audience in 1990 by C.K. Prahalad and Gary Hamel in their *Harvard Business Review* article, "The Core Competence of the Corporation."[6] In that article, they referred to core competencies as the "collective learning in the organization, especially how to coordinate diverse production skills and integrate multiple streams of technology." They predicted, quite accurately, that in the coming years managers would be increasingly rewarded for their ability to identify, enhance, and leverage their company's core competencies.

In 1994 the *MIT Sloan Management Review* published an article titled "Strategic Outsourcing" by James Brian Quinn and Fred Hilmer that further refined the term.[7] Quinn and Hilmer identified the seven characteristics of core competencies as: skills and knowledge sets, not products or functions; flexible, long-term platforms capable of adaptation or evolution; limited in number with no more than two or three per organization; unique sources of leverage in the value chain; areas where the company can dominate; elements important to customers in the long run; and capabilities embedded in the organization's systems. The connection between core competencies and outsourcing was completed with Tom Peter's frequently cited quote "Do what you do best and outsource the rest," advising executives to focus on their core competencies and outsource every other part of their operation.

For example, Chrysler and Microsoft offer two very different but equally insightful cases of how outsourcing enables companies to leverage the capabilities of outside companies and simultaneously increase the focus on their core competencies, thereby gaining a distinct competitive advantage.

In the late 1980s Chrysler was on the verge of failure, and only government-backed loans and the leadership of Lee Iacocca saved it from bankruptcy. By 1997 Chrysler was the automobile industry's low-cost producer, made the highest profit per vehicle, and was named Company of the Year by *Forbes* magazine.

How did Chrysler move to the head of the class in the auto industry? In part, by using outsourcing to improve its noncore functions while concentrating the company's internal efforts on an emerging set of core competencies.

Chrysler began by adopting the platform-team model pioneered by Toyota. Platform teams bring together designers, engineers, manufacturing, and suppliers at the moment of product inception. Instead of having each of these groups operate separately and in series, with design completing its work and then handing it off to engineering, etc., they work in parallel and as single team. As a result, the interior of one of Chrysler's highly successful LH-series was composed of just four ready-for-assembly units, each designed, engineered, and manufactured by separate suppliers working together as part of a single platform team.

Chrysler outsourced much of its services work as well. In its logistics operations Chrysler introduced the concept of "lead logistics"—designating a single outside logistics supplier to coordinate a production facility's entire inbound logistics requirements. One example was Chrysler's Jefferson North Assembly Plant where the lead logistics firm, Ryder, built a dedicated cross-docking facility, operated 65 tractors and 140 trailers, and managed all inbound logistics from upstream suppliers in Michigan, Ohio, Indiana, and Canada. For information technology, Chrysler contracted with MCI to provide and run its worldwide telecommunications network. This information technology network linked 24 manufacturing plants, 16 assembly plants, 183 Chrysler Financial Corporation offices, 4 national distribution centers, 2,000 suppliers, and 4,700 dealers. Chrysler also learned how to differentiate itself by leveraging three core competencies: product design, process design, and marketing.

At the time of its merger with Mercedes, Chrysler was generating more profit per vehicle on a $20,000 car than Mercedes was on a $40,000 car. It had also reduced its new vehicle development time from 243 weeks to 183 weeks, taking more than a full year off its product cycle.[8]

From its inception, outsourcing has been the "preferred option" at Microsoft. Its founder, Bill Gates, has often been quoted as saying he would gladly take three programmers over five support staff any time. Critical elements of product production, distribution, finance, and customer support are outsourced. Microsoft does not even maintain its own desktop environment at its headquarters, recognizing the skill and knowledge sets associated with designing and writing great software are quite different than those required to run an operational network.

What are Microsoft's core competencies? They are product design, product development, and marketing.[9]

Outsourcing is nothing more and nothing less than a management tool. It is used to move an organization away from the traditional vertically integrated, self-sufficient structure; one that is increasingly ineffective in today's hyper-competitive, performance-driven environment. Through outsourcing, the organization moves toward a business structure where it's able to make more focused investments in the areas that provide its unique competitive advantage. Along the way, the organization creates interdependent relationships with specialized service providers for many of its critical activities that must be performed extremely well, but where the organization gains little competitive advantage by doing the work itself. This not only enhances the business of the company, it creates exciting new business opportunities for other companies to become providers of outsourcing services.

Capturing Outsourcing's Benefits

At the organizational level, outsourcing represents a basic restructuring of businesses away from a model designed for the industrial age toward one that is more appropriate for today's information age. At the same time, each outsourcing decision an organization makes is a discrete transaction. Strung together, these transactions change the overall shape of the business, but each transaction has to be understood and justified in terms of its individual impact on the business's current and near-term performance. Outsourcing as an overall course of action may be a macro choice, but each specific outsourcing engagement the company enters is very much a micro choice that must be justified in its own right. (See Figure 1.2.)

The basic reason for outsourcing is to reduce costs. However the organization chooses to spend those savings, whether they are passed along to its customers, reinvested into other areas of its operations, or returned to its owners and shareholders, the need for every organization to continually drive down its costs is constant.

FIGURE 1.2 OUTSOURCING DELIVERS A HIERARCHY OF BENEFITS

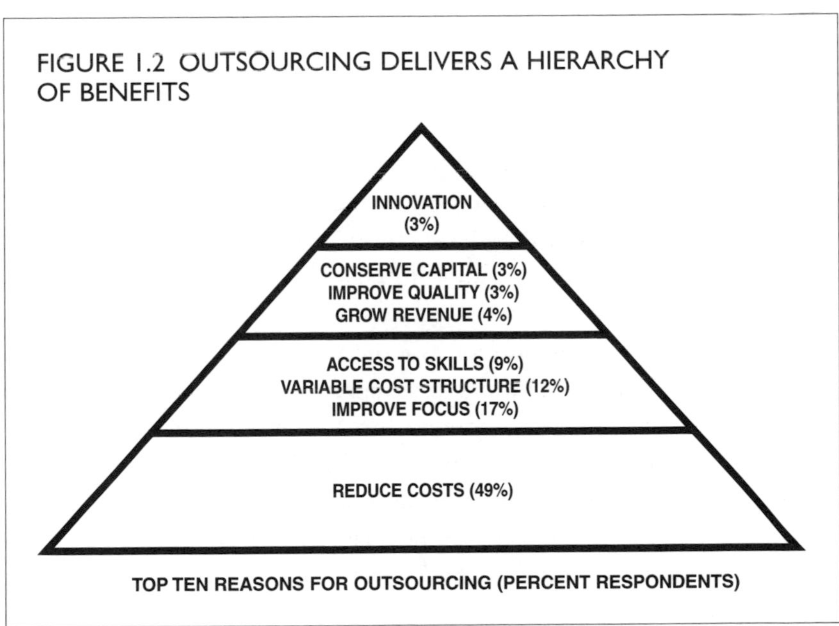

Source: The 2004 Outsourcing World Summit

About 50 percent of executives state that reducing costs is the top reason for outsourcing.[10] In most cases, the cost savings are in the 10 to 20 percent range, but can be much higher depending on how large the gap is between the company's current cost of operations and the money it will be paying the outside provider.

In some cases, this gap can be dramatic. The U.S. Department of Defense (DoD), for example, began adopting outsourcing as a management practice in the early 1990s in response to the post–cold war funding reductions that ran as high as 60 percent. Its goal was to cut operating costs faster than the budget was dropping in order to free dollars for reinvestment in modernization. As DoD began competing various internal activities against the commercial marketplace, it found that it generated, on average, a 30 percent savings. If the internal team won and the work was kept inside, the competitive process alone yielded an average 20 percent savings. If the activity was outsourced, then the average savings were 40 percent. The first 2,000 competitions DoD ran generated more than $1.4 billion dollars in annual savings. Areas outsourced included equipment maintenance and repair; base services, such as food and custodial; property construction and operations; and logistics.[11]

Another less dramatic but equally compelling example is Coors Brewing Company of Golden, Colorado. A decade ago Coors launched an aggressive program to streamline operations and focus on its core business of making and selling high-quality premium beers. It spun off a technology business, divested itself of an energy company, brought in a new nonfamily president, and began a program to redesign its internal work processes both on its own and through outsourcing.

Over the subsequent three years more than 40 noncore activities at Coors were evaluated for outsourcing. These activities represented 20 percent of the company's cost of goods sold and 18 percent of its workforce. Twenty-two of these were outsourced yielding an overall savings of 10 percent and a reduction in the company's headcount of about 600 people. Areas outsourced included sales and marketing promotion, consumer information centers, relocation services, health and welfare administration, desktop support, voicemail, accounts payables, payroll, custodial services, rail maintenance, engineering, plastics, and materials storerooms.

Outsourcing continues to be an important management tool at Coors. In 2002 the company announced a multiyear contract with Exel that extended the logistics services already being provided to Coors by

Exel. The new contract added warehousing at two new distribution centers in Golden and Ontario, Canada, part of a nationwide project to optimize Coors's distribution network. The result will be to consolidate all of Coors's existing distribution centers in the western United States into these two Exel-managed facilities.[12,13]

Although savings is an important reason for outsourcing, it is only the primary reason for half the executives who use it—meaning that for the other half something other than cost savings is the primary driver. The second most important of these is the ability to focus more company resources on the core parts of operations—activities that provide a unique competitive advantage.

For larger organizations that have built up extensive internal operations, getting back to the core of their businesses can yield real benefits. In 1988 General Motors had 3,290 people in its various accounting departments handling accounts receivables, payables, and payroll. Over the next decade, by consolidating and reengineering these activities, GM was able to reduce the number of people doing that work to 560 and reduce the total costs by 60 percent. Yet in 1998 the company outsourced these same activities and still reduced these costs by another 20 percent. Most important, GM freed executive time and attention away from accounting and gained more than $10 million in capital for reinvestment in other parts of its operations.[14] Southwest Airlines, on the other hand, is an example of a successful company that has used outsourcing since its inception, avoiding the distraction of investing in noncore areas. For example, Southwest was the first major airline to lease and not buy its aircraft. Ninety percent of its aircraft component maintenance is outsourced as well, normally back to the original equipment manufacturer (e.g., GE maintains its aircraft engines for Southwest under an innovative per-flight-hour-based contract). Southwest, therefore, can focus on its hallmarks, relentless attention to serving customers, controlling costs, and minimizing capital requirements.[15]

The next most important driver of outsourcing is the creation of more variable cost structures. Instead of having relatively fixed investments in its internal operations, the company that chooses to outsource will find that its cost structure can shift to an on-demand model. This reduces the effective cost of operations by enabling the company to adjust expenses in response to changes in the marketplace. Airline booking giant Sabre, for example, credits its variable-cost–based contract for information technology services with EDS for its ability to handle the dramatic changes in the travel industry since September 11, 2001. When Silicon Graphics outsourced its voicemail system to Avaya in 1997, it did so to bring in a specialist who could streamline a global voice network that had become unwieldy with more than 40 separate systems from multiple vendors. At the same time, Silicon Graphics changed the way it paid for this work. It pays Avaya on a per-mailbox, per-period basis as opposed to its previous, basically fixed, internal operating costs.[16]

Access to skills not available to the organization internally is another benefit attributable to many outsourcing decisions. Few organizations can hire all of the talent they need, yet few can compete successfully with a talent gap. Because service providers are more specialized and are serving many customers, they have a much deeper talent pool upon which to draw.

Measurable improvements in quality can result as well. Areas of the business that don't produce unique competitive advantage are often the last to be funded and invested in, making continuous improvements in quality difficult to achieve. When Dr Pepper/Seven Up, Inc. outsourced its mail and copy centers and shipping and receiving operations to IKON in 1998, it did so to effect a rapid improvement in what were seen as clearly underperforming parts of its operation. As a result, copier uptime quickly went from the 50 to 60 percent range to over 99 percent, while at the same time costs were cut by more than $1 million per year.[17]

Another tangible benefit of outsourcing is that not only is the need for new capital significantly reduced—since the provider often brings in the needed resources—but current assets may be sold to the provider, freeing capital dollars already invested. These dollars can then be reinvested in other parts of the business or used to improve the company's overall balance sheet and reduce its future cost of capital. In December 1992 McDonnell Douglas signed a $3 billion ten-year information technology contract with IBM. As part of the transaction, more than $100 million in information technology assets were transferred to IBM, and McDonnell Douglas received a cash payment for those assets. That money was used to help fund a corporatewide restructuring of the business and for reinvestment in core businesses. The next year earnings at McDonnell Douglas jumped by 145 percent, and non–finance company debt was cut by 45 percent. The company's stock price rose 36 percent from September 1992 through January 1994. Although ultimately acquired by

Boeing as the aerospace industry continued its unavoidable consolidation, the company's turnaround during a very difficult period was remarkable.[18,19]

Most recently, companies have begun to find that bringing in outside specialists spurs much needed innovation in their operations. Some equate outsourcing to having a dedicated R&D department; as the provider innovates new solutions they can be immediately put into practice in the company's own operations. As James Brian Quinn has put it, "No one company acting alone can out-innovate all its competitors, potential competitors, suppliers, and external knowledge sources."[20] As we'll see later, the effect that outsourcing has on innovation may be its single most important, long-term contributor to success.

Redefining Management

Another often-overlooked, sometimes difficult-to-quantify, but very important aspect of outsourcing's value is its ability to free an executive's time to focus on the "what" of the business as opposed to the "how."

For many executives, dealing with the day-to-day details of operational activities robs them of time that would be better spent externally—on customers, shareholders, investors, and suppliers. Outsourcing moves many of those "how" responsibilities to the provider, while enabling the executives to focus on defining the "what" of their businesses through a services agreement and outcomes scorecard.

Think of the CFO responsible for planning the financial strategy of the company and running a financial transaction processing shop. He or she is actually taking on two separate and very different jobs. The executive is both the "customer" of those services—using his or her output to help guide the organization's performance—and the "provider" of those services, with responsibility for all of the day-to-day operations and decision making. This may feel like control, but it actually drains executive effectiveness and focus.

As a "customer," the executive must define the business requirements, prioritize them, communicate results with the rest of the organization, monitor performance, and, of course, pay for the services. As a "provider," that same executive has an equally demanding job acquiring and training the needed people to do the work: dealing with all of the personnel challenges; evaluating, selecting, and overseeing the implementation of technology; resolving day-to-day problems; and delivering the final service.

Either one of these jobs is demanding enough, without expecting both of the same person. The time spent as provider takes away from the time available to be the customer. Often, critical customer requirements become nonstarters because of the natural resistance to the demands they will place on the same executive as the provider. The ability to truly match pay for performance is lost. Company politics often restrict the executive's ability to make the optimal operational decision as a provider.

As one experienced CFO put it, "Managing contracts is much more efficient and effective than managing employees; contracts are performance-based." And, as another observed, post-outsourcing, "My role changed from focusing on hygiene (the day-to-day maintenance of the financial operations) to really working on the business." A company's executives should only hold onto their provider role for activities unique to their company that deliver true marketplace differentiation. In all other cases, there can be real benefit from separating the two roles through outsourcing.

Overcoming Outsourcing's Challenges

Outsourcing has played an essential role in most of today's successful businesses. However, ending a review of outsourcing's history without discussing its difficulties would be a disservice.

Any change as significant as outsourcing has risk. Not all organizations execute well. Not all providers deliver well for every customer. Even when both companies execute well, other factors can keep the relationship from delivering its intended benefits.

Outsourcing Failures

Various surveys regularly report a surprisingly high rate of outsourcing failures. For example:

- A 2003 report published by IT research and consulting company Gartner reported that one-half of all outsourcing deals are labeled "failures" by decision-making executives because the results do not meet expectations.[21]

- A 2003 survey by UK-based PA Consulting Group found that 66 percent of the benefits anticipated from outsourcing were only partially realized.[22]
- A 2000 study by Dun & Bradstreet found that 25 percent of the functional areas within the 2,200 companies surveyed had prematurely terminated at least one outsourcing contract during the preceding two years.[23]

Reports like these serve an important purpose, reminding us that, in business, results are never guaranteed. Achieving the intended results requires solid planning and hard work.

When it comes to outsourcing, the particular areas of hard work and planning are: choosing the right opportunities for outsourcing; setting realistic expectations; choosing the right providers; crafting a balanced relationship that offers sustainable benefit to customer and provider, alike; properly managing outsourcing's organizational impacts; and managing the ongoing relationship.

Although problems in each of these areas can and do occur, they are preventable. There is a tremendous reservoir of experience upon which to draw. As we'll see in later chapters, the tools and techniques needed to avoid the problems companies can experience are there for executives and their teams to use, if they choose to do so.

Outsourcing's Barriers

There are also a number of barriers inside the organization—barriers that must be brought down if outsourcing is to work well.

Managers fear a loss of control. They often believe that although an activity may not be core, it may still be too critical to be outsourced. They are concerned about losing flexibility by getting locked into a long-term contract with a service provider. They are concerned about how their customers may react. They are concerned about employee, and especially union, reactions. They are concerned, particularly when it comes to offshore outsourcing, about community and political backlash over lost jobs.

Although each of these concerns is based on often strongly held opinions, more often than not they reflect more a fear of the unknown than an objective assessment of the facts.

Loss of control. It can be argued just as effectively that, when done right, organizations don't lose but gain control through outsourcing. A contractual relationship with a top service provider, with proper management reporting, tied to measurable outcomes gives executives greater control than they had over their previous, typically less formal and less well-defined internal management system.

Too critical to be outsourced. Can organizations outsource critical activities and still be successful? They can and do every day. The GM executive who outsourced payroll, for example, would go out of his way to make sure that other executives understood that the outsourcing decision was not made because payroll wasn't critical. "If we don't make payroll, the union walks. If the union walks, we don't make cars. If we don't make cars, we don't make money," he would say. GM outsourced payroll precisely because it concluded it was too critical *not* to outsource it to a specialist who could do it better and more efficiently.[24]

Loss of flexibility. Instead of reducing flexibility, outsourcing can actually increase it. Through outsourcing, the company gains access to the provider's larger resource pool. Those resources can now be tapped by the customer "on demand."

Nike has a three-tier approach to manufacturing outsourcing: developed partners, volume producers, and developing sources. Its volume producers make a specific type of shoe for Nike. As the name implies, they manufacture Nike's more mature, high-volume products. Key to the value of this relationship is the volume producer's ability to handle large fluctuations in its orders from Nike. In this way, Nike gains a reliable, highly flexible partner that helps it respond to its quickly changing marketplace. How do volume producers do it? They do it by manufacturing similar types of shoes for multiple brands. This enables them to maintain a fairly stable overall production volume while giving each of their customers the flexibility needed in their businesses. Volume producers absorb much of the shock of the very fickle marketplace for footware, enabling Nike, in turn, to better serve its customers.[25]

Negative customer reaction. Although outsourcing may be a sensitive issue for some customers, improved service quickly puts these concerns to rest. The fact that a third party is involved doesn't need to be visible at all, if the company chooses. In other cases, the provider's brand may actually enhance their customer's—think shipping and FedEx, or personal computers and Intel.

Employee resistance. Barriers also exist because of concerns over outsourcing's impact on employees and even its impact on the status and power of the middle- and upper-level managers who have direct authority over the function. This issue is particularly sensitive when the outsourcing involves offshoring. Even there, as we'll see later, organizations have tremendous latitude in preparing and assisting their people and managers through these changes.

The impacts are real, but outsourcing can also open up new career opportunities. After all, does a custodial or food services employee have a better long-term career opportunity working for a pharmaceutical company filled with Ph.D.s, clinical researchers, and sales professionals, or at a major outsourcing provider of those services, such as ARAMARK, Compass, or Sodexho? Even top managers in those functions within a pharmaceutical are still back-of-the-house support staff with limited career opportunity. At ARAMARK, Compass, and Sodexho every food service and custodial employee has a definable career path right to the chairman's office if he or she is capable. Food service and custodial employees at these companies are front-office revenue generators, not overhead.

Summary

No organization can stay competitive in today's rapidly changing global economy by relying solely on its own resources. Outsourcing is a necessary response to today's hyper-competitive environment. In this environment, no organization can afford the level investment required to be best-in-world across its entire operation, yet none can afford to be anything less. Through outsourcing, organizations solve this dilemma by focusing their internal resources on the activities that provide them a unique competitive advantage.

At the same time, each outsourcing transaction adds to the organization's overall performance and competitiveness. It saves money, redirects resources to more valuable activities, achieves a more variable cost structure, gains access to much needed skills, reduces the internal competition for capital, becomes faster and more responsive, and even increases its level of innovation. Managers and executives themselves are able to better focus their energies externally, on customers, as opposed to internally, on day-to-day operations.

Although outsourcing's ability to create these benefits for companies and their customers and shareholders is well documented, challenges and problems do exist. These are highly complex, sophisticated relationships that require care in their planning, execution, and management. Failures do occur. However, this simply doesn't have to be the case—the experience is now there for others to learn from if they are willing to make the investment.

Chapter

2

FROM OUTSOURCING TO BUSINESS PROCESS OUTSOURCING

We traditionally think of companies in a hierarchical way, with people and the work they do organized into departments. Each department reports to a manager. These departments are then grouped into larger business units along functional or geographical lines reporting to executives. These executives, in turn, report to a handful of top executives with responsibility for the company's overall operations and performance.

Understandably, outsourcing has followed this traditional hierarchical structure as well. Outsourcing along department and functional lines has made it easier to describe the work being performed, who's doing it, the inputs and outputs, and costs. Prospective customers can describe the scope of the work to be outsourced in fairly straightforward terms, and service providers can bid for, win, and perform that work under a commonly understood structure. This approach also has simplified decision making and responsibility, since the same functional executive responsible for the work before it is outsourced is generally responsible for it afterwards. The hierarchy of the business, therefore, was not changed, just the way it sources the work of a particular department.

As a result, manufacturing executives can outsource subcomponents of their product, or their logistics or warehousing departments. CIOs can outsource data centers, the work done within them, and often the equipment needed. Facilities executives can outsource the mailroom, cafeteria, and janitorial departments. CFOs can outsource payroll and receivables departments.

There are, however, other ways to think about how the work taking place within a company is organized and, in turn, how it might be outsourced. One way is with a more lateral process perspective. Processes cut across an organization's departments and functions, ending where they produce an output that is valued by the organization's customers. (See Figure 2.1.) Customers care about outcomes, not about the internal operations of the company they are buying from, let alone its internal departmental structure. They care about ease of ordering and having that order accurately filled. They care about the accuracy of the invoice they receive, the timeliness and accuracy of the confirmation of their payment, and the speedy resolution of any questions or problems. Ultimately, they care about the end points where the company delivers something of value to them. Customers care about the products and services they receive and how well they fit their needs and expectations.

This process-oriented view, seen as ending at the points where the organization delivers value to its customers, has proven to be quite effective as a tool for improving most company's overall performance. Mike Hammer, who more than a decade ago launched reengineering with his

FIGURE 2.1 BUSINESS PROCESS OUTSOURCING MEANS WORKING ACROSS THE ORGANIZATION TO DELIVER VALUE TO CUSTOMERS

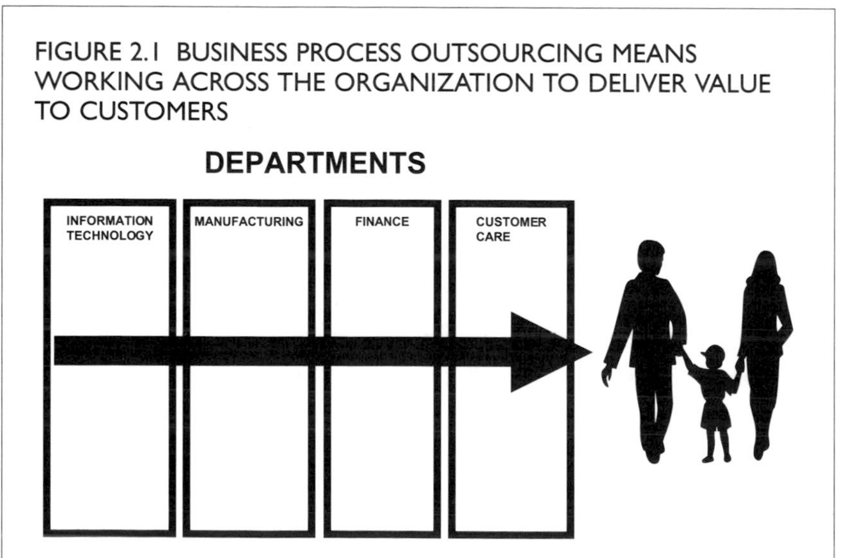

breakthrough book *Reengineering the Corporation: A Manifesto for Business Revolution,* is today one of the leading proponents of this process-centric view of the organization; what he calls the *process enterprise.*

Process enterprises develop a cohesive approach to understanding, performing, managing, and measuring the groups of related activities that produce the outputs customers value. As opposed to operating the business as a hierarchy of departments where each is responsible for performing its own tasks, process enterprises embrace a program for understanding and operating their businesses as a collection of end-to-end business processes. In a process enterprise, executive leadership, education, responsibilities, measurement, and reward systems are all recalibrated to this fundamentally different view of the business. Solid results have been reported at organizations both large and small that have adopted the process enterprise approach, and it is one of the most important new management systems available.[1]

When process thinking is applied to outsourcing, it becomes business process outsourcing, or BPO. BPO shifts the focus of traditional outsourcing and the way the relationships with outside specialists are defined and implemented—within discrete departments—toward a process-centric, end-to-end view of the business's activities.

Because BPO cuts across many parts of the organization's operations, the outside specialist becomes a much more integral part of their customer's overall business. The provider not only assumes responsibility for performing specific pieces of work, but for helping to design the overall business process, its outcome measurements, the technologies that enable it, and the supply chains that feed into it. With business process outsourcing, providers operate across the customer's value chain—often straight to the customer's customer. This can have a profoundly positive effect on the business, how it operates, and how it creates value for its customers. Business process outsourcing may have its roots in traditional outsourcing, but the results can be dramatically different. You don't have to look very far for examples, and they're not just in the mega-corporations. BPO can be found in practice at great companies of all types and sizes. Specialty retailer Manhattan Fruitier may not be a corporate giant, but it's a great company with a great product. Its gift baskets have been highly praised by Zagat and others and are sold at the company's storefront in New York's Gramercy neighborhood and online all around the world. It's also a great example of business process outsourcing.

You would probably expect a small retailer like Manhattan Fruitier to use UPS or another carrier to ship orders to its customers—an example of traditional outsourcing of a discrete activity. But Manhattan Fruitier has gone further than that, making UPS an integral part of its entire end-to-end order-fulfillment process—from taking customer orders online to scheduling, tracking, delivering, recordkeeping, and even measuring its performance. Manhattan Fruitier has built UPS's software and services into its front-end Web site as well as its back-end operations. The company has used business process outsourcing to make UPS, a logistics powerhouse, its partner in meeting the needs of its customers. Manhattan Fruitier has accomplished more than just outsourcing package delivery. The company has eliminated the costs of developing and maintaining essential software systems; it's able to provide through UPS a better, more responsive customer experience on its Web site; it's saving more than $2 every time a customer checks an order online instead of calling the store; and it's able to grow its business quickly by plugging new business operations, like a new West Coast distribution center, right into UPS's systems and processes.[2]

To make BPO work for companies ranging in size from Manhattan Fruitier to giants such as British Petroleum and General Motors, there are a number of unique elements that need to be built into the relationship from the start.

The first is a focus on the end-to-end business process and the results that process delivers to customers. The second is a replacement of the typical boundaries within and between the internal silos of the business, and between it and its providers, with a penchant for blending and reengineering across all of these boundaries. The third is a drive to work with the provider to achieve scale and efficiency gains across the supporting supply chains. The fourth and final element is to unlock the value hidden inside the company's current operations through commercialization. This chapter discusses each.

Working from the Customer In

Business process outsourcing begins by sitting down with the clients, the actual users of the services, and asking them what *they need.* It means understanding what the client needs and then examining the points of contact—the moments of truth—where those needs get met. The internal activities of the business, and how BPO can enhance them, are then looked at from this perspective. The question becomes, how can we use BPO and the skills, resources, and capabilities of outside experts teaming with us across our business processes to deliver greater value to our customers? Instead of viewing outsourcing as a sourcing decision affecting an internal operation, it's seen as a value-enhancing decision directly connected to the needs of the customer. BPO shifts the focus of outsourcing from inside-out to outside-in.

Working in this way—from customer-in and following process, not department, boundaries—produces very different results. A great example of this, one that anyone in any business can easily relate to, is found at HealthNow NY, a Buffalo, New York–based health insurer with more than 750,000 members and an annual revenue of more $1.5 billion. For an insurer, new subscriber enrollment is an end-to-end process that delivers unique value to customers. Within that process, a critical subprocess is providing new subscribers with enrollment packages that explain their services and how to get them.

Traditionally, these enrollment packages were hand-assembled at HealthNow NY. Seven full-time employees hand-picked new-member information and stuffed the various pages into envelopes for mailing. Documents of all different shapes, sizes, and styles were combined, making both quality control and the actual use of the information by the new customer difficult at best. Because of this, new members were just as likely to pick up the phone and call customer assistance to get answers to their questions as they were to look through the pile of materials they had been sent. This led to delays in getting needed information to the new member and higher costs for HealthNow NY.

HealthNow NY addressed the need to improve this deliverable not by outsourcing the hand-assembly department, but by bringing in an outsourcing provider, in this case Xerox, to help them first examine and reengineer the entire process, and then take over selected aspects of it. The result was the redesign of the enrolment package into a print-on-demand kit, custom produced for every subscriber. Each kit now contains only the information that that subscriber needs, based on his or her specific plan options. The kit is now a single, professionally designed book with laminated pages and a four-color glossy cover. Xerox provides the supporting information and print technologies, manages many elements of the supply chain feeding into the kit's physical production, and operates the center where the kits are created.

The results have been remarkable: a fourfold increase in customer satisfaction with the enrollment kits; a reduction in calls and costs at the company's customer services center; and a reduction in total costs of the entire process of 40 percent.[3,4,5]

Using a customer-in approach to work across the hierarchical structure of the company makes outsourcing that much more powerful a tool. Companies often debate whether or not outsourcing is being done to cut costs or improve service. If approached from a business process outsourcing perspective, the debate ends fairly quickly. Decisions are made from the customer's perspective, with improved outcomes leading to higher customer satisfaction and increased revenue. As was the case with HealthNow NY, operational savings take place almost as a by-product of improving the process. If it's better, faster, and more effective for the customer, then it's likely to save time and money for the company, as well. Approached this way, business process outsourcing becomes the equivalent of the maxim: *Quality is free.*

Business process outsourcing also combines outsourcing and reengineering into a single, cohesive effort. Many executives struggle with the question of whether to reengineer first and then outsource or to first outsource and then reengineer. Business process outsourcing essentially means doing both at the same time. While outsourcing "what is" can provide important benefits, simultaneously redesigning the process and outsourcing "what should be" delivers even greater benefits faster. Business process outsourcing means working with the outside specialist to first examine and document the current process, reengineer it, and then deploy and manage the newly reengineered process—all as part of the same initiative. It means teaming with outside specialists throughout the reengineering effort to bring their expertise to the table from the beginning.

Functional Process Outsourcing

A company's business processes end at its true customers, the people paying the bills. There are, however, many internal processes that feed into these business processes but exist essentially to support the people within the company, its internal customers. Human resources, finance and accounting, information technology, travel, and facilities services, such as hoteling, are all examples of these internal processes.

These internal processes often exist entirely within the boundaries of a functional area of the business—they often don't cut across as many parts of the business's operations as is the case with business processes that flow all the way out to the end customers. However, using a process-centric approach to the outsourcing of these activities, what is called *functional process outsourcing*, can still deliver greater results than if the activities were outsourced along strict departmental boundaries.

Take, for example, all of the work within a finance department involved in maintaining its company's books: reviewing and verifying receivables and payables, making deposits, reconciling bank statements, entering updates into the company's financial system, and producing timely reports for management (the internal customer of the process). Outsourcing this type of work within a finance department has produced real benefits for many companies. They gain significant savings by leveraging the scale and scope of the provider's operation. They gain access to a more flexible workforce, one that can be ramped up for quick quarterly and year-end processing and then regulated back down for the rest of the year. The company can tap specialized financial skills it only needs occasionally. All of the work of recruiting and staffing personnel and dealing with day-to-day operational issues are assumed by the service provider. As a result, internal skills can be freed, making more time available for financial planning, what-if analysis, and forecasting. All of these are real benefits from outsourcing within the finance department that many companies have done in the past.

At the same time, the traditional approach to outsourcing results in several other opportunities for improvement getting missed. The software systems being used are still owned and operated by the company. These systems are limited by the money and skills the company can and is willing to devote to them. They may be adequate to support the current operations of the company, but are probably not at the leading edge of what can be done with technology to automate and streamline the overall process. Improvements to the supply chain may be being missed as well. The company is still individually purchasing banking and other financial services. It's contracting as a single purchaser for external audit services. In effect, elements of the work may have been outsourced, but the process itself has remained essentially unchanged.

Functional process outsourcing means outsourcing all of the work of an internal process but adds in the technology that supports it and the supply chains that feed it. The German-based chemicals company BASF used functional process outsourcing to streamline, reduce costs, and improve services within many of its human resources processes. The operations and underlying technology for its benefits administration process is outsourced as an end-to-end process serving the company's internal customers—the company's 13,000-plus North America employees and their managers.

The first step was to outsource to the service provider the call center supporting the company's employees. Next, responsibility for the software systems that provide employees self-service access to their 401(k), benefits plans, and enrollment services were outsourced to the same provider. Other aspects of the process outsourced included employee care, inbound and outbound document handling, imaging, management of benefits suppliers, and financial reconciliation and control.

As these enhanced services came online, not just incremental, but order-of-magnitude improvements occurred. For example, calls to the self-service center that had previously taken ten minutes, on average, were answered online in less than a minute. Other improvements included a reduction in the overall HR-to-staff ratios, fewer errors and less staff time devoted to problem resolution and more consistency in the responses provided employees on benefits issues. Additionally, the HR department staff could then spend more time working in a consultative role with the company's business unit heads on such topics as staffing, recruiting, compensation and benefit redesign, and change programs, such as plant openings, closings, and business acquisitions.[6,7]

Breaking Down Barriers

A process-centric approach to outsourcing, whether it's across an end-to-end business process or within a functional process, offers greater opportunities for improving the business's performance than traditional outsourcing. Key to obtaining this value is breaking down the barriers that separate the traditional vertical silos of the business.

Two of the most important silos are the functional departments themselves and the technology department that supports them. For functional process and business process outsourcing to work, these two silos need to be able to be operated as one so that decisions about outsourcing and reengineering can be made seamlessly.

This can be a challenge for many companies because these silos are headed by separate executives, each with their own responsibilities, pressures, goals, and budgets. Various joint management and steering committee structures, as well as changes to how budgets are owned and managed, are frequently used tools for breaking down barriers. Another way barriers can be eliminated is by restructuring certain functions under a shared services model. (See Figure 2.2.)

With shared services, common support activities, such as human resources, finance, purchasing, facilities operations, information technology, and the like, are brought together, reporting to a single management team. This team takes on the role of an internal outsourcer, providing these services to their customers—the other departments and functions of the company.

Shared services centers allow the organization to consolidate activities previously performed separately within individual business units. Prior to moving to a shared services structure it would not be uncommon to see multiple human resources, finance, and information technology depart-

FIGURE 2.2 SHARED SERVICES CREATES AN INTERNAL BPO BUSINESS SUPPORTING INTERNAL CUSTOMERS

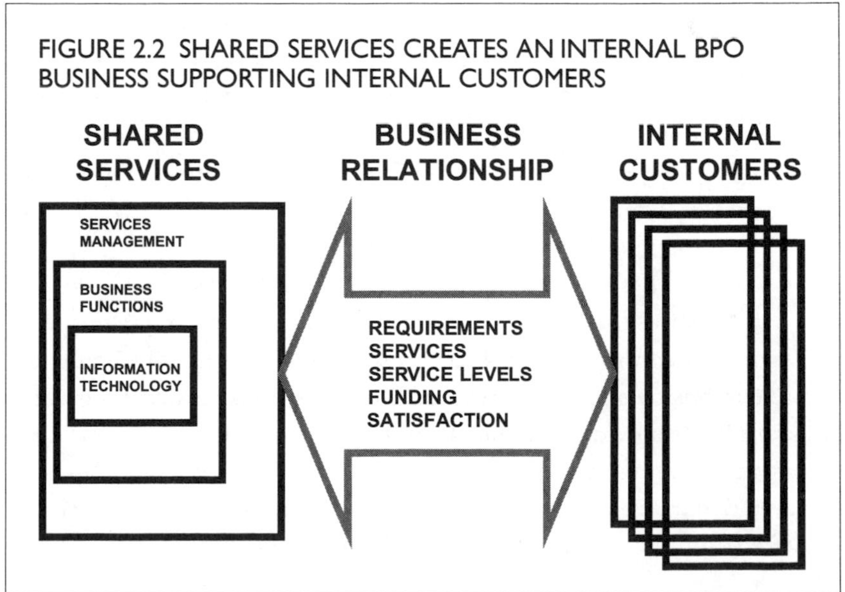

ments operating across the organization. This traditionally has been the case for many large organizations and can be even more prevalent for companies operating in multiple regions of the world or serving multiple customer segments where these operations have developed fairly autonomously. Bringing these functions together under a single shared services umbrella leads to a clearer focus on the actual processes being performed, their true costs, and how best to serve the internal customers. Once organized into a shared services structure, the previous boundaries between these departments and functions can be broken down as the management team seeks ways, in a very commercial, very competitive-minded way, to deliver greater value to what are now its customers.

A classic example of this is BHP Billiton. With its global headquarters in Melbourne, Australia, BHP Billiton is the world's largest diversified resources group, with businesses in the aluminum, base metals, coal, diamonds, petroleum, and steel industries. The company's 2003 revenue was $17.5 billion. BHP Billiton has adopted a shared services model to support its global operations that creates an internal marketplace for the company's finance, human resources, procurement, and information technology services. Each of these services is evaluated and deployed using a three-tier structure:

- Services are *embedded in the business unit* when they are applicable only to that unit, are more effectively delivered in that unit, or provide that business unit a unique competitive advantage.
- *Shared services*—what the company calls internal outsourcing—is used where the services can be leveraged across multiple business units and performance can be improved through common processes, common systems, and improved customer focus in the planning and delivery of the service.
- *Outsourced services* are used where the shared services unit is either not cost-competitive or cannot deliver at the needed quality levels.

The company operates four shared services centers around the world in Adelaide, Australia; Houston, Texas; Santiago, Chile; and its most recent center in Johannesburg, South Africa. These centers operate as an integrated global network where services are requested through a single front-end and the work can then be performed locally, across time zones, globally, and virtually, while maintaining a single point of presence for the internal customer of those services.[8,9]

By 2000, it was estimated that at least 50 percent of Fortune 500 companies had implemented shared services,[10] and today those numbers probably have risen to 80 to 90 percent. At the same time, savings of from 20 to 40 percent have been commonplace.[11] Using shared services to break down the barriers between functional silos controls costs and creates a more process-focused and customer-focused approach.

In many cases, the most effective way to create the shared services environment can be through business process outsourcing. That is, bringing in an outside organization to manage the consolidation of these operations and simultaneously to redesign the processes and deploy the enabling technologies. In other cases, once brought together into the shared services structure, internal management can begin an ongoing program to evaluate which services are best performed internally and which are better sourced from the outside. With either approach, adding functional process and business process outsourcing to the shared services model can increase the intended benefits and accelerate their realization.

Transactions, Technology, and E-sourcing

The outsourcing of transaction-intensive processes is at the center of much of what's possible through business processes outsourcing.

As consumers, we initiate transactions with companies every day: a bank account inquiry or withdrawal, a purchase at a store, the registration of an automobile, a call to a toll-free number to check the status of a payment. Transactions like these are simple, straightforward, and all around us. In each case, the transaction includes verifying the activity to be performed, performing the work of the transaction, and creating a permanent record of the completed work.

Transactions, by their very nature, are clearly defined sets of related actions making them easy to describe, measure, and monitor. They are information-intensive and repetitive. While they are certainly critical to the operation of any business, they seldom offer much opportunity for creating competitive advantage—they simply have to be done correctly, every time, and within a specific time frame. It's that simple.

There is a tremendous opportunity to improve the speed and lower the cost of transaction processing through the application of technology. Much of the work of a transaction is placeless and can be performed anywhere. Because transaction volumes are subject to peaks, valleys, and seasonality, the average cost per transaction can be lowered significantly by having a variable-cost, as opposed to a fixed-cost, structure—perfect for an outside organization paid on a per transaction basis.

It is also possible to separate where the information systems are located from where the staff involved in initiating, reviewing, verifying, and auditing the transaction are located. Not only can staff be physically separated and working anywhere in the world, but the work can be taking place in more than one company.

MedPlans Partners, for example, is a privately held company that processes claims for health care insurers. The company operates two claims processing centers, one in Fort Scott, Kansas, and the other in Louisville, Kentucky. Although few outside the industry have heard of MedPlans Partners, its customers are some of the best-known names in the insurance industry.

MedPlans Partners employees adjudicate and process claims on behalf of these clients and do so at a per-completed-claim price. The company can take on any required volume of claims from its customers either as an ongoing assignment or for a fixed time period. Clients can use MedPlans Partners as part of their ongoing claims processing capacity, or to level out seasonal fluctuations, reduce a backlog, or help them through a technology migration. MedPlans Partners claims processors are trained on all of the most common software systems for this work and are connected over private networks directly to their clients' systems. Sometimes these systems are run internally by the client, in other cases, the systems are outsourced to specialty technology providers who design, host, and manage the application—thus making it accessible to both the client and any of its outsourced providers, like MedPlans Partners.

Speed, Scalability, and Accessibility

In many ways, business process outsourcing is resulting from the convergence of three very powerful forces—the Internet, robust software applications, and process-centric thinking. Essentially, the Internet is doing for software systems what it has already done for data—making them widely available, affordable, and even ubiquitous.

One term for this convergence is *e-sourcing*. The central idea is quite simple: Take software applications, host them, make them network-accessible, and allow users to run the application directly through the browser software on their PC or other network-enabled device. It's software as a service supporting transactions that can be initiated from anywhere in the world and on-demand. Just about any software application, from the most essential data archiving application to the most sophisticated e-commerce application, can be deployed and accessed this way.

This e-sourcing approach of driving transactions through common systems accessible to multiple users anywhere in the world addresses a fundamental need in business today: the need for speed. Speed has emerged as an essential factor in the success of any business, and leveraging common systems over the Internet is one approach that can dramatically cut the time it takes to bring them online.

Scalability—the ability to ramp up a solution quickly as the business grows—is another key advantage. As a company's customer set grows, as the number of purchasing transactions or types of buys it makes increase, as the number of products in its product line expands, and as the number of sites it operates increases, an organization needs to have business processes and enabling technologies that can grow quickly and incrementally. If the business is run as essentially a global technology infrastructure to which various inside and outside organizations are connected, then much of the needed scalability is achievable.

This approach is also very important to functional process outsourcing. Here, the issues are access to capital and to the needed information technology resources to implement new Web-enabled, customer and employee self-service applications. Functional process leaders in areas such as human resources, finance, and purchasing often find themselves unable to get the applications they need because of the internal competition for information technology resources. Payroll, for example, is an application of utmost importance to a company, but it can't be the number one technology project for most. E-sourcing enables business executives to work collaboratively with their technology team while at the same time purchasing much of the desired capability as a service through an outside provider.

Speed, focus, flexibility, connectivity, scalability, and price are all leveraged and taken to Internet-time through e-sourcing. And e-sourcing is inextricably linked to functional process outsourcing, business process outsourcing, and the resulting expanded opportunities to create value for organizations.

Scaling and Integrating Supply Chains

Streamlining supply chains is yet another major focus for many organizations. Moving from thousands of suppliers to hundreds not only reduces the costs associated simply with managing that many relationships, it enables the company to get better pricing based on a closer relationship with its suppliers as well as larger volume discounts. It also creates a more strategic relationship between the companies; one that can bring to the table not just the supplier's products and services but additional expertise they are willing to share only with their best customers. In these ways, well-executed supply chain improvement programs commonly save companies from 5 to 15 percent while shortening cycle times, improving overall supplier relationships, and enhancing product quality.[12]

Business process outsourcing often includes supply chain consolidation. Often the supplier, because it is managing the same supply chain on behalf of all of its customers, can deliver greater levels of scale, integration, and savings than any one customer could individually. Take the example of Morrison Management Specialists. This company, a U.S. unit of the UK's Compass Group, manages food services, both cafeterias and in-room meals, for hospitals. A typical large U.S. hospital system is likely to be operating four or five hospitals, in one or two states, with an annual food purchasing volume of perhaps $4 million. Morrison, on the other hand, is purchasing and managing the supply chain for food on behalf of its 600 clients in 28 states. Its total annual purchasing is in excess of $350 million.[13] This gives Morrison the ability to streamline and integrate food purchasing at a scale that no single hospital system could ever achieve on its own. Additionally, the company has an investment in and a strategic relationship with Foodbuy, which has an annual purchasing volume of more than $4.9 billion, making it one of the largest food products buyers in the country.[14,15]

The same kind of power to streamline, integrate, and consolidate supply chains through business process outsourcing can be seen in many functional process outsourcing arrangements, as well. Exult, a provider of human resources outsourcing, manages services on behalf of more than 600,000 employees at its various client organizations. This makes Exult's collective purchasing power for benefits, training, relocation services, outplacement, and the like, second only to the largest employer in the world, Wal-Mart, and a handful of other large providers in its field against which it competes.[16]

There are a number of discrete activities that make up supply chain management and that are commonly integrated and enhanced through business process outsourcing. Purchasing is certainly one, but so are supplier quality performance, planning, order fulfillment, warehousing, logistics, and transportation. It is the integration and transformation of the goods and services coming in through this supply chain that enables a company to deliver its goods and services to its customers. Through business process outsourcing, the outsourcing provider becomes an integral part of the customer's operation and takes on many of these responsibilities at a scope and scale far beyond what's possible through the customer's own operation.

Commercializing Hidden Value

Because both business process and functional process outsourcing address end-to-end processes, not merely stand-alone departments of work, the scope of what's outsourced is far more comprehensive and complete. These end-to-end processes, along with all their supporting technologies and supply chains, essentially represent complete businesses in their own right. For example, whether or not outsourced, the internal shared services center of most large corporations already have within their operations most of the competencies, capabilities, and resources that would be required to provide their services not only to the current parent company, but to others as well. They could become commercial enterprises delivering finance, human resources, procurement, information technology, and other services on a paid basis.

This idea of using business process outsourcing as a vehicle to "commercialize" existing internal operations is a very powerful one. It offers companies an opportunity to not only gain the operational advantages they seek through outsourcing, but to generate additional economic value from their existing operations. This economic value can come in the form of lower prices, new revenue streams, equity in a new business venture, and sometimes all three.

Several examples of this exist. Early, foundational clients, such as BP and Bank of America, received equity stakes in their human resources outsourcing provider, Exult; similarly, Commonwealth Bank of Australia received an equity share in EDS Australia as part of its information technology outsourcing contract with that company. AMR spun-off Sabre as a new business. General Motors did the same with Delphi (automobile parts), Cincinnati Bell with Convergys (call centers and telemarketing), and American Express Company with First Data (transaction processing).[17] Bell Canada used outsourcing to commercialize its logistics operations by forming and later selling a company named Progistix-Solutions, its network installation operations through Expertech, and its residential installation and repair business through Entourage Technology Solutions.[18] In all of these cases, profitable, growing businesses were created. In other words, business process outsourcing was used as a vehicle to commercialize a company's existing internal operations.

Of course, just because the opportunity for commercialization exists does not mean that it applies to each and every business process outsourcing opportunity pursued. There are, after all, a number of principles that are key to its success. Some have to do with the current management: Is it committed to the venture and entrepreneurial in its approach? Others have to do with the viability of the business being created: Where will its competitive advantage come from? What unique technologies and processes does it possess? Does it have the capacity for funding and growth over time? Still others have to do with the marketplace: Is there a growing market for its services? Who are the competitors, and how will this new commercial enterprise distinguish itself from them?

The central point is that business process and functional process outsourcing, because they represent a much more comprehensive approach to the activities being outsourced, create a natural base upon which a new commercial enterprise can be built. It's another way that business process outsourcing expands and redefines outsourcing as a management practice.

Summary

Business process outsourcing represents an important expansion in where and how organizations are using outsourcing. Instead of focusing exclusively on neatly defined departments of work, business process outsourcing looks across the company to improve it, working in from the customer's perspective. It combines a process-centric view of the business with reengineering, technology, and supply chain consolidation to deliver not only a more efficient operation but a higher-value outcome for the customers.

Much of the focus of business process outsourcing is around the transaction-intensive parts of a company's operations, everything from processing a receivable to filling a customer order. These types of transaction-intensive processes lend themselves to outsourcing. They are high in volume, but add minimal value; they are technology-driven and placeless; they are discreet, variable in volume, and measurable in outcome. These are frequently pieces of work that the company is already consolidating into shared services centers; often supporting its global operations.

Outsourcing also opens up new commercial opportunities for many organizations. It enables them, either on their own or through various forms of joint ventures, to leverage their existing internal investments into new commercial offerings.

Business process outsourcing fundamentally repositions outsourcing from its traditional role as a tool for cost-cutting to one for process improvement, better customer service, and creation of new sources of revenue and business growth.

Case Study: Microsoft Courseware

Courseware is an essential part of Microsoft's business. It's how technology professionals learn about the company's products, get certified as specialists, and get excited about what its products can do for customers. Delivering the latest courseware to hundreds of certified technical training centers run by the company's channel partners is critical to Microsoft's ability to achieve these goals. It's also an end-to-end business process that Microsoft has successfully outsourced for years.

The business process begins with Microsoft delivering courseware content to its provider, Bertelsmann, and ends with cash remittance back to Microsoft from the sale and delivery of that courseware to the learning centers. It is an integrated management system that includes not just processing and preparing the courseware master files, but jointly forecasting demand and materials requirements. Working from this integrated planning process, Bertelsmann then designs and manages all of the downstream process activities between the process's two end points—courseware and cash. Activities performed include administering the programs and providing customer care; manufacturing, packaging, and distributing the courseware materials; and performing billing and collections.

As courseware has increasingly become an on-demand product, Microsoft and Bertelsmann have teamed with additional companies like Océ to meet specialized production requirements. For example, Bertelsmann produces 60,000 to 80,000 customized training kits every month, ranging from a few dozen to more than 1,000 pages. Software developed by Microsoft in conjunction with Océ, working with Océ document-finishing equipment, is an integral part of the entire process. This network of providers delivers an integrated business process solution for Microsoft in an area that it would otherwise need to invest in and develop its own capabilities.[19,20,21]

Chapter

3

THE OFFSHORE DIMENSION

Taking parts of a company's operation offshore, or *offshoring* as it's commonly called, is certainly not a new idea. The MADE IN CHINA label has appeared on products for decades. As Western companies took their process expertise overseas, and as the global transportation infrastructure developed to make shipping of raw materials, subassemblies, and finished products practical and cost effective, offshore manufacturing became commonplace.

What is new is that the global digital infrastructure built in the 1990s is now making it just as possible to perform information-based activities anywhere in the world and to instantaneously deliver the results anywhere else in the world. This development has essentially made much more of the work of the modern organization "placeless." Designs can be drawn, programs written, bills generated, and customer calls answered just as easily halfway around the world as they can be across the street. The resulting offshoring of knowledge-based work is quickly becoming just as cost-effective and commonplace as it has proven to be for manufacturing in the past.

Companies ranging in size from corporate giants, such as American Express and General Electric, to mid-size CPA firms, software companies, and hospitals are all finding that offshoring, whether through outsourcing or through company-owned captive centers, can dramatically reduce costs while improving quality and increasing an organization's speed, flexibility, and overall capabilities.

Global Markets—Global Sourcing

Today's companies operate and source globally to increase their revenue, reduce their cost structure, increase their company's capabilities, and, in many cases, accomplish all three. Procter & Gamble (P&G), which competes globally and generated about half of its 2003 revenue from its operations outside the Unites States, is a great example of this.[1]

P&G began a pilot program in 2001 to explore the advantages of globally sourcing some of its information technology work, particularly software development. The goal was to create $100 million worth of capability around the world that could be leveraged on-demand by its individual business units. Through the pilot, the work of about 600 people was relocated to lower cost P&G locations in places like Manila, the Philippines, and Warsaw, Poland. Additionally, hundreds of contractor positions were consolidated and taken offshore through outsourcing.

What P&G found was that offshore labor rates were, on average, about one-fifth of those in the United States and other more advanced economies. For example, a contract Java programmer that might cost $98 an hour in Cincinnati costs $20 to $22 dollars an hour in India or the Philippines.

But P&G found that it wasn't just lower local labor rates that created the cost difference; it was also the competition between outside organizations bidding for P&G's work.

The company found that productivity differences were an important contributor as well. Highly educated and well-trained individuals at these locations are extremely motivated to work hard to improve their standard of living—individually, for their families, and for their countries. They are often on the job at 7:00 A.M. local time, handling e-mails before beginning their regular work at 8:00. Similarly, internal meetings and training are typically deferred until the evening hours in order to maximize customer time during the day. It was the rates, competition, and work ethic that combined to create an offshore cost advantage.

Other benefits occurred as well. P&G was able to build a more dynamic operating structure. Resources could be added and removed more quickly. Flexibility, as measured by the percent of the company's information technology workforce that could be ramped up and down on short notice, increased. Economies of scale were created because the program centralized purchasing for skills that could be used by multiple business units. With the ability to objectively measure a provider's processes against standard industry benchmarks, quality increased.

Overall, during the first 12 months of the pilot, P&G saved an estimated $28 million dollars—an important benefit to any company in any economy.[2]

It's a Corporate Campus, Not the Center of the Universe

As P&G found, the sophistication and resources of any one company pale when compared to the world outside its corporate campus.

Microsoft employs about 55,000 of the best and brightest programmers from around the world.[3] But that's still only a tiny fraction of the estimated ten million programmers worldwide.[4] Microsoft's recent investments in offshore capabilities in Hyderabad, India, and in Beijing, China (where one-third of Microsoft's 180 new programmers have Ph.D.s from American universities), reflect its emerging acceptance that Microsoft's Redmond, Washington–based headquarters is not the center of the programming universe.[5]

Bill Gates has said that outsourcing mission-critical work offshore is now "a commonsense proposition."[6] Does that mean that the Redmond campus will shrink dramatically over the coming years? Not likely. What it does mean is that Microsoft will learn from its experiences and expand its offshore program in a consistent, thoughtful way—as long as it continues to add value to the company's business.

General Electric, with its 315,000 employees worldwide, has been offshoring for sometime now. The company began setting up operations in India in the late 1990s. By 2003 there were 22,000 people working for GE in India, processing financial transactions such as receivables, payables, and credit verifications, handling customer calls, and developing software.[7,8]

Companies have to be looking off-campus for solutions. And off-campus has to mean down the street, in a nearby country (what is sometimes called *near-shore outsourcing*), and halfway around the world.

Cost Savings . . .

Cost savings are clearly the most compelling driver for offshoring at this moment. The largest portion of these cost savings typically come from the wage differential between employees in highly developed Western countries and those in the emerging economies, such as Asia and Eastern Europe.

Typical examples of this are:

- Architects, developing blueprints from sketches, earn $250 per month in the Philippines as compared to $3,000 per month in the United States.[9]
- Java programmers in India earn $5,000 per year verses $60,000 per year in the United States.[10]
- Aerospace engineers in Russia earn $650 per month as compared to $6,000 per month for their U.S. equivalents.[11]
- A top electrical engineering graduate in India earns $10,000.[12]
- U.S.-trained and -licensed radiologists in India read X-rays, MRIs, and CT scans for less than half their U.S. counterparts.[13]

Although direct labor costs for offshore workers may be as little as one-tenth those in developed countries, companies should not be seeking savings of the same magnitude. After all, wages are just one part of total labor costs and labor costs are just one part of total costs. Start-up costs are incurred along with additional management and communications costs. On the other hand, certain locations, such as Ireland and Ontario, Canada, offer tax incentives for companies that establish operations there. Taking all of these factors into consideration, net savings are typically in the 20 to 40 percent range—still quite impressive by any measure.[14] British Airways saves nearly $23 million per year for every 1,000 jobs it relocates to India. The company has currently outsourced or established captive offshore centers for most of its call center and ticketing operations. The company's Passenger Revenue Accounting (PRA) operation has become so efficient that it has commercialized its operations and now provides these services for other airlines. Recognizing the ongoing capital requirements of what is now a new growing commercial concern, investment banker Warburg Pincus recently became a majority owner of this previously internal operation.[15]

It's important for everyone—inside and outside Western companies—to note that the underlying wage differentials are not, however, likely to remain what they are today. Upward wage pressures in developing countries combined with competition-driven downward wage pressures in developed countries will work together to reduce the gap. In fact, indications of this can already be seen. For example, the average raises for information technology workers in India in 2003 were 14 percent, the largest in any of the developing countries. This already reflects the growing competition for experienced technology workers in that country.[16] At the same time, a newly formed Vermont-based consortium of independent programmers is billing customers at the very competitive rate of $35 to $50 per hour. This is still two to two and one-half times their Indian counterparts, but one-third to one-half the rate of their large city competitors.[17]

The current appeal of offshoring will continue only as long as it creates value for organizations. Eventually, the companies in India and elsewhere that are the recipients of today's work will find their cost advantage eroding. Some believe that current wage differentials between the West and India will be completely gone by 2020.[18] If changes in exchange rates are added to the equation, it could be even sooner. The natural dynamics of supply and demand, emergence of the next low-cost labor pool, government actions, and the constant drumbeat of new and better technologies will at first reduce and eventually eliminate the current wage differentials.

. . . and More

So, although wage-based cost savings is a strong motivator for looking offshore, it cannot be the only benefit sought. Other benefits must be realized.

One of the most important benefits to offshoring is the creation of an operating structure that can "follow the sun." Global companies are operating somewhere in the world every hour of the day. Customer calls need to be made and received. Invoices need to be generated and payments processed. Software problems need to be worked on in real-time, regardless of the time zone of the user who first encountered it. Restructuring the business's operation into a global web helps do this.

Another benefit that has to be sought is quality. One example where offshoring can produce higher quality, despite the often negative press coverage, is in call centers. Not only are the net costs lower, primarily because the lower wages are far from offset by increases in other costs, but in India, for example, customer service jobs are far more highly prized than they are in the West. While most American call center operators are high school graduates, in India most have college degrees.[19] This reflects the different value that societies at different stages in their development place on various kinds of work. This educational difference, along with a service-oriented culture, enables the best service providers in India to deliver both higher levels of customer service and lower costs.

Competition is another important way that offshoring leads to lower costs and better service. As discussed in Chapter 1, outsourcing by itself yields benefits through the competition of existing operations against well-established providers. When locations around the world are included in the mix, each with its own unique advantage, the bar is raised even higher for everyone, and improvements through competition flourish around the globe.

Offshoring can also create a presence and knowledge in the region that yield other very important advantages—advantages that accrue back to the company's home country, customers, employees, and investors alike.

Offshoring's Value Model

Traditionally, organizations have a home base of operations—a region or country where they began and where their first customers are located. This home, whether in the United States or not, is that organization's reference point when it comes to offshoring. The company views the comparative value to be gained through offshoring relative to that home. This is just as true for a company in China as it is for one in the United States.

In going offshore, the company has the opportunity to change its business in two primary ways: its net costs and its net capabilities. Net costs refer to all of the aspects of its costs that might be impacted by the change, such as labor, support, technology, communications, infrastructure, legal, insurance, and taxes. The resulting cost differential can be positive (it can produce a lower net cost for the organization) or negative (it can produce a higher net cost). At the same time, offshoring will also affect the organization's net capabilities. Capability means all of the operating characteristics of the business, including the volume of work that can be processed, its quality, speed, and flexibility. The effect on the organization's overall capability can also be positive (increase its capability) or negative (decrease it). The combination of these two dimensions—cost and capability—produce four distinct offshore sourcing strategies, each with its own intended impact on the business. (See Figure 3.1.)

The first and most frequently employed strategy is *strategic sourcing*. Strategic sourcing means that the business is seeking both a positive effect on its net costs and a positive effect on its net capabilities. To do this, the location an operation is being moved to must offer a lower overall cost structure for performing that work while not increasing other costs within the business by a greater amount. To increase the business's capabilities, the offshore location must also offer a sufficiently large, highly skilled, and well-supported workforce—one that is able to deliver superior results. Also, the company must be able to effectively manage that

FIGURE 3.1 OFFSHORING OFFERS A RANGE OF STRATEGIC VALUES

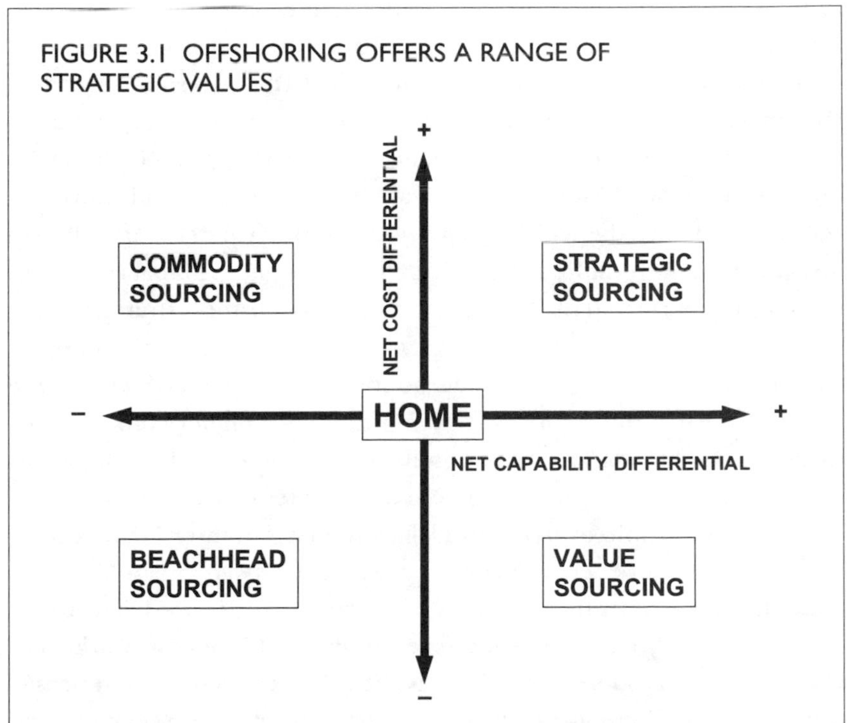

remote operation and successfully integrate it into its overall business structure.

The second strategy is *commodity sourcing*. As the name suggests, here the business is not seeking a simultaneous improvement in costs and capability, but may be quite willing to capture the lower costs even if there's a trade-off resulting in some diminution of its capabilities. Even so, this can be a sound business decision in areas that have become commoditized and where current costs at home are simply out of line with what the market will bear. Commodity sourcing may also be appropriate as a transitional stage where it's expected that, over time, the net capabilities will improve—that is, commodity sourcing leading to strategic sourcing.

Of course, things can work out the other way: a project intended to be strategic fails to deliver the value and devolves into a pure commoditization of the work. This may lead the company to bring some or all of an operation back on-shore or to another locale where a smaller net cost differential may exist but the intended increase in capability is realized. In December 2003 Dell Computer very publicly brought some customer support for its corporate clients back to the United States from India in response to customer complaints over the quality of service they were receiving.[20] Does this mean that Dell is abandoning offshoring and outsourcing? Certainly not. What it means is that Dell is responding to its customers, adjusting its business, learning from the experience, and planning for future improvements. Insiders say that Dell actually didn't reduce its overall workforce in India at all. At the same time this work was brought back into the United States, work in other parts of its call center operations were shifted to India. Dell was flexing its global resources, not moving away from offshoring as a necessary business strategy.

There are also two valid strategies where the net cost differential is negative but offshoring still makes good business sense. *Value sourcing* takes place when the company is willing to absorb higher costs in order to gain access to an improvement in its net capabilities. The company is willing to pay a premium to gain access to greater capabilities.

A great example of this is the Chinese manufacturer Haier Group and its recently opened refrigerator manufacturing plant in Camden, South Carolina. Essentially, Haier is offshoring to the United States. The company actually pays U.S. workers ten times what it does its workers in China, and while some of that cost is offset by reduced shipping costs, not all of it is. There are really two key benefits Haier is seeking. First, proximity enables the company to respond more quickly to American retailers who stock little inventory and expect just-in-time delivery of product. Second, the company is gaining important brand visibility in the United States—visibility that will be critical to the company as it begins to go head-to-head in the consumer appliance market with major American household labels, such as Whirlpool and Maytag.[21]

The final strategy created by the blending of costs and capabilities is *beachhead sourcing.* Here, the company initially expects neither a net cost nor a net capability advantage. Then why go offshore at all? The reason, as the name suggests, is that the organization is seeking to establish a beachhead in that offshore location. It believes that, over time, it will be able to work toward a net positive cost differential, net positive capacity differential, or both, and that when it achieves these ends the investment will prove well worth it.

It's a Tool, Not a Panacea

The fact that offshore operations and outsourcing, used separately or in combination, can add to the success of an organization is well established. However, just because the potential is there doesn't mean that every organization will realize it. Offshoring and outsourcing are not panaceas—they carry their own set of challenges and risks. Problems can and do occur, and, as already discussed, companies can get less or more out of the program than they expect.

When American Express first began outsourcing its call centers, it found that the performance of the outsourced operations for high-end customer interactions was quite poor, abandoned the project, and pulled the work back in-house. On the other hand, it found that the performance of outsourced call centers for simpler customer interactions was actually better than at its internal centers. In particular, these outside operators did a better job of up-selling callers on additional American Express products and services. As a result, that part of the project quickly took root and grew rapidly.[22]

The right questions then are: How might offshore outsourcing specifically create value for my company at this time? How can we test the approach and build experience? Are we prepared to abandon failures while increasing our investment in successes?

In the end, organizations should probably not outsource unless they are prepared to make an ongoing investment of time and talent to learn how to create and leverage long-term relationships with outside companies—relationships that will become an integral part of their strategic, tactical, financial, and social fabric. Similarly, organizations should probably not go offshore unless they are prepared to make the investment needed to learn how to successfully integrate elements of businesses running at significant distances and under differing cultural and legal frameworks. It goes without saying, then, that they should not outsource offshore unless they are prepared to do both.

Most successful companies take a longer-term view of the value of offshore outsourcing and are building toward advantages that go well beyond near-term cost savings. When GE entered the Indian market more than a decade ago, it went there to make and sell products locally. The company recognized that it could not be competitive in India at the cost levels prevalent in its other operations. It also realized that India was an emerging market and that the local capabilities would develop over time. It turned out that GE's business in India never really developed as expected. However, what the company did find was a base for strategically sourcing back-office operations that today is central to its worldwide operations. GE became a pioneer in offshoring because it sought one advantage, didn't find it, but, by creating a presence, was able to recognize and capture and unanticipated advantage that has, in the long-run, proved extremely important to the company's overall success.[23]

Finding the Value

Where should you be looking to find the value from offshoring?

The answer to that question is unique to every company and every situation. Later chapters will provide more specific guidance on working through the evaluation and selection process. There is, however, a great deal to learn from the collected experience of others. Figure 3.2 captures this experience on a single chart for information technology and information technology–enabled activities, such as back-office operations and call centers. It reflects the experience of others along two dimensions: (1) the attractiveness of locations based on such factors as cost, infrastructure, culture, language, stability, outsourcing experience,

FIGURE 3.2 INDIA IS TOP OFFSHORE DESTINATION—TODAY

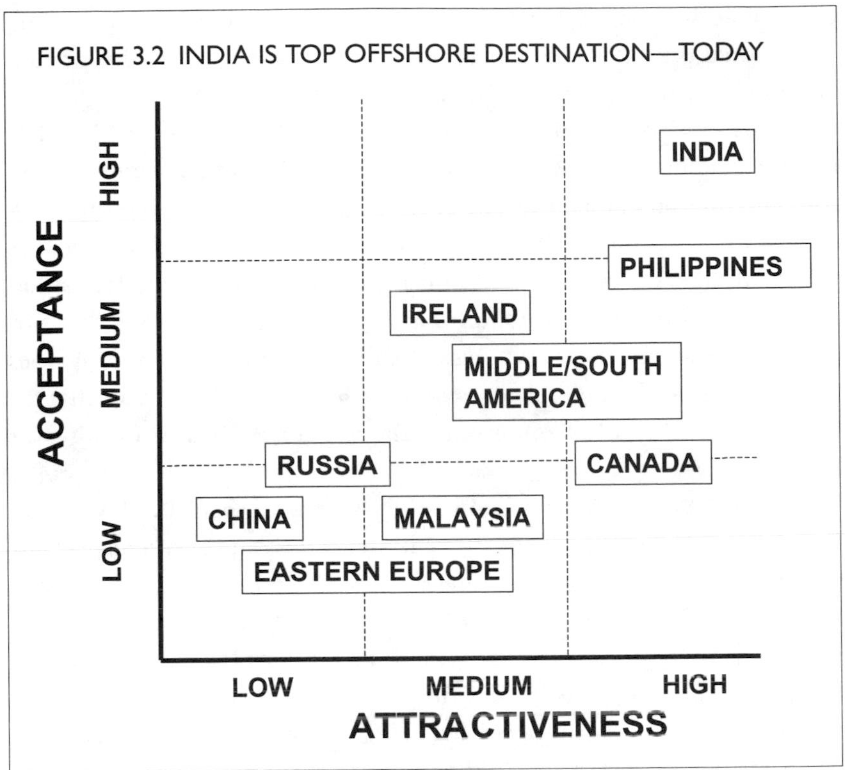

Source: Composite for IT and IT-enabled services, developed from multiple sources, including A.T. Kearney, The Capco Institute, ISANI, JDalal Associates

local management skills, tax implications, intellectual property, security, and the size of the labor market; and (2) the acceptance by Western companies of outsourcing to these countries based on the country's share of the current offshore market for these services.

India is clearly the preferred destination of most companies, rating the highest in both attractiveness and market share. Most experts rate it very high for its cost, quality, availability of skills, language, infrastructure, and experience. At the same time, it dominates the market from the customer's perspective with as much as a 70 percent market share in many studies.

Second in offshoring preference is the Philippines, with great language skills, infrastructure, and cultural compatibility but fewer skilled individuals, a slightly higher risk profile, and less experience as an outsourcing destination. However, since no one likes being second, the

Philippines is becoming increasingly competitive toward India creating exceptional opportunities for companies looking for aggressive pricing and other terms.

Canada is possibly the most overlooked "offshore" destination, but that is changing quickly. Canada has lower costs than other Western countries and, although it may not be able to match India on this score, it offers all of the cultural, risk, infrastructure, and security characteristics that a Western executive would find in his or her home country. Additionally, provinces such as Ontario are offering tax incentives that further lower the effective costs of establishing operations for certain types of businesses. It's reasonable to expect offshoring to Canada, or what for U.S. companies would be more near-shoring, to grow dramatically over the next years.

Ireland, Central America, and South America, especially Mexico and Brazil, are in the mid-range for both attractiveness and acceptance. They are, however, moving in opposite directions. Ireland has been losing share, especially in the call center field, to India, whereas South America is just beginning to gain acceptance among Western businesses. Malaysia is another emerging country offering cost levels similar to the other developing countries, currently with far less outsourcing experience.

Russia, Eastern Europe, and China are also emerging countries in this field. Although there are challenges in each of these countries, each is receiving a great deal of attention, and Western companies are establishing beachheads in these locations in anticipation of rapid growth and other future advantages.

Of course, generalizations like these hide many details. The countries themselves are not homogeneous. The opportunities in St. Petersburg are very different than in Moscow. In India, the cities of Bangalore, Chennai, Mumbai, and Delhi offer very different opportunities. Most recently, companies are beginning to examine opportunities in tier-two cities in India—cities such as Jaipur, Chandigarh, Kochi, Mangalore, and Jalandhar—where wage rates are still extremely low.[24]

There are also a wide range of other locations to consider that haven't been mentioned, many established and others still developing, including Australia and New Zealand, the Caribbean, South Africa, and Iceland. Every country has its own unique advantages and opportunities. A company can follow the well-traveled path to India, the Philippines, or China, or it can try less-traveled but possibly more rewarding alternatives.

As one would expect, the opportunity map looks very different for different services. It also looks very different depending upon the company's home country. For example, for Japanese companies, China is a near-shore locale with a very different profile in terms of culture, language, and risks than what's seen from the United States or Europe. In fact, many believe that China's first big moves in outsourcing will be as a near-shore destination for companies in the Asia-Pacific region. China may then use these early successes to build up the needed capabilities to eventually rival India among Western companies.

All of these developments can directly affect the types and timing of opportunities for Western companies and how they should be thinking about the future shape of the emerging global outsourcing economy. Early involvement, even if only on a limited scale to gain a presence and understanding, can quickly become a springboard for significant opportunities.

Putting the Jobs Issue in Perspective

For all the reasons discussed, taking operations offshore, in general, and offshore outsourcing, in particular, are receiving unprecedented attention—in the executive suites of both customer and provider companies; in the reports and recommendations of consultants; in countries like India that are recipients of much of the new business; in the Western media; and in U.S. politics. Some argue that offshoring is one of the most important opportunities for improving businesses performance and therefore the overall economy available today; others argue that it's yet another example of companies seeking short-term gains at the expense of both employees and customers.

The impact of lost jobs and the very real problems and emotions that result are painfully real. There is nothing anyone can say to someone who is out of work, not sure where his next job will be, and is having trouble paying the bills that will convince him that what is happening is "good." At the personal level, it is wrong and insensitive to even attempt to do so. Companies are beginning to recognize this and to set aside some of the savings from offshore outsourcing for retraining and transition services for former employees. For example, IBM has a $25 million fund set aside for this purpose. It's a start, and it represents the kind of practical, right-now action needed to help those caught in the middle of these changes.

Acknowledging this, we do, however, also need to be looking at macroeconomics. When we do, the issue seems to come down to this question: Do productive, competitive companies create economic growth and jobs, or does protecting current jobs best ensure a strong economy and prosperity? In many ways, it's a debate between the institutional form of capitalism more prevalent in Europe—where businesses are protected as institutions, and where jobs are treated as acquired rights—and the entrepreneurial form of capitalism that has been the hallmark of the United States—where any business that no longer meets the needs of the market vanishes to be replaced by a new one, and where employment-at-will dominates the job scene.

Entrepreneurial capitalism is more vibrant but less predictable. And, though we can't predict exactly what the future will look like, we can gain comfort from the past. We've been at inflection points like this before, most recently as manufacturing jobs went offshore over the past three decades and were replaced by today's services industries. What happened? Not only did the U.S. economy not falter, it powered ahead in dramatic fashion. (See Figure 3.3.) While the number of services jobs more than doubled over that period (with manufacturing jobs declining on both a percentage of employment and in real terms), the U.S.'s GDP almost tripled. Spending on research and development went up two and one-half times, and per capita income rose by more than 80 percent. While some may argue that the offshore migration of manufacturing jobs was bad for the U.S. economy, the data simply doesn't support the argument. One thing we can be sure of is that the entrepreneurial spirit is still alive and well and will flourish if allowed.

The economic success of offshoring means that in addition to directing some of the savings toward enabling workers to be part of the future, it's equally important that companies use savings from outsourcing and offshoring to not just maintain, but to increase spending on research and development. Costs of current operations in developed countries are beginning to eat into R&D spending, which could have a disastrous impact on individual companies and developed economies overall. One warning sign of this can be seen in recent data on R&D spending by U.S. software companies. The level of R&D spending by software companies actually fell by 2 percent in 2002 after having consistently grown by 15

FIGURE 3.3 AS MANUFACTURING WENT OFFSHORE, THE U.S. ECONOMY BOOMED

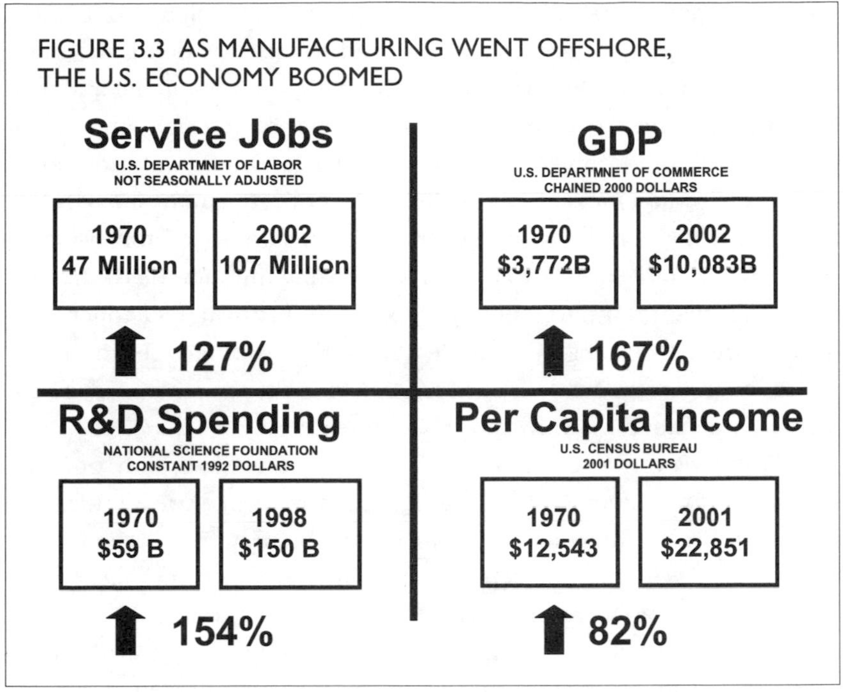

percent per year throughout the late 1990s and early 2000s.[25] One reason for this drop-off is that software companies are being squeezed by the escalating support costs of maintaining their current installed base. Outsourcing and offshoring lower-end tasks to low-cost locales will free critical dollars and talent for reinvestment.

While the arguments for economic doom and gloom are simply not supported by the facts, and historical precedent suggests that exactly the opposite will be the final outcome, many individuals are faced with the hard reality that jobs are being eliminated and that their skills may not be as competitive in an increasingly globally sourced job market as they had been in the past. We need to understand and address this problem in very real, very personal terms. Just as companies have no guarantee that they can sell the same products and services tomorrow at the same prices they do today, none of us, as employees, have a guarantee that we can command the same salary tomorrow for the same skills we now have. Competition may be uncomfortable, it may even be painful, but it also forces all of us to get better and smarter.

Some may not be willing or able to rise to the challenge of competition in a global job market and will find themselves doing the same work for less money. But many more will find ways to compete and win. They will earn their current and higher salaries by getting better, learning new skills, and doing so ahead of the pack. Others will move away from the more technical parts of their jobs entirely toward elements of their jobs where they add greater value, for example, customer-facing activities. Still others will find themselves moving into new fields that use their skills in entirely different ways. For example, through October 2003 health care and social services added 255,000 jobs, while jobs in private educational services increased by 56,000 during the same period.[26] These are just two examples, with many more to emerge.

If history is any teacher, there will be a period of disruption, one that will be painful. But, in the end, the U.S. economy will, if we let it, generate even more exciting, higher-paying jobs within new fields. The United States enjoys a uniquely entrepreneurial form of capitalism that sets the country apart from many others. Along with focusing tremendous energy on working through the change, comes the need to let go of the past. Think of the labor force transitions the United States has seen in the past 150 years—from mining to factory work to developing computer software. With each transition has come incredible progress and a greater understanding of the benefits of change.

Most of all, we need the leaders in the private and the public sectors to be open and honest with everyone, especially employees, about current trends, expectations, and plans. We need to begin to come together to develop a blueprint for moving forward. We need to encourage real debate about how we go about building the future. Leaders need to help workers honestly assess their marketability in an increasingly global economy. And we all need to be asking ourselves if we have the right skills for tomorrow and how we are going to develop them. Full transparency on all of these issues is the only way we can move forward, together.

What really matters is how leaders use the current opportunity available to them to build more productive and more competitive organizations and to help individuals prepare for the future. Done right, the result will be organizations that are able to continue to generate economic growth into the future, and a workforce that continues to be the envy of the world.

Summary

Organizations are leveraging capabilities around the world to improve their operations and the products and services they deliver to their customers. Offshoring began with manufacturing, but over the past few years it has quickly spread to information-based work. The result is that most of the work of the modern organization is now "placeless." Just as offshore manufacturing increased the amount and quality of products we enjoy while simultaneously reducing prices, the same is happening as these new areas go offshore.

Wage differentials are a big driver for offshoring, but not the only one. Global operations need to run seamlessly 24 hours a day, seven days a week. This follow-the-sun strategy of global operating centers fits the needs of most multinationals. Quality can also be improved when better skilled workers can be employed for jobs that are not as highly valued in Western countries. Offshoring can create a presence enabling the company to sell more products and services into that market than it could otherwise.

There are a wide range of locations and value propositions for outsourcing that must be evaluated. As organizations look offshore, they need to decide how best to capture the comparative value—by creating operations of their own, what are now commonly called captive centers, or through outsourcing. Offshoring is now an integral part of outsourcing, and outsourcing is an integral part of the globalization of businesses.

Offshoring is not, however, without controversy. Many individuals and groups in the West vehemently oppose the practice, primarily because of its impact on jobs. Although protecting current jobs may feel like the right thing to do, protectionist approaches have never worked to the benefit of the economy overall, and the same is true for offshoring. The far better approach is to use this opportunity to make our current organizations and overall economy more productive and competitive. In so doing, we create more prosperity and jobs, not less.

Outsourcing, in combination with business process outsourcing and offshoring, provides executives the most powerful tools yet for creating rapid and dramatic improvements in their businesses. Options abound in terms of what to offshore, and how and where to create the relationships.

Subsequent chapters map out the practical approaches for capturing this value. But for now, the following are clear:

- Offshoring represents an irrefutable opportunity for organizations to reduce costs and improve other aspects of their operations.
- The benefits are not automatic, and management needs to exercise real care in the planning and implementation of these initiatives.
- The impact on Western economies and workers is far from all bad, as many in the media would have us believe.

Case Study: Thomas Cook

U.K.-based Thomas Cook, owned by Lufthansa, is the leader in leisure travel in Europe, and it is one of the top three companies in the world in its industry. The company provides between 16 million and 20 million holidays per year.

In 2001 Thomas Cook, although a leader in its industry, was operating at a loss. Its recent exit from the financial services business had left it with a cost base that was unsustainable in the leisure travel business where margins are wafer-thin, often in the 1 to 2 percent range. In response, a companywide transformational program was launched, including changing the company's leadership, its strategy, its core processes, revitalizing its 162-year-old culture, restructuring its business operations, and increasing its investment in marketing and branding.

Shared services, strategic sourcing, and global business process outsourcing all played an essential role in this overall change agenda. Shared services meant centralizing many of the company's business functions along with control over their costs. Strategic sourcing meant dramatically reducing the number of suppliers the company worked with—there were, at the time, 37,000—and getting those that the company retained to operate as business partners with a shared interest in helping Thomas Cook not only recover, but grow. Global business process outsourcing meant selecting strategic partners with global reach who could leverage skill and cost advantages from around the world to Thomas Cook's benefit.

Thomas Cook entered into global business process outsourcing relationships with a number of companies. Accenture was selected as the company's strategic partner for its shared services center, for selected processes within that center, and for its migration to SAP. Netherlands-based PinkRoccade was selected for information technology desktop management. Syntel, an Indian-based technology firm, was selected for legacy computer system maintenance.

Thomas Cook also offshored and outsourced its ticketing and invoicing processes to Lufthansa's center in India. Other more traditional outsourcing relationships were created for catering, facilities maintenance, mail distribution, and other parts of the business.

In total, these programs yielded savings of £140 million in their first year and an improvement in the company's pretax profits of £93 million. The offshore relationships with Syntel contributed a 53 percent savings to this, and the relationship with Lufthansa yielded a 41 percent savings.[27]

Chapter

4

A NEW OUTSOURCING VALUE MODEL

The opportunities available through global business process outsourcing are immense. Increases in productivity and competitiveness in the order of 10- to 100-fold are achievable. Capturing this magnitude of improvement, however, requires a far more strategic approach to outsourcing than has been common in most organizations so far.

Traditionally, outsourcing has been approached as a reactive, operational-level intervention. That is, outsourcing has been connected to specific initiatives for change, such as reductions in costs, headcount, or improvements in returns on invested capital. These initiatives, in turn, have been typically justified by the need to respond to changes in the organization's competitive environment, its revenues, or its level of funding. At the same time, the specific outsourcing decisions made have tended to be operationally driven. While senior management has certainly encouraged outsourcing and has been called upon to approve the selected candidate areas, it is less likely to be involved in setting the framework and guiding the analysis leading to those recommendations.

This relatively tactical approach to outsourcing has certainly been effective in achieving the specific outcomes sought. At the same time, it has done little to capture the immense power global business process outsourcing has to create truly differentiating competitive advantages across an organization. This traditional intervention-based approach to outsourcing has also contributed to much of the organizational resistance we see to it. If outsourcing is simply a tool chosen to affect a specific outcome, why was it selected over others available? Seldom has outsourcing been explained as an integral part of creating sustainable competitive advantage in today's hyper-competitive global economy. The failure to position outsourcing this way has caused some to see it as an arbitrary choice that is perhaps based on other, even hidden, agenda items.

Today's increased awareness and visibility of outsourcing actually creates a unique opportunity for leaders to change this thought pattern. Outsourcing is now part of the public mindset. It's an open debate that is taking place around every water cooler and on every TV news show. A more comprehensive and integrated approach to global business process outsourcing is now possible, and companies like American Express, Dell, P&G, Cisco, Ericsson, GE, and others who have already done so are seeing real rewards.

New thinking and new approaches to global BPO are needed. If global business process outsourcing is to become a source of competitive advantage, then it has to become part of every organization's strategic planning process. If half of executives believe that the greatest value of outsourcing is something other than cost savings, then a more robust value model is required. If more than 70 percent of the typical organization is likely to be outsourced within 10 to 20 years, then perhaps zero-based and just-in-time sourcing needs to take its place alongside zero-based and just-in-time budgeting as a management principle. If organizations are going to be competing internal operations against outside sources, then a more market-driven approach to making these decisions is needed. Finally, if global BPO is truly the future shape of business, then outsourcing management needs to become a discipline in its own right.

This new set of management principles are a natural and necessary outgrowth of the enormous and increasing importance global business process outsourcing will have on the operations of organizations of every kind. (See Figure 4.1.) Taken together, these principles represent a comprehensive approach to rethinking the entire sourcing model of the organization. Some of them stand alone and others overlap and complement each other. Adopting them will help to move the organization toward a more focused operating structure—one that is better suited for today's and tomorrow's realities.

FIGURE 4.1 FIVE PRINCIPLES FOR CAPTURING THE VALUE OF GLOBAL OUTSOURCING

1 - **SOURCING AS STRATEGY**
SEEKING COMPETITIVE ADVANTAGE FROM INTERNAL SOURCES, EXTERNAL SOURCES, AND THE COMBINATION OF THE TWO

2 - **EXPANDING THE VALUE MODEL**
GBPO VALUE = ((BUSINESS CASE) x (ACCELERATION + FLEXIBILITY)) ^{INNOVATION}

3 - **ZERO-BASED SOURCING**
SOURCING DECISIONS MADE FROM A BASE OF ZERO EVERY PLANNING CYCLE

4 - **MARKET-DRIVEN DECISIONS**
ESTABLISHING BEST SOURCE THROUGH OPEN COMPETITION

5 - **OUTSOURCING AS A MANAGEMENT DISCIPLINE**
INVESTING IN TRAINING, PERSONAL DEVELOPMENT, AND TOOLS AS WOULD FOR ANY VALUED MANAGEMENT SKILL

Sourcing as Strategy

Traditionally, organizations have seen only one source of competitive advantage: their internal operations. However, outsourcing opens up brand new sources of competitive advantage. Some of these new competitive advantages come directly from the outside partners, others come from the competition-driven continuous improvement that outsourcing generates in the organization's support functions, and still others are found in unique ways the organization blends its inside and outside operations to create new solutions for its customers. All of this can happen, however, if and only if sourcing is elevated to a level of importance where it becomes part of the organization's overall strategic planning process.

Strategic planning basically is the process of determining what's happening today and what is likely to happen in the future in the markets the organization may serve. From there, it goes on to determining which segments of those markets the organization will serve and how, and just as importantly, from where its competitive advantage in doing so will come. This strategic plan then guides the organization's operating plans and investment decisions.

In establishing their competitive advantage, organizations typically look to a cost-based advantage, a differentiation-based advantage, or a focus-based advantage—one that enables them to combine elements of both in meeting the needs of a specific customer segment. Cost advantages generally work best in markets where customers are not likely to perceive a differentiation in the product or service for which they are willing to pay. In cost-driven markets rapid commoditization—achieving ever lower and lower prices—becomes the competitive edge most organizations seek. Differentiation, on the other hand, generally works best in markets where customers are likely to recognize a distinctive quality of the organization's products and services for which they will pay a premium. Design, features, performance, quality, ease of use, prestige, speed, customer service, and unique product or service guarantees are all examples of the kinds of differentiation-based competitive advantages an organization might seek. Focus-based strategies work best when the organization believes it can achieve a sustainable competitive advantage by performing different activities than its competitors or performing similar activities in a different way—ways that will be particularly well tuned to that specific set of customers' preferences and loyalties. In these markets the organization often seeks a mix of competitive advantages based on both cost and differentiation.

What sourcing as strategy does is change when, in the strategic planning process, the question of the sources of these competitive advantages gets asked. Is the source of the organization's competitive advantages only its internal knowledge, know-how, and resources? Or, is the source of its competitive advantage found in the combination of its unique internal capabilities with those developed through its network of outside relationships? To make sourcing a strategy, organizations map the markets they plan to serve, the competitive advantages they seek, and the sources of those competitive advantages, both inside and outside the organization. (See Figure 4.2.) This makes sourcing as strategy a powerful tool for improving the organization's ability to serve its customers, to compete, and to grow.

Sourcing as strategy also means that by asking these questions as part of the strategic planning process, the answers guide the organization's investment decisions. Internal investments are made only in those areas that deliver a unique competitive advantage when done internally; external investments are made only in those relationships that provide

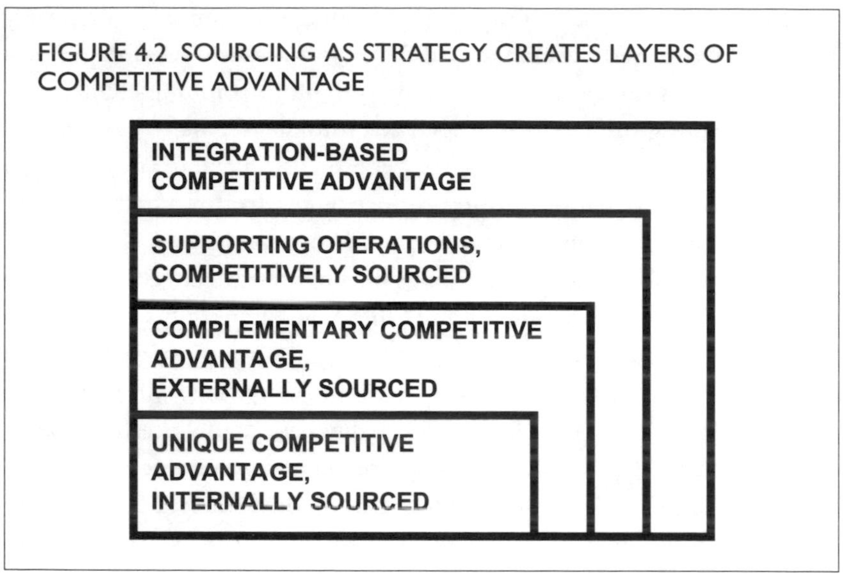

FIGURE 4.2 SOURCING AS STRATEGY CREATES LAYERS OF COMPETITIVE ADVANTAGE

added, complementary competitive advantages; and additional investments get made in activities that enable the organization to uniquely blend the two. All other activities that are necessary but offer little or no opportunity for competitive advantage are operationally sourced on a strictly competitive basis. If the most efficient source is internal, then that's where the work gets done; if it's external, then that's where it goes.

The result of sourcing as strategy is that the organization no longer broadly allocates resources across its entire organization, leaving the sourcing decisions up to the downstream operational managers. Instead, the senior leadership directs sourcing decisions as part of the organization's overall strategy for competitive advantage in the markets it intends to serve.

One example of this kind of thinking can be found at American Express. American Express has one of the most recognized and highly respected brands in the world. The American Express brand conveys quality, unparalleled and guaranteed dependability, and prestige, as well as other attributes that make it one of the company's most highly valued sources of competitive advantage. As a result, when American Express examines its sources of competitive advantage, activities that directly strengthen the brand's image and raise brand awareness are top areas for internal investment. At the same time, the company strategically invests in outside relationships that provide it highly valuable and complementary competitive advantages in selected market segments. The company's relationship with airline partners, such as Delta Airlines, and selected publications, such as *Fortune* magazine, provide it complementary competitive advantages in research and development, product design, marketing, and sales for those specific customer segments.[1]

Sweden-based Ericsson is another example of sourcing as strategy. Over the past few years the company has repositioned its internal source of competitive advantage away from its product design and manufacturing operations toward its services operations. It has brought in Sony as a strategic partner for the design of its multimedia products, Flextronics as its manufacturing partner, and IBM and Hewlett-Packard have been brought in to operate its information technology systems. At the same time, the company has invested internally in its services capabilities, thereby developing a new source of unique competitive advantage that is enabling the company to win major multiyear contracts operating telephony networks for its customers. Similarly, companies such as IBM and Nortel have used sourcing as strategy to move selected manufacturing operations to specialized partners while redirecting internal investments in other areas of unique, internally sourced competitive advantage.[2]

Organizations that fail to adopt sourcing as strategy often find themselves underperforming the competition. Whereas their competitors get better and better at creating competitive advantage by leveraging the capabilities available through a global network of resources, these firms continue to compete for the same customers using only the competitive advantages they can generate from their own internal operations.

In a later chapter, we'll see how companies go about making outsourcing part of their organization's strategic planning process.

Expanding the Value Model

Each decision an organization makes needs to be justified financially. Most decisions are justified because they reduce costs, increase revenue, improve return on assets, or accomplish some combination of these. Financial models for projecting these benefits and for guiding management decision making range from straight dollar comparisons to return on investment, internal rates of return, return on assets, scenario planning, economic value added, and many more. Each method is intended to focus management's attention on the factors most important to the organization's success. Because of this, organizations tend to select one or more of these methods for their financial decision making—ones that are consistent with their unique operations and preferences.

As discussed in Chapter 1, at the macro level, global business process outsourcing is part of a necessary restructuring of organizations. However, at the micro level, or at the level of each specific outsourcing decision, the benefits to the organization must be carefully projected and measured. Chapter 1 also introduced the important idea that outsourcing does not deliver just a single benefit—cost savings—but a hierarchy of benefits that includes costs savings, greater focus on core processes, a more variable cost structure, access to skills, speed to market, improved quality, capital conservation, revenue growth, and innovation.

Depending upon the financial analysis tools used by an organization and the assumptions it makes, many of these benefits may be captured in the base business case for outsourcing. At the same time, some of the most important benefits of outsourcing may not be captured at all. For example, how much value does the business case place on achieving a more variable cost structure, accelerating the overall operation thereby enabling it to introduce future improvements faster, and increasing the level of innovation producing brand new ideas and methods? If these factors are not reflected in the business case for outsourcing then they can essentially become footnotes to both the decision itself and to the way the relationship is managed over time. What organizations measure, they achieve. What goes unmeasured goes unmanaged.

For outsourcing to be approached more strategically, an expanded value model that captures some of these more important and yet hard to quantify benefits is needed. The following value model offers one way of understanding, measuring, and capturing these much larger business benefits. It is not intended to change the formal business case that the organization uses to book its financials, but it is intended to help executives put a quantifiable dimension on the full potential available to them through outsourcing. By bringing this greater level of quantification to the entire hierarchy of outcomes, better decisions can be made and management attention can be better directed toward ensuring that the intended benefits are actually realized.

This expanded model for gauging the value of global business process outsourcing is:

$$\textbf{GBPOV} = [(\textbf{Business case}) \times (\textbf{Acceleration} + \textbf{Flexibility})]^{\textbf{Innovation}}$$

That is, the full value of global business process outsourcing (GBPOV) is the traditional business case multiplied by the ongoing improvement to the organization's acceleration and flexibility, all raised to the power of innovation.

The traditional business case captures the project's impact on costs, revenues, and assets in whatever form the organization would normally use. (Approaches for developing this based business case are presented in Section II.) Acceleration is, then, one of the two factors that can have a multiplying affect on that base business case. Acceleration comes about through global business process outsourcing when new technologies, processes, and skills become available to the organization faster through its relationship with the service provider than if it had to operate on its own. One way of gauging this acceleration is to look at where the organization has been operating historically on the technology curve for that activity: Has it over the past few years, been ahead of, at, six months behind, or many years behind the state-of-the-art technologies available for doing the work? Where will it be in the future through its outsourcing relationship? Will it be operating at that same spot in the technology curve, or will it be operating at a point that is closer to the state-of-the-art, at the state-of-the-art, or even slightly ahead of it? The same questions can be applied to the other factors of process and skill.

This approach makes gauging the value of outsourcing a forward-looking process. The immediate improvements in these areas have already been built into the base business case. The focus here is on how ongoing improvements will create additional value for the organization in the future. This is a crucial point for several reasons, chief of which is that it focuses the expanded business case, management attention, and the provider's attention on sustaining a continuing level of investments in technologies, people, and processes that produces an ongoing acceleration of the business's ability to integrate and leverage new capabilities. Using this approach, outsourcing decisions can be made based on the ongoing value to be created, not just on the current gap between where the organization is and where it could be.

Flexibility is the second multiplier of the base business case. Flexibility is measured in terms of the percent of the organization's resources that can be increased and decreased in response to changes in its business and needs. This flexibility to adjust to future changes helps ensure that the originally anticipated benefits are actually realized. After all, how often are the benefits of a project never fully realized because changes in the environment offset those benefits before implementation even occurred? Flexibility projects the increased capacity of the organization to change in response to its environment. It's a highly desirable, yet seldom measured characteristic and one of the most important potential benefits of outsourcing. Taken together, acceleration and flexibility act as multipliers of the base business case.

The final factor added to the expanded value model is innovation. Innovation can be measured as the number of new ideas that are identified and implemented over a given period of time. When two or more organizations are brought together through outsourcing, they bring separate and distinct specialties to the relationship. These specialties interact in new and unanticipated ways. The result, if sought and managed properly, can be an ongoing flow of new solutions to old problems and unexpected solutions to problems and opportunities yet encountered. Innovation is included in the value model as an exponential factor. Although the level of increased innovation must be conservatively forecasted—its impact can be dramatic.

What is the result of using the expanded model for considering the business impact of outsourcing? Let's say that the base business case is $25 million, but that new technologies, peoples, and processes are projected to come online twice as fast as what the organization has been able to do in the past. Similarly, assume that the operation will become twice as flexible, that it will be better able to ramp up and down in response to changes in the business. Finally, a 10 percent increase in the number of new ideas generated and new ways of doing things may be expected. The net effect of these factors in terms of business value from this global business process outsourcing decision makes the business case not the $25 million base case, but almost $160 million in total potential value:

$$[(\$25\text{mm}) \times (2 + 2)]^{1.1} = \$158.5\text{mm}$$

What an expanded value model does is give executives a way to project and measure the total effect of outsourcing on the business. It helps them manage the project toward achieving not just the direct savings and revenue improvements anticipated, but the possibly even more important effects of acceleration, flexibility, and innovation.

There is some risk, however. Historically, outsourcing projects have been justified and executed without any real attention to the importance of acceleration, flexibility, and innovation. If these factors are not made part of the value equation from the beginning—and if the project is not managed to achieve them—then they are likely to go unrealized. The basic savings and revenue goals may be achieved, but a lot of hard work will be done to realize essentially the same value that other more traditional approaches might have generated. This means that if the effort cannot be structured so that acceleration, flexibility, and innovation are included, then the justification for moving forward with outsourcing is significantly less. The business may still get the cost savings or the revenue boost, but it may have been able to get there following a much easier path.

Even worse, if outsourcing is approached and managed in such a way that the company's acceleration, flexibility, and innovation are actually reduced, then the value of the savings and revenue improvements achieved will be reduced as well. Global business process outsourcing will have become a trade-off of one set of benefits for another set of limitations. In the most extreme cases, if the project ends up slowing the business, making it less flexible or less innovative, then the real value realized may drop below zero.

Finally, the suggested value model is not intended to provide results that the CFO can book, nor directly reflect in the company's balance sheet—that's the purpose of the base business case. What using the expanded value model does do is provide executives a more quantifiable way of thinking about, planning for, and capturing the full potential impact that outsourcing can have on their business. It focuses attention on the entire value-creation potential of the project, helps executives rank their projects in a more holistic way, maintains focus on the whole value proposition, and provides a vehicle for measuring and comparing results against expectations.

Zero-Based Sourcing

The third new management principle that flows from a more strategic approach to global business process outsourcing borrows a page out of the budgeting text book and is called *zero-based sourcing.* Just as organizations have used newer budgeting approaches, such as zero-based budgeting, to improve the linkage between their goals and how they spend their money, new approaches to how organizations go about making sourcing decisions are needed as well.

Sourcing, just like budgeting, has traditionally been done assuming that the recent past is a good predictor for the near future. That is, that future types and levels of internal sourcing will generally match current ones with some incremental adjustments up and down in response to specific changes in the business climate. But, just as this traditional approach to budgeting has given way to newer ones, global business process outsourcing requires that organizations rethink this traditional approach to sourcing.

Zero-based budgeting requires that the funding of each and every part of the organization's operation be fully re-justified at each planning cycle from an assumed base of zero. Zero-based sourcing, then, means that the sourcing decision for each and every aspect of the business's operation be re-justified at every business planning cycle from a base of zero. The fact that an area of the business's operation is internally sourced today does not predetermine how it will be sourced in the future. With zero-based sourcing, the source for every part of the business's operation is routinely retested against the business's needs and the marketplace of available sources, and that retesting takes place with every business planning cycle.

The question then becomes, If we were starting this business from scratch today, how would we source that work? Are new competitors internally sourcing the same things we are, or have they identified new, external sources to leverage their competitive advantage?

Adopting zero-based sourcing as a management practice can help move the organization down the path toward an optimal sourcing strategy much quicker. It frees the organization from the need to justify changes against an assumption of the status quo. It puts every part of the organization on notice that its subject to the same testing at every planning cycle. Just as brand-new parts of the organization are sourced from a blank piece of paper, existing parts of the operation are sourced the same way. Outsourcing is no longer positioned as an intervention directed toward specific parts of the business because of implied problems; it becomes seen as part of the regular strategic planning process, just like capital allocation and budgeting.

Zero-based sourcing is, of course, not the only new approach that can be borrowed for the world of budgeting. Another one is just-in-time sourcing. Here, the organization adopts a continuous sourcing analysis that is performed throughout the planning period and takes place on a project-by-project basis. Current sourcing decisions are considered to last only as long as the projects that created them. In fact, shared services centers are often managed exactly this way, with the organization's internal customers free to take their business on a project-by-project basis to the source they believe can best contribute to the outcomes they seek—whether inside or outside the organization. Shared services centers essentially compete for the internal customer's business on a day-in and day-out basis.

These approaches suggest that all parts of a business's operation—including those internally and externally sourced—need to be constantly tested against the marketplace of sources emerging worldwide. Any delay in identification and consideration of these new sources can contribute to higher costs and reduced competitive positioning. Adopting zero-based sourcing can accelerate the process of change and, thus, better recognize any rapidly emerging opportunities.

In evaluating which of these sourcing approaches to adopt, organizations first should look at how quickly their business environment is changing relative to the costs of re-justifying its current sourcing decisions. Certainly these newer approaches will not be the best use of resources for every organization. But for those organizations that already recognize the need to respond to an increasingly hyper-competitive environment, these approaches can accelerate the needed changes and bring about an understanding and adjustment to the new business realities that much sooner.

Market-Driven Decision Making

A market-driven approach to sourcing means that the organization's sourcing decisions are in direct response to the capabilities of the marketplace of available providers. Where the organization's internal capabilities are superior to the marketplace of providers, the activity is performed internally; where they are not, the activity is performed externally.

In performing this analysis, it's important that all factors be considered, especially the level of ongoing investment. Investments in technologies, processes, and people is what gives an organization its ability to deliver superior results, and as a result, a market-driven approach to outsourcing considers these factors.

Take, for example, the computer software development department in a typical Fortune 500 company. Companies of this size have about 700 employees performing this work. They are likely to have been drawn from a mix of individuals with specialized backgrounds and training, as well as nonspecialists from other parts of the organization who have moved into the department. The company is likely to invest about 40 hours of training per year in this staff, with about three-quarters of it focusing on company-specific issues and topics. Overall, the operation is likely not to have been taken through any form of formal certification, against common industry standards, of its processes and techniques. As far as the tools being employed, the company is likely to have made a one-time investment in fairly generic software development technology and in selected development methodologies, such as rapid application development. Overall, a software development department like this might be allowed to spend about 3 percent of its budget on its entire non-project–related spending, including its management and R&D in new technologies and approaches. This is a typical large organization, spending levels in smaller organizations would be that much less.

Compare this to the typical provider of software development on an outsourced basis. Most larger providers staff more than 7,000 software developers, who have been almost entirely recruited from the best talent available. Training on a per employee basis is typically 80 hours per year, with most of it focused on technical skill development. The company is likely to have gone through formal review and certification of its development processes against the highest industry standards. Investments by the company in new development technologies and R&D are typically in the 8 to 10 percent range every year.[3]

When comparing internal operations against a marketplace of providers like this, these disparities in the level of investment in people, processes, and technologies create real competitive advantages for providers and disadvantages for in-house operations. But this is exactly the competitive environment against which the organization needs to be testing its internal operations if continued sourcing inside the organization is to be justified. To not do so, means giving up incremental levels of performance and capability across the organization.

Another example of the importance in investment can be found just as easily in the facilities operations of these same organizations. The typical Fortune 500 company operates in about 20 million square feet of space. It employs about 400 people in its real estate department and existing contractors, and would provide coverage across a fairly diverse set of geographies, demanding a fairly wide set of skills. Minimal investments in supporting technologies are likely to be found. Trammel Crow Company, one of dozens of providers in the field, has an operation spanning more than 600 million square feet at more than 31,000 properties. It has 6,200 employees, of whom 4,100 are in its outsourcing business. It has relationships with hundreds of specialty firms, from custodial to construction. It has made investments in excess of $30 million in software and Web-based systems to create a global virtual support network.[4]

Market-driven decision making as a principle simply means allowing these comparisons to take place between an organization's internal operations and the marketplace of providers, and then encouraging executives to base their sourcing decisions on the competitive differentiations and the specific performance results they enable. It means bringing the power of the free market economy to bear to improve the internal operations of the firm.

Outsourcing as a Management Discipline

About 30 percent of companies report that they spend 1 percent or less of the annual cost of an outsourcing contract on managing the relationship between their organization and the service provider. Seventy-four percent spend 5 percent or less. Is this the right level of investment? Perhaps not. These same executives say that on average they are losing 13 percent of the value of the contract because of problems in the working relationship with their providers. Thirty percent say the loss is 20 percent or more.[5]

It is fair to conclude that increased investments in outsourcing as a management discipline would provide most organizations a significant return on investment—at least 300 percent and probably many multiples of this. This suggests that in most organizations there is a pressing need to elevate the status of outsourcing to that of any other valued management discipline and to make the co-requisite investments in training, development, and management tools.

One approach to answering this need is to add outsourcing training to the management development curriculum. This simply means putting this new management discipline on a par with others, such as human resources, finance, technology, and strategic planning. Given that the level of outsourcing across organizations is only going to increase, the sooner these investments begin, the better.

Another approach organizations can employ in the mean time is to bring their most experienced practitioners together into centers of excellence, supporting the entire organization. This can be done on a companywide basis or within specific functional areas where outsourcing is being used most extensively. American Express, GlaxoSmithKline, Freddie Mac, General Motors, Microsoft, the U.S. Department of the Navy, Thomas Cook, and Sabre are all examples of organizations that have done this successfully. Similarly, some organizations are recognizing new positions, such as external enterprise manager, strategic sourcing executive, or even chief resource officer. Whatever title is chosen, these moves recognize the reality that outsourcing is becoming an essential skill set for most organizations.

There are eight skills that comprise this new management discipline:

1. Developing a global business process outsourcing strategy
2. Optimizing the opportunities
3. Creating and leading successful project teams
4. Engaging the marketplace
5. Developing the financial case
6. Pricing, contracting, and negotiating
7. Managing people and change
8. Managing the transition and the outside relationship

Each has a natural affinity to a step in the sourcing process, but they are not themselves steps. At some level, each discipline plays itself across the entire process. For example, discipline eight, managing the transition, is certainly most related to the implementation step in the sourcing process since this deals with communicating and with transitioning employees, but it is also an integral part of the strategy step, where sourcing options, financials, and management relationships are evaluated.

Section Two is devoted to the management discipline of outsourcing.

Summary

Leaders can no longer afford to approach outsourcing as a tactical response to specific change initiatives. To stay competitive, they need to make it an integral part of how they think about and run their operations.

Doing this requires the adoption of a new set of management principles. These principles change the strategic planning process, expand the way the value of global BPO is projected and measured, apply zero-based thinking to sourcing decisions, bring the power of the free-market economy into the internal operations of the business, and elevate outsourcing management to that of a recognized, trained, supported, and rewarded discipline. Embracing some or all of these principles will dramatically accelerate the pace of change in most organizations.

Section Two

THE DISCIPLINES OF OUTSOURCING

Chapter

5

DEVELOPING A GLOBAL STRATEGY

The previous chapter made the case that for outsourcing to be truly effective, it needs to be integrated into the organization's overall business strategy. This means shifting from a view of outsourcing as a reactive tool—where opportunities are sought only in response to external pressures for change or a consultant's report on the latest opportunity—to one of weaving outsourcing into the very fabric of the business's decision making and operations. This chapter explains how this is done.

The first approach is the top-down approach. It treats sourcing as strategy and integrates the business's strategic plans with its sourcing plans. The second approach discussed is the bottom-up approach. This approach, building upon the idea of zero-based sourcing, is a methodology for identifying those areas of the business that are least likely to be providing unique competitive advantage when done internally. Both approaches work and can be used simultaneously.

This chapter also introduces two other important management ideas. The first is that of an outsourcing framework. The outsourcing framework provides a structure for mapping the activities of an organization so that they can be consistently examined from a sourcing perspective, whether that perspective is the top-down approach, the bottom-up approach, or both. The other key idea introduced is the often overlooked opportunity for creating competitive advantage through unique ways an organization combines its internal and external sources.

Top-Down Approach

Strategy is essential to the success of any organization. It answers the critical questions about what's happening in the environment and marketplaces the organization serves, how it makes a unique and competitively viable difference in serving the needs of the customers in those markets, and how it allocates and invests its resources toward the achievement of those ends.

As introduced in the previous chapter, many organizations view sourcing as an operational decision made only in response to the business's strategy. Sourcing as strategy suggests that, instead, outsourcing is an integral part of the development of that strategy; that an organization's sourcing decisions are essential to its ability to create competitive advantage. This changes when in the strategic process the question of the sources of competitive advantage gets asked and answered. Sourcing as strategy is, then, a top-down approach to identifying the sources of competitive advantage—both internal and external—and then ensuring that the organization's investment and execution plans are aligned with this strategy. Instead of positioning business process outsourcing as an outcome of the organization's investment decisions, sourcing as strategy positions it as an essential driver of those decisions.

Figure 5.1 shows the steps of this top-down strategic process. Later chapters deal with the staffing of the team responsible for this work. For now, we'll deal just with the process itself.

The first step of the process is to *segment* the organization's marketplace. This segmentation is typically done by identifying the combinations of customers served and the products and services with which they are served. These groups may then be further broken down by geographies or other delineations unique to the markets that the organization operates in or intends to operate in. When complete, this segmentation may result in as little as two or as many as dozens of segments. The identification of these segments is the essential first step in developing the organization's strategy and is the basis for all the steps that follow.

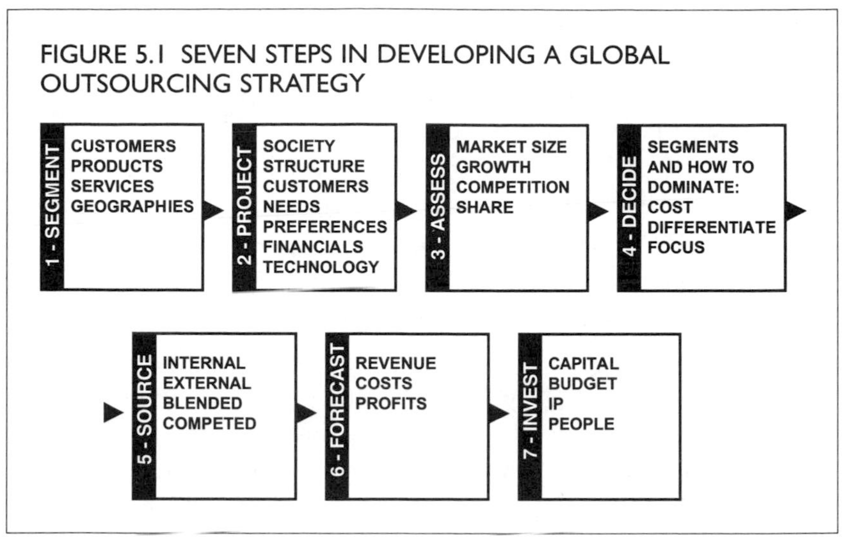

FIGURE 5.1 SEVEN STEPS IN DEVELOPING A GLOBAL OUTSOURCING STRATEGY

The second step is to *project* the changes in these segments over the planning period. Typically, this planning period can be no more than two to three years. This shortened strategic planning time frame is a direct result of the hyper-competitive environment. It is also a key reason that internal investments, which typically require much longer periods to achieve a full return, can no longer be the default option for organizations. The potential changes in the environment are looked at in terms of projected changes in society, business, and their overall structures; changes in the customers themselves, including their needs, preferences, and financial situations; and, of course, changes in technology and its potential impact on all of the other factors being considered. There need not be only one projection. Scenario planning can be used to describe more than one possible future along with the unique characteristics and probabilities of each.

The next step is to *assess* each of the segments in terms of their overall size and growth. Just as importantly, each segment must be looked at in terms of the current competitors, likely future competitors, and how each competitor may fair in terms of its market share.

The fourth step is to *decide,* based on the opportunity available to the organization, which segments to pursue and what it will take to dominate in each. The former means selecting those segments that are most attractive in terms of growth and opportunity. The latter means deciding what competitive advantages the organization needs to have in order to not only successfully compete, but to move itself toward a position of leadership.

These needed competitive advantages should be stated in specific, measurable terms. If cost is an element of advantage, then what cost points does the organization need to hit to be successful? If differentiation is the road to dominance, then specifically what will that differentiation be? Will it be design, features, performance, quality, ease of use, prestige, speed, customer service, guarantees, or other characteristics? And, how are they to be objectively measured?

At the end of step four, the organization has created a list of market segments it desires to serve and what it believes is needed to compete and win in those segments. The fifth step, *source,* is then the essential link between the market-facing side of the organization's strategy and the sourcing side. It is the mapping of the required competitive advantages across the operational activities of the business to determine where and how each advantage will be created. Some of these competitive advantages may be found in the organization's internal operations, but others are just as likely to be sourced through external relationships, while still others may come from unique ways the organization blends its internal and external sources. All other activities—those that need to be done and done well but offer little or no opportunity for creating a competitive advantage—are nonstrategic and should be sourced at the operational level on a purely competition-driven basis. Sourcing as strategy is a senior-level executive process, competing nonstrategic, commodity activities is an operational-level process.

The sixth step is to *forecast* the business outcomes from these decisions about segments and sources of competitive advantage. For commercial organizations, this forecast is in terms of revenue, costs, profit, and other key financial indicators. For noncommercial enterprises, these outcomes may be forecasted in different terms, such as budget targets and the number of constituents served. This is the process of taking the strategic plan and turning it into a set of forecasted outcomes. This can be expected to create a slight iterative loop where the segments served and sources of competitive advantage get adjusted to bring the forecasts in line with intended outcomes.

The seventh and last step of the top-down process is to *invest* in execution. This means allocating all the forms of investments available to the organization: its capital, its operating funds, its people, and its intellectual properties. This alignment—this fit, if you will—between the organization's strategic plan and its execution plan is the essential step in transforming strategy into action.

This seven-step process makes sourcing an integral part of strategic planning. It expands the view of the sources of competitive advantage available to an organization, thereby enabling it to better compete in the market segments it chooses to pursue. It also elevates the organization's outside relationships so that the ones that contribute competitive advantage are treated as an integral part of the organization's strategic planning process and as part of its network of strategic assets.

The top-down approach also requires that the strategic plans of the organization and of its key outside sources be connected. The result is a weaving together of a network of relationships at the highest levels of the organization.

Bottom-Up Approach

The bottom-up approach does not mean that decisions are made at lower levels of management. What it does mean is that the process used for identifying outsourcing opportunities focuses on selecting activities that do not contribute a unique competitive advantage, and then competing these commodity-type activities against the marketplace of providers. It represents a zero-based sourcing approach where all areas that do not deliver a unique competitive advantage are evaluated from a competitive sourcing perspective.

Since they were first introduced by the author in 1996, the following three questions have been used by hundreds of organizations to determine the areas of the business that are least likely to deliver a unique competitive advantage:

1. If starting from scratch today, would we really build the capability inside?
2. Are we so good at it that others would hire us to do it for them?
3. Is this an area of the business from which our future leaders will come?

If the answer is yes to all three questions, then the activity is either a source of unique competitive advantage or close enough to one to remain internally sourced until evaluated from a more strategic, top-down perspective. If the answer is no to any of the three, then looking at what the marketplace of external service providers has to offer is appropriate.

The first question of the three-question test captures the essence of zero-based sourcing. It asks what the organization would do if it was being formed today. Would it invest in creating the capability internally or would its leaders' first inclination be to look for sources available in the external marketplace? It also tests the organization's existing sourcing choices against what new competitors entering its marketplace are doing. Are new competitors also building this capability for themselves, thereby validating its unique contribution or suggesting that adequate external sources are not available, or are they acquiring the capability from the outside and then focusing their internal investments elsewhere?

The importance of this single question in properly shaping a company's investment decisions has recently been revalidated by the venture capital market. Many venture capital firms now require that companies they plan to invest in externally source all of their nondifferentiating functions, such as finance, accounting, human resources, and basic information technology services.

The second question gets at the very heart of organizational hubris. Successful organizations are, often because of their very success, filled with a belief that because they are successful, they must be good at everything they do, and that the unique ways they do things directly contribute to that success. This belief is often reflected in statements such as "we are different" or "we are unique." One great way to challenge this hubris is to simply ask if other companies would hire yours to perform that internal function for them. Could your company sell this activity as a service in an open, competitive marketplace? Could it successfully compete against the marketplace of service providers that do it for a living? Would another company hire yours to process its receivables, payables, or payroll? Is there a marketplace for your organization's real estate portfolio management services? Are your assembly and test capabilities markedly superior to the norm for the industry? Are they superior to the top companies that perform that work for your competitors?

Finally, the third question establishes just how valued the skills needed to perform the activity are to the organization. Are they the skills that are so highly prized that they are reflected in the knowledge- and experience-set of the company's top leaders? In its chief executive officer? Activities that are based on highly valued skills naturally receive the lion's share of internal funding for their development and support. The people in those areas are likely to be able to see a career path leading to the company's corner office. The organization is likely to be attracting the best and brightest in those fields.

Whereas the top-down approach examines sourcing as a contributor to competitive advantage, the bottom-up approach sets out to separate the areas that the organization is performing internally more out of habit than out of need. It results in the creation of a list of activities that should at least be tested more thoroughly as potential areas for improved performance through business process outsourcing. How to select the very best activities to focus on for business process outsourcing is the subject of the next chapter.

As pointed out earlier, the bottom-up and the top-down approaches are not mutually exclusive. The bottom-up approach can be used to quickly move the organization in the direction of better leveraging its assets through outside relationships. The top-down approach can be used to turn sourcing into a competitive advantage.

Two examples, both drawn from the health care industry, illustrate the difference between these two approaches as well as the ability of each to produce important benefits.

The first is El Camino Hospital, located in Mountain View, California. El Camino is a 426-bed, locally owned and governed community hospital. Being in the heart of Silicon Valley, the hospital's strategic plan called for distinguishing itself by being on the forefront of tomorrow's "smart hospital." This meant developing and deploying technologies on the leading edge of the health care field. Information technology is naturally one of these areas. In developing its strategic plan and sources of competitive advantage, El Camino decided to acquire some of this needed competitive advantage through strategic outside relationships. In one case, the hospital selected health care technology specialist Eclipsys Corporation as its partner. Besides gaining operational improvements in costs and service levels, the hospital is using this relationship to accelerate the introduction of new information technology systems in such areas as medical records and computerized physician order entry.[1]

On the other hand, St. Louis, Missouri–based BJC Health System is a great example of the bottom-up approach. The system was first formed in 1993 by bringing together the operations of previously separate health care providers into a single system serving 200,000 individuals with 35,000 caregivers at more than 200 sites. The immediate goal of the integrated system was to demonstrate its ability to reduce overall costs. Outsourcing was a key management tool for accomplishing this. Improvements in purchasing, especially based on the integrated system's larger buying power, consolidating service across the sites, and the sharing of best practices were other techniques used.

Using a bottom-up approach to identifying the outsourcing opportunities, BJC outsourced its medical supplies, food services, laundry, esoteric laboratories, and emergency room operations. Total savings from these and the other initiatives through 2000 exceeded $190 million.[2]

Mapping Activities

Whether the top-down or the bottom-up approach is used, the outsourcing framework, depicted in Figure 5.2 and covered in more detail in the Appendix, is an effective tool for mapping an organization's activities. This activity map can then be used as the basis for identifying and evaluating the organization's activities using either the top-down or the bottom-up approach.

FIGURE 5.2 AN ORGANIZATION IS A NETWORK OF SERVICES DELIVERING VALUE TO CUSTOMERS

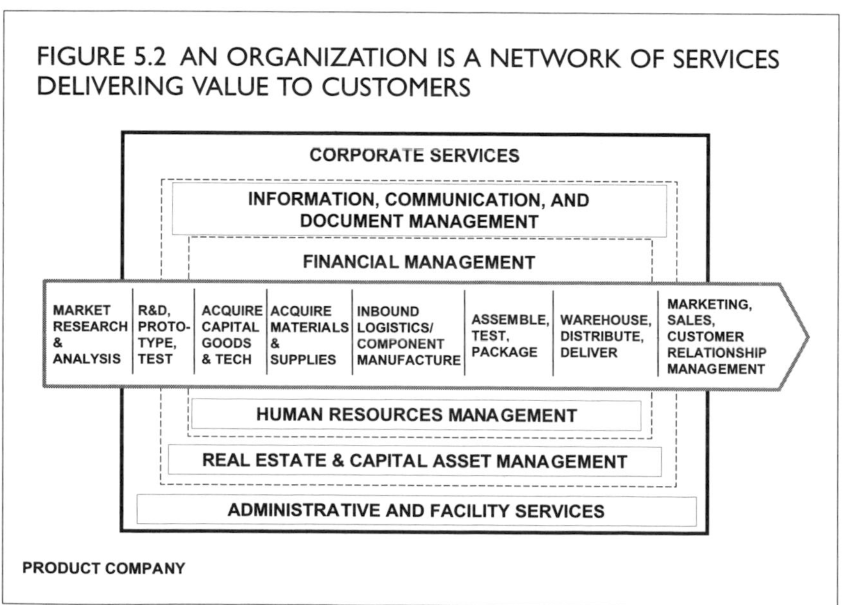

Some of an organization's activities take place along what is called the *value chain* of the organization. That is, the series of activities that begins with the conceptualization of a product or service and ends with its delivery and support for a customer. (The value chain for a service company is naturally different than that of a product company and is shown in Figure 5.3.) The rest of the organization's activities actually surround that value chain and are the management and support activities that enable the work of the value chain to be done. These include, for example, the activities within the human resources function; within finance and information technology; within corporate services, such as legal and purchasing; and within the other support areas of the business.

In the top-down approach Step 4 is where each activity is evaluated for its ability to provide one or more unique competitive advantages if sourced internally, complementary competitive advantages if sourced externally, or additional competitive advantage from unique ways internal and external sources might be blended. In the bottom-up approach each activity is evaluated using the three-question test, and through that analysis, selected as an activity for consideration for outsourcing.

Each organization will naturally want to modify the generic framework provided here to match its unique operations. Modifications typically are done by adding more specific activities under the framework's lowest common level and by replacing the framework's generic terminology with more industry- or company-specific terms, as needed. For example, a pharmaceutical company would replace the generic "product prototype and test" activities provided with the specific phases of drug development and trial. Separate maps may also be needed for each of the organization's business units with distinct value chains.

Figure 5.4 shows an example of the result of this customization for a credit card company. The value chain activities have been renamed to match industry and company-specific terminology. Additional detail has

FIGURE 5.3 VALUE CHAIN OF A SERVICES COMPANY

MARKET RESEARCH & ANALYSIS	R&D, PROTO-TYPE, TEST	ACQUIRE CAPITAL GOODS & TECH	ACQUIRE MATERIALS & SUPPLIES	HUMAN RESOURCE ACQUISITION & DEVELOPMENT	DELIVER SERVICES TO CUSTOMER	MARKETING, SALES, CUSTOMER RELATIONSHIP MANAGEMENT

FIGURE 5.4 VALUE CHAIN ANALYSIS PROVIDES SOURCING BLUEPRINT—CREDIT CARD COMPANY EXAMPLE

VALUE CHAIN ACTIVITIES

STRATEGY DEVELOPMENT	PRODUCT RESEARCH & DEVELOPMENT	DESIGN & PRODUCTION	WAREHOUSING & DISTRIBUTION	SALES	NEW CUSTOMER PROCESSING	TRANSACTION PROCESSING	CUSTOMER SERVICING
– BRAND MANAGEMENT – RISK MANAGEMENT	– MARKET RESEARCH – PRODUCT DESIGN – PRODUCT MANAGEMENT	– ADVERTISING – CATALOGUES – DIRECT MAIL – ACCOUNT STATEMENTS – SALES MATERIALS	– DATA & MATERIAL STORAGE – INVENTORY MANAGEMENT – FULFILLMENT – SHIPPING	– DIRECT SALES – TELEMAR-KETING – ONLINE	– PROCESSING – APPROVAL – ACCOUNT SET-UP	– CHARGES – PAYMENTS – SETTLEMENT – PAYABLES	– INBOUND – CORRES-PONDENCE – COLLECTIONS – AUTHORIZ-ATIONS – DISPUTES – CARD REPLACE-MENTS
SOURCING STRATEGY							
UNIQUE COMPETITIVE ADVANTAGE, INTERNALLY SOURCED	UNIQUE COMPETITIVE ADVANTAGE, INTERNALLY SOURCED - AND - EXTERNALLY SOURCED	SUPPORTING OPERATIONS, COMPETITIVELY SOURCED	SUPPORTING OPERATIONS, COMPETITIVELY SOURCED	UNIQUE COMPETITIVE ADVANTAGE, INTERNALLY SOURCED - AND - EXTERNALLY SOURCED	SUPPORTING OPERATIONS, COMPETITIVELY SOURCED	SUPPORTING OPERATIONS, COMPETITIVELY SOURCED	SUPPORTING OPERATIONS, COMPETITIVELY SOURCED

been added. Finally, the map has been expanded to show the sourcing approach the company has selected for each of these sets of activities.

This form of activity mapping produces an effective blueprint for moving the organization forward in its evaluation of the optimum source for each of its activities.

The Integration Advantage

The opportunity to create additional competitive advantages through the unique ways that an organization blends and integrates its operations and those of its providers is often overlooked.

For example, when General Motors outsourced receivables, payables, and payroll in the late 1990s, the executive team moved about 100 of its top people into new positions as knowledge engineers. Their role was to work on an ongoing basis to further integrate and reengineer all of GM's processes, working side by side with its new service provider.[3]

Chrysler, on the other hand, uses the platform team approach to make its suppliers part of the design of its new products from the moment of inception. Suppliers work with Chrysler to help it achieve the costs and product differentiating characteristics it's seeking for the specific customer segment targeted.

The chief executive officer of New Zealand–based Meridian Energy has made the senior executives for his company's major outsourcing relationships—facilities operations, information technology, and customer care—part of his inner circle by having them participate in every other meeting of his direct reports.

As discussed in greater detail in Chapter 12, PricewaterhouseCoopers and Procter & Gamble are additional examples of companies that have implemented specific management programs to capture and leverage the power of integration to produce significant added benefit for their companies.

These are just a few examples of how organizations can use outsourcing relationships to create new sources of competitive advantage. To do this, however, teams of people from all of the organizations involved need to be able to work together during the strategic planning cycle to jointly understand the areas of competitive advantage sought and to jointly identify ways to get there. It is no longer a matter of the customer calling the shots and measuring the provider's performance against expectations; it's a matter of working together, with full access to each others' capabilities and strategic plans, to build something new and exciting.

This is a critical element of sourcing-as-strategy and an important new opportunity for competitive advantage in today's world.

Summary

The days when an organization could create competitive advantage simply by capturing internally the benefits of economies of scope and scale have passed. Mass production of standard products using amassed physical assets is no longer the advantage it once was. In today's environment, organizations are finding that they need to be much more focused on the market segments they will serve, how they will differentiate themselves in those markets, and how they will source their operations to gain those advantages.

Companies can use a top-down approach to identify outsourcing opportunities, where the sourcing decisions are made as an integral part of the business's strategic decisions. They can take a bottom-up approach, where the identification of external sourcing opportunities begins with those areas that offer little opportunity for creating competitive advantage. They can also seek new forms of competitive advantage in the unique ways that blend their internal and external sources. Whatever approach, or combination of approaches, is chosen, the most important factor is to elevate sourcing to the level of an important management decision.

Chapter

6

OPTIMIZING OUTSOURCING OPPORTUNITIES

Using the outsourcing framework in combination with the top-down souring as strategy approach, the bottom-up zero-based sourcing approach, or a combination of the two, results in a list of potential areas where competitive and operational improvements may be possible. The next question has to be: Of these, which ones offer the greatest advantage at this moment in time? To answer this question, the candidates need to be refined in terms of scope, and prioritized in terms of risk and reward.

Experience has shown that the best candidate areas are likely to be those where there is (1) a robust marketplace of providers and (2) solid proof points of success from the experiences of others. This is not meant to suggest that a me-too approach should dominate an organization's thinking or that there are not exceptional returns available for trailblazers, but it simply emphasizes the point that marketplace dynamics and experience do play important roles in helping to ensure that the value sought is the value gained.

Another key factor in refining and prioritizing the list of candidate opportunities is to shape the scope of the opportunity from a process-centric perspective. That is, to include in the candidate opportunity under consideration not only the discrete set of activities derived from the outsourcing framework, but all of the activities, technologies, and supply-chain management work that make up and feed into the end-to-end business process. By crafting opportunities in process terms, all of the value creation potential discussed in Chapter 2 comes into play.

The final selection and prioritization of these opportunities is often in response to pressing needs for changes in the business's overall operations. Some of these come from the need to make significant new investments, especially in technology, to either keep pace with the competition or to take advantage of a new opportunity. Outsourcing can be a natural alternative to making the investment internally and tying up the capital. Another immediate need can be the relocation of current operations or the opening of new ones. Changes in regulations or industry standards also create these kinds of inflection points. Acquisitions, divestitures, and product line launches and discontinuations are other examples. Outsourcing is often triggered in response to these kinds of business demands.

Whatever the drivers, candidate opportunities need to be prioritized in terms of the potential size of the impact on the business and in terms of their risks. Outsourcing is no different than any other management tool; an investment is required to plan and execute the project. Given this, the organization's resources will be best focused on the opportunities most likely to produce the highest return at the lowest cost and risk. In the end, organizations are perhaps even more likely to outsource when the risks can be kept low as they are when the rewards may be potentially high.

This chapter outlines a repeatable management process for prioritizing outsourcing opportunities. It closes by examining special considerations that should go into outsourcing at the customer interface—where a provider's employees will be working directly with an organization's customers.

Riding Outsourcing's Waves

By the end of 2004 organizations around the world will be spending $6 trillion on outsourcing.[1] This spending, and therefore the maturity of the marketplace, is not, however, evenly distributed across all areas of the business. About 50 percent of the spending is in manufacturing. The other half is concentrated in a number of fairly mature areas and some rapidly expanding ones.

One of the first steps in evaluating any outsourcing opportunity is to match that opportunity with what other organizations are already doing and against the maturity of the marketplace. Mature segments of the market offer proven results, while emerging areas offer opportunities for organizations to catch a wave early and gain a unique advantage. Mapping and scoring the opportunities an organization is considering in terms of where the marketplace is in its maturity curve can be a very effective first step in the process of selecting the best candidates. (See Figure 6.1.)

Overall, the most mature outsourcing markets—those in which the largest percentage of organizations outsource and where the marketplace of providers is the most robust—are in the physical parts of a business's operations. Activities such as facility services and maintenance, cafeterias and mailrooms, manufacturing, warehousing, and shipping are all examples of this.

These physical activities are already routinely outsourced by most companies. Manufacturers commonly outsource 70 percent or more of their product content. Upwards of 75 percent of companies outsource basic facility services, from cleaning to cafeterias. (The percentage of

FIGURE 6.1 IT'S IMPORTANT TO RIDE OUTSOURCING'S WAVES

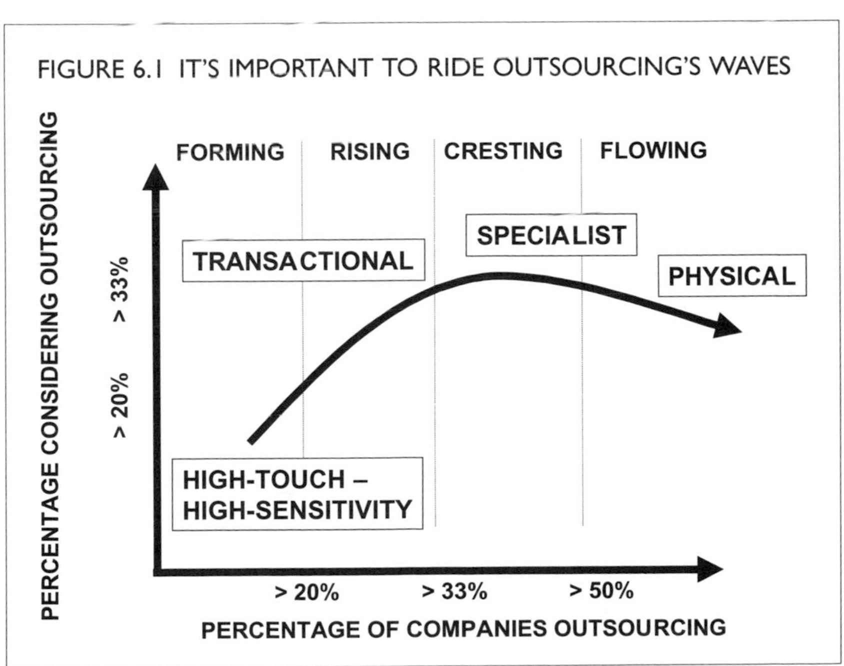

companies outsourcing and considering outsourcing selected activities across businesses is shown in Figure 6.2.)

The providers of these services are very mature, highly successful companies with extensive reach and capability, such as ARAMARK, Dana Corporation, EMCOR, IKON, Johnson Controls, Pitney Bowes, Ryder, Solectron, and Xerox. Hundreds of other companies, including many smaller, specialty providers, exist. Any organization not outsourcing in these areas already should certainly consider adding them to their short list.

What might be called outsourcing's second wave, one that is continuing to expand and mature, is in the specialist areas of the business. Think about all of the specialized professionals from across a wide range of disciplines—from advertising to travel to information technology—who work within the typical company. These individuals and their departments have an affinity to their specialty that is just as great, if not greater, than their affinity to the particular company they work for. Bringing these specialists together into separate outsourcing companies has been a natural and rapidly growing area for many years.

Highly sophisticated service providers exist across all of these specialized areas, such as Olgilvy & Mather in advertising, American Express Company and Carlson Wagonlit Travel for travel services, and ADP and Paychex for payroll.

Organizations from the largest to the smallest now routinely outsource many aspects of their information technology operations to spe-

FIGURE 6.2 WHAT COMPANIES ARE OUTSOURCING

Activity	**Type**	**Percent Outsourcing**	**Percent Considering Outsourcing**
Food and Cafeteria Services	Physical	77%	Less than 10%
Facility Engineering and Maintenance	Physical	75%	13%
Component Manufacturing	Physical	62%	14%
Product Warehousing, Distribution, and Delivery	Physical	62%	10%

Activity	Type	Percent Outsourcing	Percent Considering Outsourcing
Mailroom Services	Physical	62%	8%
Travel Services	Specialty	75%	Less than 10%
Legal	Specialty	66%	12%
Advertising	Specialty	57%	22%
Payroll Processing	Specialty	53%	26%
Document Design and Layout	Specialty	53%	6%
Internet Services	Specialty—IT	52%	22%
Software Development and Maintenance	Specialty—IT	46%	27%
Data Center Operations	Specialty—IT	45%	22%
Help Desk Services	Specialty—IT	42%	24%
Desktop System Management	Specialty—IT	36%	22%
Telemarketing	Transactional	41%	21%
Customer Service and Inquiry Handling	Transactional	36%	18%
Customer Order Processing	Transactional	32%	18%
Financial Accounting and Reporting	Transactional	32%	11%
Employee Benefits Administration	Transactional	31%	42%
Product Research and Development	High-Touch, High-Sensitivity	38%	7%
Field Service Delivery	High-Touch High-Sensitivity	37%	14%
Human Resource Strategy Development	High-Touch High-Sensitivity	35%	15%
Product Prototype and Test	High-Touch High-Sensitivity	34%	24%
Field Sales	High-Touch High-Sensitivity	27%	18%

Source: 2002 Survey of 410 Global Executives, The 2002 Strategic Outsourcing Study, Michael F. Corbett & Associates, Ltd., December 2002 cialized providers ranging in size from CSC, EDS, and IBM to thousands of smaller, niche players.

Outsourcing's third wave, and the one that is creating a very robust and rapidly emerging market, is in the transactional parts of the business—activities such as telemarketing, customer order processing and inquiries, employee benefits administration, and receivables and payables. As discussed in Chapter 2, these all represent repeatable, process- and technology-centric activities. They offer the opportunity to simultaneously reengineer and outsource the business process, along with the technologies that support it and the supply chains that feed it.

New providers for these services are emerging daily, often backed by significant venture capital. At the same time, well-established companies in related fields are quickly launching new business units to satisfy this expanding area of customer demand. Outsourcing in these transaction-intensive areas of the business can offer unique, early-mover advantages, such as favorable contract terms, the ability to more directly craft the way the services will be provided, and even the ability to gain an equity stake in the provider's business.

The final area, what might be called outsourcing's fourth wave, is just beginning to form. It is in the high-touch, high-sensitivity areas of the business—activities that play a more direct role in the organization's relationship with its customers and that are more central to the planning and development of future products and services. Service delivery, field sales, and research and development are all examples of these high-touch, high-sensitivity areas. Unexpected opportunities can be found here, as well.

Seeing Opportunities in Process Terms

The second step in scoping and prioritizing the opportunities is to redefine them in end-to-end process terms and to evaluate the total opportunity from that perspective. This means looking at the entire process that the activity under consideration is part of and mapping the complete series of activities, working from the customer touch points in.

For example, a fast-growing company can easily find itself supporting customers in tens of countries all around the world. The result is often the creation of geographically scattered customer support centers, each performing its own discrete functions. One center may be created to take orders, but a different center may handle problems or inbound service calls from customers. Outsourcing one or more of these centers, even if it involves taking the center offshore, may have only a limited impact on costs, and certainly does little to change how the process operates as seen from the customer's point of view. On the other hand, examining the entire customer relationship management process yields a different view; one that leads to a different set of opportunities. In one case like this, the client, working with its business process outsourcing partner, created a "virtual global contact center" model. By tying all of the client's centers together through common technology, all customer touch points were consolidated, customer information was centralized, and better-trained, better-managed agents were able to handle a wider range of customer needs. The result was within just a matter of weeks achieving a 98 percent-plus quality target on call handling, and over the first year a 40 percent reduction in labor costs, a 50 percent increase in operator productivity, and millions of dollars in savings.[2]

The benefits of this type of process approach to outsourcing are significant. The organization gains a clear understanding of how the various pieces of its operation connect to, reinforce, or take away from its ability to deliver value to the customer. The key performance indicators for the work can be defined in terms that are meaningful from a customer perspective, not simply from the perspective of an internally focused performance standard. Finally, all of the underlying technologies and supply chains are clearly identified and can be evaluated for inclusion in the scope of services to be outsourced.

The actual work of developing a process diagram is well documented in the many texts on business process analysis and reengineering. Generally, the most successful approach is to hold a series of modeling workshops with participation from the subject-matter experts involved in the process and facilitators to help describe and depict the process using consistent terminology and documentation.

This is often done as an iterative process that typically begins with a "white board" exercise that captures the activities and their relationships. From that, a common set of diagrams using a consistent symbolic language as well as supporting textual descriptions are created. These textual descriptions follow a consistent template that, for each process, subprocess, activity, and task, describes its purpose, triggers, timings, durations, and resource requirements. All required resources are identified, including skills, technology infrastructure and applications, and physical environment. Data flows are captured in the same template-driven manner, including the sources, destinations, characteristics, and inputs and outputs for each activity. Key performance indicators are documented, as well. These establish the base for determining how well the process is operating overall in relationship to the customer value it's intended to create.[3]

This process analysis and mapping forms the basis for all subsequent planning and decision making, including defining the scope of the work to be outsourced, determining current costs and performance, quantifying the measures of success and how it is managed.

Prioritizing the Best

Once the candidate areas have been listed and scoped in process terms, they need to be prioritized. The goal is to ensure that the opportunities that afford the organization the greatest return at the lowest level of risk get pursued first. The prioritization scheme can and should be kept in mind as the list of opportunities and scoping is done, thereby ensuring that resources are continually migrated toward the most important opportunities.

This prioritization is based on a number of factors. These factors and the weight given each can change over time, even for the same organization. Typically, the factors considered are the size of the operation as measured in financial terms, the marketplace of service providers, the potential benefits to be realized, the ease with which the project can be executed, and a preliminary assessment of the risks involved. Organizations can develop a very formal score sheet for evaluating and ranking opportunities, or they may choose a more iterative, discussion-driven approach.

In either case, gauging the size of the opportunity in financial terms is often the first factor considered. Unless the opportunity is affecting a large enough portion of the business's operations, it may simply not be worth the effort to pursue. This is why establishing the scope, especially in process terms, is important to identifying and pursuing the best opportunities. What's large enough? That depends on the organization, but a threshold based on minimum dollars spent, revenue impacted, or number of employees involved is common. Opportunities above the threshold receive further consideration. Those that do not are set aside or reexamined within the framework of a larger opportunity.

The second factor is an assessment of the marketplace of suppliers. Do suppliers of sufficient size and expertise exist for this opportunity to be pursued? Very large companies may find that there is simply not a provider large enough to absorb their operations. This is, of course, less frequently a problem today, and certainly not in the more mature parts of the market. On the other hand, organizations may conclude that unique advantages can be created and captured by becoming the anchor client for a new provider in a new field.

The third factor is a preliminary assessment of the potential benefits to be realized. What level of savings is likely? How would any freed up resources be redeployed? How much can the flexibility of the organization, as measured by the percentage of costs or resources that can be ramped up and down quickly, be increased? How large is the gap between current internal quality levels and where the marketplace of service providers is performing? What level of capital spending can be avoided? Opportunities that have the greatest potential for delivering against the business's goals represent the smartest ones to pursue.

Another factor is ease of execution. How well is the process understood, defined, and measured? Who are the customers? How easy will it be to migrate them to the new environment? Who are the stakeholders, and how easy will it be to bring them into agreement on the changes proposed? Is there a positive perception of how earlier outsourcing projects of this type have gone? How many employees will be affected? What will be the impact on them, and how prepared is the organization to work with those individuals throughout the process? These and other factors affect the ease with which the organization can execute. Organizations that do not have a proven track record of success with outsourcing will often place a higher priority on opportunities that are easier to execute. Once a track record of success has been established, it is easier to take on more challenging projects.

Gauging and Overcoming Risk

If, however, the business case for outsourcing, business process outsourcing, and offshoring is as compelling as we think, the question has to be asked: Why isn't everyone doing it across almost every part of their business? Why are we not already at a 70 percent outsourced level? Certainly the ability of the provider market to absorb that much work is one factor, but there have to be other factors slowing outsourcing's progress, as well. The risk and the confidence an organization has in its ability to manage risk are the top factors.

When companies evaluate outsourcing, they are constantly balancing perceived benefits and perceived risks. Outsourcing's risks come in many different forms. And it's these risks that keep companies from concluding that they "must" outsource. Additionally, these risks are viewed quite differently when evaluating offshore outsourcing versus domestic outsourcing.

There are four major classes of risks that organizations evaluate.[4] The first is *strategic risks*. Strategic risks include the loss of control over future business decisions; loss of knowledge, especially protection of intellectual properties; future changes in the service provider's business that may impact the customer's; and, particularly when offshore outsourcing is involved, risks associated with cultural differences and geopolitical risks.

There are also *operational risks*. These can include risks associated with the impact of outsourcing on the organization's people, both those who may be transferring to the service provider and those remaining with the company; risks associated with integrating the provider's processes into the business's; risks from poor performance; and, particularly with offshore outsourcing, risks associated with impact of future legislation and changes in regulatory compliance.

The third category of risks is *result risks,* that is, will the intended results be realized? Governance and the ability of the organization to manage collaboratively with the provider to achieve the intended benefits is the big consideration here.

Finally, there are *transactional risks*. Termination clauses, both for cause and convenience, dispute resolution, liability, indemnity, warranties, asset transfers, intellectual property ownership, and payments are all examples of transactional risks.

An assessment of these risks and how well prepared the organization is to manage them is an inseparable part of selecting the best candidates for outsourcing. To do this, the organization needs to first use the examples presented here to develop a comprehensive and complete list of the risks. Next, it needs to perform a preliminary evaluation of the magnitude of each, what would be needed to mitigate the risks, and how easy or difficult it will be to put those mitigation plans into action. Here again, the analysis may be performed more through a process of internal discussion and debate or may be done using very formal scoring sheets and templates. Regardless of the particular process used, the key requirement is to ensure that the risks and required actions are identified and captured.

This is another reason why outsourcing has moved through business in waves. The risks associated with outsourcing physical and specialist activities are well understood and have been successfully mitigated at organization after organization. As a result, the confidence an organization has in its ability to truly capture the expected benefits is higher. Newer areas, such as transactional activities and high-touch and high-sensitivity work, as well as offshoring, are less well understood, making the risks effectively greater.

Due diligence before the final selection of scope and providers, careful relationship and contract structuring and negotiation, and ongoing governance are all key elements of outsourcing risk mitigation. This process doesn't end once the relationship goes operational but continues throughout its life.

Outsourcing at the Customer Interface

The relationship between an organization and its customers is perhaps the most critical of all of its activities, demanding great care in its planning and execution. Placing a third party between an organization and its customers—outsourcing at the customer interface—naturally requires special consideration. This applies whether the interaction is face-to-face, over the telephone, via mail, or electronically. It does not suggest that outsourcing shouldn't occur at the customer interface, but it does mean that there are unique considerations to be evaluated during its design and execution.

After all, as one executive put it when referring to a service provider's interactions with its customers, "In 60 seconds they can turn off somebody to us for life." Does that mean that companies don't outsource at the customer interface? Not at all. In one case Xerox uses Ryder System to deliver, install, and complete the training of its customers on new equipment. Prior to this business process outsourcing relationship a salesperson would sell the product and coordinate its delivery, a separate technician come to set up the machine, and then the salesperson would return to provide the final training. These multiple steps have now been collapsed through outsourcing into one strategic relationship. Additionally, Ryder's management of the supply chain, from warehousing to delivery, enables Xerox to leverage its provider's capabilities and reputation to its competitive advantage. Outsourcing that "last mile" of the customer experience has shortened cycle times and improved customer satisfaction.

When evaluating outsourcing at the customer interface, it is useful to examine the activities involved along two dimensions. The first is to consider the level of judgment required during the interaction. Interactions that last for an extended period of time; are complex in nature, that is, involve the exchange of a great deal of information or have many alternative paths; and ones that require discretion on the part of the individual performing the work, require a high level of judgment. The greater the level of judgment, the greater the potential risk—this is true whether the interaction is outsourced or not.

The second dimension to look at is how much value the customer places on the interaction. Was the interaction customer-initiated? Is it central or peripheral to the value the customer is looking for from the overall relationship with the company? Is the interaction key to customer retention? Just as with the level of judgment required, interactions that represent a high level of customer value also represent a higher risk. Looking at both dimensions at the same time, highly valued interactions requiring the greatest judgment are the most sensitive of all.

This does not mean that these more sensitive customer interactions should not be considered for outsourcing, but it does suggest (1) that it may make the greatest sense to build from outsourcing lower-risk to higher-risk interactions as experience is gained and unexpected situations are resolved; and (2) that even greater care, planning, and monitoring should go into the execution of outsourcing for these more sensitive interactions.

Some considerations that go into this planning and monitoring are, first, the design of the interaction. Will the end customer be made aware that the service is being performed by another organization? Generally, customers are not made aware of the fact that the service they are receiving is outsourced. However, in some cases, the provider's brand may actually increase the customer's perception of value. Second, how seamlessly can and will the customer interactions be handled? Making the flow between internal and external operations seamless usually requires a significant level of process and technology integration. The more important the interaction, the greater the investment the customer and provider should be prepared to make to ensure that the activities are seamless to the end customer.

A final design consideration for outsourcing at the customer interface is identity. The more sensitive the interaction, the greater the investment made to ensure that the provider's employees fully identify with their client and with their client's customers. A close sense of identification increases their ability to respond to unexpected situations in a way consistent with what their client would have done.

The key consideration in all of this is to recognize that when outsourcing at the customer interface, the organization is not outsourcing responsibility for defining and ensuring the "customer experience." The organization maintains full control over what services its customers receive and the nature and character of that experience. What it is doing is leveraging its assets along with those of its service providers toward the delivery of those experiences. Maintaining full responsibility and control of the experience, while outsourcing its execution, is the key to success when outsourcing at the customer interface.

Nothing is more important than defining and managing the customer experience. Leading organizations, such as the Ritz-Carlton, Hewlett-Packard, and Dell, place tremendous emphasis here. The Ritz-Carlton, winner of the 1998 and 1999 Malcolm Baldrige Quality Awards, has identified almost 1,000 touch points for an overnight guest, each representing a point where a problem can occur. Each touch point has been carefully broken down and analyzed to both prevent and respond to any problem. Hewlett-Packard has a Business Customer Organization with accountability for managing and constantly improving the total customer experience for HP's business customers in all its segments. Dell Computer's CIO led that company's customer experience initiative, including the development of a customer-centered warehouse that allows Dell to measure and track the quality of the experience at every touch point, whether performed by Dell employees or outsourced.[5]

Summary

Optimizing the effect of business process outsourcing requires a consistent management process where potential opportunities are prioritized in terms of impact, benefit, and risk.

One way to do this is to ride outsourcing's waves by focusing the organization's outsourcing efforts on those activities that are already outsourced by many others. This ensures a robust market with well-understood benefits and already mitigated risks. At the same time, some of the greatest benefits can accrue to organizations that are first to outsource in a new area and gain favorable terms and competitively differentiating positioning. Organizations should consider both.

Organizations only outsource when they feel the risks are well understood and manageable. Until then, almost no amount of discussion of potential benefits can move them forward.

As part of their regular strategic and operational planning processes, organizations should produce agreed to, senior executive–backed lists of prioritized opportunities to pursue. By focusing attention and energies in this way, organizations maximize their abilities to reduce costs, improve quality, and gain competitive advantages through outsourcing.

Case Study: British Petroleum

Beginning almost a decade ago, British Petroleum (BP) began the process of developing a consistent, repeatable management process for identifying the highest priority opportunities for outsourcing, and then crafting and executing contracts for each.[6]

BP operates more than 100 separate business units, each focused on their own business opportunities and customers. To support these business units, common functions were brought together into a centralized shared services organization that is responsible for integrating all of these activities and supporting many business units. This created a natural platform for evaluating outsourcing opportunities in a consistent, repeatable manner.

The focus at BP is to identify, retain, and enhance those roles that are the most strategically important and operationally important. At the same time, strategic partnerships are used to enhance areas seen as being of greater strategic importance but of lower operational importance, and traditional outsourcing contracts have been used to enhance areas of less strategic importance but of greater operational importance.

Over time, BP has entered into outsourcing and business process outsourcing contracts for finance and accounting services—both the work itself and the information technology systems and support for that work—and similarly for its human resources administration, facilities management and services, information technology infrastructure services, payroll services, and other elements of its shared services operation.

As the company has refined its process and learned to manage the risks, it has come to find that outsourcing is no longer viewed as an exception to the norm, but as its primary strategy for creating change and innovation within these areas of its operations.

Chapter

7

CREATING AND LEADING SUCCESSFUL TEAMS

Taking outsourcing from opportunity identification through to implementation and ongoing management requires both structure and leadership: structure in terms of a repeatable management process that is understood and followed by all, and leadership in terms of executive sponsors, project team leaders, and effective project team members. This chapter focuses on the process of outsourcing and its key participants.

Outsourcing tests every facet of the organization. As has already been discussed, at the level of strategy a new layer of analysis is introduced. The default option of creating competitive advantage exclusively through internal investments is replaced by a broader view that competitive advantage comes from blending both internal and external sources. At the implementation level, outsourcing looks very much like a divestiture, spin-off, or an acquisition. As such, it affects everyone—both inside and outside the scope of the specific services involved. It demands careful planning and implementation, not only at the operational level, but also in terms of contracting with the provider and managing the impact on people. Once implemented, the effectiveness of the ongoing management of the relationship between the companies is the ultimate determining factor of the results achieved.

Because of these multifaceted, multidimensional characteristics, outsourcing is almost always approached as a multistage project with teams of individuals playing critical roles at each of its stages.

The Process of Outsourcing

The process of outsourcing begins with strategy, moves through assessment and implementation, and then continues into the management of the relationship. It forms a closed loop as the management of the current relationship sets the stage for what's strategically possible in the future. (See Figure 7.1.)

Done well—accomplished in a way that is consistent with the expanded value model presented in Chapter 4—it's a value-creation loop; done poorly, it can become a value-destruction loop. A solid process and the right management leadership and teams are what make the difference between the two results.

At the same time, outsourcing is affecting the organization at multiple levels: at the corporate level, at the business unit and location level, and within various functions and departments. It demands multidisciplinary skills, such as business, process knowledge, technology, finance, human resources, and legal.

A model for this process is shown in Figure 7.2. The overall process has been broken into five stages. The end of each stage is thought of as

FIGURE 7.1 OUTSOURCING DEMANDS A CLOSED LOOP LINKING STAGES AND TEAMS

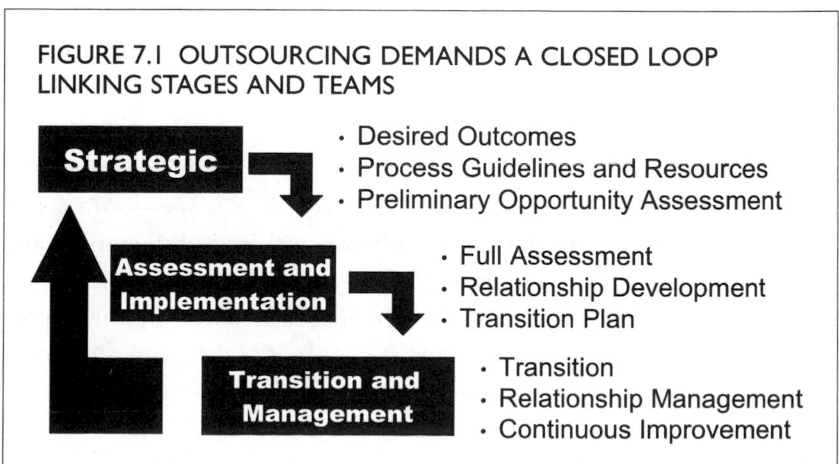

FIGURE 7.2 OUTSOURCING'S FIVE STAGES

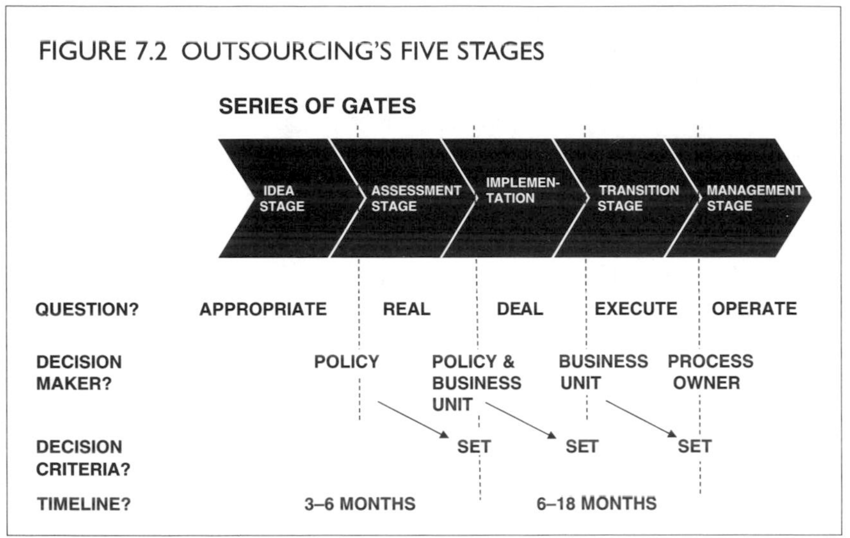

a *gate* that the project must successfully pass through before it enters the next stage.

The first stage answers the essential question: Is outsourcing this business process appropriate for this organization at this time? If deemed appropriate, the second stage is an in-depth assessment of the opportunity. That is, the development of the business case and analysis of the provider marketplace to confirm that the anticipated benefits are, indeed, real. If the opportunity is found to be real, then the next stage answers the question: Can we reach agreement on a deal with one of the qualified providers? If so, then the subsequent stages of the process cover its implementation and ongoing management. Each stage has a clearly defined and straightforward question it seeks to answer. And that answer is the starting point for the next stage.

Resistance to a change of the scope and impact of outsourcing from within and across the organization can be significant. Overcoming this resistance requires that not only the stages and gates be defined, but that a forward-leaning management approach be adopted. To do this, the decision makers at each gate, and the decision criteria used, must be clear to all involved. The question of appropriateness often needs to be answered at the level of senior executives with overall policy-making responsibility. After all, the factors that go into answering this question are complex with long-term implications, and, once made, the project will consume significant resources. Policy-setting decisions of this impact are typically made at the level of the CEO and his or her direct reports, or even at the level of the board of directors. It's important to note that the process being recommended places the "appropriate" decision early in the process, so that neither significant internal or external resources are consumed performing detailed analysis, negotiation, or implementation planning on a proposal that may ultimately be rejected by senior leadership as inappropriate. At later stages, the decision-making authority moves downstream to the strategic business unit heads and the owners of the actual function or process.

Another key element of this staged but forward-leaning approach to making and executing outsourcing decisions is that as each decision gate is passed, the criteria for the next gate is established. In other words, when the policy decision is made that an opportunity is appropriate, the policy-level decision makers also establish the specific criteria to be used for the assessment decision. The parameters for this next decision gate are established in terms of anticipated benefits and acceptable risks. It might be phrased along the lines of, "This opportunity is real if upon detail assessment we find that. . . ." The reason it is important to establish the exit criteria for the next gate as part of passing through the previous one is to short-circuit the natural tendency of those coming onto the project at a later time to revisit the "wisdom" of the decisions that preceded them. For example, the goal of the individuals involved in the deal stage is not to reassess the appropriateness or the viability of the opportunity, it's to do their very best to complete a deal that fits the criteria established during the assessment stage.

Finally, it's important to set reasonable time frames for the project. Although certain organizational changes can be planned and implemented in a matter of weeks or months, significant outsourcing projects will require between 3 and 6 months for scoping and assessing the opportunity, and then 6 to 12 months for putting the relationship together with a provider and transitioning to the new operating environment. It certainly can happen faster, but only if the level of executive attention and organizational resources applied are up to the task. Setting reasonable time frames for each stage, whatever they are, is an important part of maintaining momentum while not forcing the work to be done in such a compressed manner that shortcuts get taken, leading to poor decisions and even poorer execution.

The Outsourcing Teams

Most outsourcing projects will require that a series of teams form and evolve over its life.

One such team, of course, is the policy-level team already described. This group has responsibility for determining the appropriateness of an opportunity. Another important team is the one tasked with generating ideas for review by the policy-level team. When the top-down, sourcing-as-strategy approach is used for identifying opportunities, the team working on the organization's business strategy will, as a natural course of its work, be identifying opportunities for consideration. Many of the organization's senior executives will likely be involved in that work creating a natural feed into the policy team.

When a bottom-up approach is used, it is often more effective to create an independent project team specifically chartered with the responsibility to look across the organization, develop the preliminary activity and process analysis discussed in the previous chapter, and bring the most promising ideas forward to the policy level for consideration. This team, what might be called the *idea team,* works best when it is small, led by a well-respected, experienced person, has good quality technical and business-people assigned to it, and does not report directly to the management of the operations being examined for outsourcing. It can be extremely difficult for individuals working from within a function or department to objectively assess and generate ideas for improving that operation through outsourcing—the sense that outsourcing implies failure is often too hard to overcome. Therefore, individuals doing the work should be extremely knowledgeable and respected, but should be operating independently.

As an idea moves from the idea stage to the assessment stage, a larger team is needed. Often one or two members of the idea team will continue as members of this team to provide much needed continuity. An executive from the policy team is often selected as the executive sponsor for the project at this point. A functional or process executive typically becomes the assessment team leader, joining functional managers; process experts; information technology experts; representative customers or end-users of the process; and purchasing, legal, finance, human resources, and, possibly, external consultants. The key is to make sure that the assessment team possesses all of the functional disciplines and process knowledge needed to perform a complete analysis of both the opportunity and its implications for the organization and its people. The assessment team typically morphs into the implementation and transition teams, adding and subtracting team members based on the needs of the particular project. The management team will be discussed in detail in a later chapter.

A note on the role of consultants: Consultants often play an important role in many outsourcing and BPO projects. Consultants can bring templates for much of the work that is common from one project to the next. They bring the experience gained from multiple projects, which can enable the team to move forward more quickly and avoid common mistakes and pitfalls. Consultants often know the provider market extremely well and can speed the process of bringing the right providers to the table. As an "honest broker" they can represent the interests of their client in discussions and negotiations. Consultants are also bringing resources to the project, thereby reducing the amount of internal time needed for the project—time that might better be spent elsewhere.

At the same time, consultants bring their own biases to the process. This can sometimes complement the interests of the customer, but it can also conflict. Because consultants have looked at the marketplace and the issues many times before, they may not be as alert to new ways of doing things or new providers. At the same time, certain providers can have a natural affinity for or against certain consultants.

Eventually, the consulting engagement will end. This means that the most important factor to keep in mind is that it is the customer, not the consultant, who must lead the project. The customer must be, throughout the process, the one defining and shaping the relationship; a relationship the organization will ultimately be managing.

In the final analysis, each project team needs to evaluate its skills and resources and the type and role they want and need external advisors to play.

The Outsourcing Project Leader

As with all business activities, the team leader has a critical role. Driving an outsourcing project is a complex task requiring strong leadership skills. In selecting individuals for this position, the following characteristics should be considered:

Ability to embrace and champion change. Outsourcing is, first and foremost, a tool for organizational change. The managers leading these efforts must not only be able to embrace the changes that outsourcing entails, but be able to champion them across the organization. They must be able to communicate not only what is happening, but why and how it will benefit the organization, its customers, and its stakeholders.

Earned credibility across the organization. To be an effective change agent, the individual must have a high degree of credibility across the organization; credibility that typically has been earned through a proven track record of contribution to the organization and its success.

A desire to manage, not to do. Another critical leadership skill is the desire to manage, not to do. The leader must be results-focused. He or she should excel in the ability to accomplish results through others. Any attempt to engage the marketplace in a way that is proscriptive detracts from creativity and the ultimate value of the end results. The outside organization is selected because of its unique expertise. The provider must then be free to control the "how" of the work while the client organization's management focuses on defining and leveraging the results.

The ability to build trust. There are a number of characteristics that can build trust throughout the formation of the relationship with the provider. Consistency, fairness, objectivity, principle-based decision making, open communications, and a demonstrated desire for both organizations to succeed are some of the most important of these. Managers entrusted with evaluating and crafting outsourcing relationships need to possess these characteristics. If they do, the relationship between the organizations will be well grounded and poised for success; if they don't, both trust and, ultimately, results will suffer.

Strong communications skills. All of the skills discussed so far clearly demand strong communications skills. Communications is required throughout the process both externally and internally. Communications includes all media: written, verbal, small and large groups, traditional and electronic forms.

Strong negotiation skills. As Dr. Roger Fisher, author of numerous books on negotiation and head of the Harvard Negotiation Project, observes, "Each negotiation is an opportunity to strengthen the relationship between the organizations."[1] Negotiation is not just a matter of getting the best deal, it's a matter of maximizing the value of the relationship for the client organization while, at the same time, fairly meeting most, if not all, of the needs of the provider. Negotiation is an acquired skill, one gained through practice and, in many cases, training. It is not just something that occurs while the deal is being crafted. Negotiation takes place every day, at every level of the organization, as both parties constantly adjust to changing situations. Nor is negotiation something that takes place only with the service providers, but it occurs constantly inside the organization, as well.

Strategic planning skills. When opportunities are being driven from a top-down approach, the need for strategic planning skills is obvious. However, they're also needed when opportunities have been identified using the bottom-up approach. A disciplined, consistent style in evaluating each decision as to its future implications is needed, as well as an ability to communicate these considerations throughout the organization and, of course, to the service provider.

Project and team management skills. This is obvious, but still worth stating. The project leader needs to be able to integrate the activities of a diverse group of professionals toward the common goal. Project management is the ability to manage the relationships between these activities, deal with the constant changes, and in so doing, maximize the outcomes while minimizing the resources consumed. Leaders of an outsourcing team are, by the very nature of the work, operating in a team environment. Many individuals representing different disciplines and functions are involved on the customer side. Just as important, the provider's representatives are operating as a team. The leader must be able to effectively bring both of these groups together, keep them focused, recognize and reward each individual's contributions, and balance everyone's interests.

Marketing skills. All of this requires a strong dose of marketing skills. The ability to use communications, negotiations, and many of the skills just discussed to support and gain commitment and action from others is the essence of marketing. The leader of an outsourcing team constantly markets the value of the project within the organization, ensuring that interests are understood and met, dealing with exceptions, and overcoming resistance.

Process expertise. The project leader must have knowledge of the work being done, how the process works, what represents best-in-class performance, and how it is achieved. This does not imply that the project lead can or needs to match the expertise of the other team members or the provider. But it does mean that expertise on the process and process analysis enables the leader to understand the issues being faced, the value of what's being accomplished, and the ways that results are achieved.

Summary

Successful outsourcing efforts require support and leadership from the top of the organization; a well-defined, forward-leaning planning and implementation process; and participation of a multidisciplinary team. Organizations should not underestimate the complexity of the project or the level of internal resistance that a change of this magnitude can enjoin. Only a strong, fully supported process will overcome these challenges.

A multistage process—with each stage being thought of as a gate that the project passes through—works best. These stages ask and answer the basic business questions: Is the opportunity appropriate? Is it real? Can we craft a good deal? Can we execute? And finally, can we manage? It's important to identify ahead of time both the decision criteria and the decision makers for answering each of these questions.

Strong project leaders are important, and the key skills needed by these individual are:

- The ability to embrace and champion change
- Earned credibility across the organization
- A desire to manage, not to do
- The ability to build trust
- Strong communications skills
- Strong negotiation skills
- Strategic planning skills
- Project and team management skills

- Marketing skills
- Process expertise

As outsourcing becomes more prevalent, outsourcing management is becoming a recognized discipline in its own right, and it is able to command premium salaries. Whereas only 25 percent of executives are outsourcing 25 percent or more of their budgets today, 51 percent expect to be doing so by the end of 2005.[2] At the same time, almost 80 percent of hiring managers indicate that they would pay a salary premium of from 6 to more than 20 percent for managers with prior outsourcing experience.[3]

Case Study: Bell Canada

Bell Canada has made managing outsourcing a core competency.[4] Since 1995 the company has extensively used outsourcing across a wide range of activities, including account receivables processing, customer service, logistics, network installation, office support services, operator services, real estate, and telemarketing. Early in its use of outsourcing, a central team was created to provide corporate control over the development and management of outsourcing arrangements at Bell Canada with the objectives to bring a disciplined approach to the management of outsourcing arrangements; to ensure best-in-class value aligned to changing corporate needs; and to ensure that new opportunities are identified, implemented, and renewed.

Working from that charter, a management tool kit was developed to guide the company's outsourcing work, including a how-to guide that outlines a six-phase process. The phases and the steps in each are as follows:

1. Identify outsourcing opportunity.
   - Develop concept.
   - Perform high level strategic review of operations.
   - Identify corporate direction.
   - Develop "high insight" reports on outsourcing competitive intelligence.
   - Perform business comparative or situation analysis.
   - Identify outsourcing potential.
   - Get executive concurrence and sponsorship.
   - Assign steering committee.

2. Perform preliminary opportunity assessment.
   - Identify current processes.
   - Understand user needs.
   - Identify internal baseline costs and organization.
   - Develop process requirements.
   - Perform risk assessment analysis.
   - Explore supplier alternatives.
   - Develop preliminary outsourcing business case.
   - Present to business prime.
3. Develop and evaluate business case.
   - Finalize business case.
   - Verify customer approval.
   - Verify board approval.
4. Establish outsourcing relationship.
   - Implement request for proposals process.
   - Develop outsourcing contract.
   - Finalize human resources plan.
   - Finalize deal structure.
   - Negotiate contract.
   - Ratify contract.
   - Execute contract.
5. Implement the solution.
   - Communicate project, team, and leadership.
   - Develop detailed transition plan.
   - Finalize communication plan.
   - Implement new organization structure.
   - Transition activities.
   - Monitor transition and implementation.
6. Manage ongoing relationship.
   - Perform daily management activities.
   - Monitor performance.
   - Implement relationship management processes.
   - Complete annual outsourcing business plan.
   - Change management process.
   - Assess strategic review.

- Reconfirm business case.
- Review outsourcing performance assessment model.

Each of these steps is supported by additional tools in the tool kit, including a decision model, business case template, generic contract, outsourcing business plan, outsourcing assessment model, and strategic review plan.

Chapter

8

ENGAGING THE MARKETPLACE

Outsourcing can only happen when there is a marketplace or developing marketplace of high-quality service providers in the business of performing the process for multiple clients. Selecting the right provider in that market is the single most important decision the organization will make. This task becomes even more complex and difficult when the outsourcing is taking place on a global scale.

Unfortunately, the model that most organizations use for engaging the marketplace for outsourcing services is a traditional purchasing model. Although purchasing has evolved dramatically over the past decade, when most businesspeople think of purchasing, they think of a process that is prescriptive and cost-centric; prescriptive in that the customer engages the market with as set of tightly defined specifications. Cost-centric in that the goal is to acquire each unit that meets the specifications at the lowest possible total cost. A purchasing approach also implies that payments take place on delivery and only when the customer agrees that what was delivered matches the specifications.

Outsourcing is a completely different type of business relationship. It is more akin to a strategic alliance or joint venture than to a traditional purchase of a product or service. One of the key differences is that the outsourcing provider is being engaged by the organization specifically because it believes the provider knows more about how to perform the process well than does the organization itself. Prescribing the way the work is to be done makes little sense, and actually works against the organization's best interests. Second, the relationship is not at all like taking receipt of a product and ensuring that what's delivered matches the specifications. Outsourcing is an ongoing and continuous exchange of services and value for money, extending over a period of perhaps many years. As a result, building the right relationship with the right provider will prove to be far more important than getting the best "deal" in today's market. Outsourcing is not a series of transactions; it is an ongoing, highly interdependent business relationship.

These essential differences lead to the conclusion that from the very beginning the way an organization engages the marketplace for outsourcing needs to be very different than the way it has "bought" products and services in the past. These differences and the key underlying principles that shape them are the focus of this chapter.

More Like Hiring Than Buying

A better model to use in developing an organization's approach to outsourcing is the one used to recruit and select a senior executive.

When companies outsource, they really are hiring both a senior executive and his or her entire department to do the actual work. This includes the planning and operational team, as well as the resources, technologies, and intellectual properties they are going to use. This doesn't suggest that the identification and selection of the provider should be based solely on the individuals who will be assigned to the customer, although it is certainly a factor. It does suggest, however, that the overall approach should follow more a recruiting mindset than a buying one.

Think about it. When recruiting, an organization begins by detailing the responsibilities of the position, the results it expects, and the types of experience and backgrounds that are likely to be good indicators a candidate can be successful in the job. It examines "hard" factors, such as the candidate's background, demonstrable skills, job and salary history, and record of accomplishment. But it also considers a number of "soft" factors, such as personality, values, motivations, and, ultimately, how it "feels" about the individual.

A successful organization also doesn't begin the search by saying, "Let's find the lowest-salary person willing to take the job." Instead, it begins by understanding its internal pay scale and where this position fits within it. It gets input on the relevant salary ranges for the job under consideration especially given the experiences and skills it thinks are required to do the job well. It goes to the market with this clear view of what it is looking for, the range of salaries and benefits that are appropriate, and even a plan for the types and levels of bonuses and incentives needed to attract and motivate top candidates.

This is a far more appropriate model to use in engaging the marketplace for outsourcing services than the traditional purchasing model. It means that the organization needs to first develop a clear understanding of its requirements. This is done by working with the end users; the actual customers of the process, whether internal employees or external customers. It takes a series of meetings with these users, as well as process experts, to define the current process, and, just as important, to get a clear understanding of the required results. It also means doing the hard work needed to understand the types of competencies and capabilities an outside organization taking over the process will need to have to be successful. What competencies and skills, industry experiences, technologies, and type of track record of continuous improvement is it going to take? These are the questions that need to be answered before even beginning to actually engage the marketplace. It also means developing an accurate and complete baseline of current costs and performance levels for current processes as well as best-in-class metrics that capture what other organizations, including service providers, are achieving. It means looking out over the strategic planning horizon and considering how the very nature of the process may need to change in response to changing customer preferences, technologies, and competitors.

This process of first defining customer needs, then engaging the marketplace of providers, and ultimately selecting the right provider requires a well-orchestrated interplay of internal assessment and consensus building, coupled with an effective, practical, and at times hard-nosed interaction with the marketplace of potential providers.

There are a number of ways to go about identifying potential providers. One of the best and often overlooked ways is to open a dialogue with outside organizations the company is already doing business with. These are the companies already providing either a product or service within the scope of the process under consideration or that are providing a solution for a related process. They should be companies with which a solid and successful relationship has been developed over a period of time.

Many if not most of today's best-known providers actually began their outsourcing businesses in response to interest expressed to them by an existing customer in a traditional business line. Building upon successful, trusted relationships is outsourcing's equivalent to "promoting from within."

The next way to identify potential providers is to use the organization's professional network to find out what others are doing and who they are working with. This network can be at the level of the company's board, where board members may have direct experience themselves or may sit on the boards of other companies that have outsourced some or all of the business processes under consideration. Board members who have seen other companies achieve good results through outsourcing often play a catalyst role in helping an organization take a serious look at the opportunities available. This professional network also includes trusted advisors, such as accounting companies, law firms, professional associations, and other senior-level relationships, as well as, of course, the company's own operating executives' professional networks. Just as with the recruiting of an executive candidate, the organization's business network is a powerful tool for identifying the right companies to engage in early conversations.

A third approach is direct research. Direct research includes reviewing articles in the press, scanning advertisements and the Web, and attending conferences. Information on who is in the industry, the types of organizations they are working for, and at least a preliminary sense of the results being achieved can be easily gained in this way.

Finally, many companies will use consultants, what might be called *experienced guides,* to help them identify potential providers. Certainly, these individuals and organizations can bring to the process their collective experience of having worked with many organizations as they crafted their relationships. They can also bring insight based on a substantial investment made in researching the marketplace over an extended period of time.

All of these techniques can, and probably should, be used in concert. It's also important to keep in mind that even at these very early stages the organization is beginning a process leading toward the creation of a long-term relationship between itself and an outside company. The very nature and character of that ultimate relationship is shaped at each and every step along the way. How the outside organizations are contacted and communicated with, at what level, by whom, for what stated purpose, the type and amount of information the customer is willing to share, the knowledge and sophistication the customer demonstrates, and its overall approach to strategic relationships are all communicated directly and indirectly. Each contributes to the character of the final relationship and how it works. Again, it's a process far more akin to executive recruiting than to purchasing.

As organizations are identified and engaged in preliminary conversation, their strengths and weaknesses are analyzed, and a short list of three to six organizations is developed. These are the organizations that will essentially be invited to review the opportunity in detail and propose a solution. The types of items being considered, which will be covered in greater detail later in the chapter, include not just the work these companies are currently doing or might be able to do, but their financial viability, management strength and culture, customer references, cost models, quality processes and results, and their overall industry leadership in terms of process design, execution, and technology.

Developing and Communicating Requirements

There are a range of approaches that organizations can use to capture their requirements internally and then communicate them externally. Both aspects of the process are of equal importance, and the approaches available for doing this range from the very formal to the very collaborative.

A more formal process typically follows a defined purchasing model. It can begin with the use of a prequalification letter as a first step in the customer's process of establishing what it's looking for in the companies it may choose to outsource to. The prequalification letter states the customer's basic requirements for any potential provider. These requirements might include the length of time the provider has been in business, its financial health, its current suite of services, its experience in the customer's industry, and its current clients. Prequalification letters are typically sent to a fairly long list of potential providers with each requested to respond with the information demonstrating that the company meets the customer's stated qualifications.

Even companies following a formal process often skip the prequalification letter step, however, and begin with a more comprehensive and robust request for information (RFI). Like the prequalification letter, the RFI is, implicitly, a statement of what the customer is looking for in the providers that will receive full consideration. The request for information goes further, however, in that it will ask for a wide range of information not only about whether the organization meets specific qualifications, but its overall operations, including how it does what it does. A request for information will often ask about the size and scope of the various elements of the provider's operations, its process for transitioning into a relationship and managing it on an ongoing basis, how it allocates its resources, and how it evaluates and minimizes its business risks. Essentially, the request for information focuses on any and all aspects of the potential provider's operations that might have a bearing on the customer's ultimate selection decision.

The final step in a formal process for engaging the marketplace is typically a request for proposals (RFP). A request for proposals is a very detailed description on the part of the customer of its business requirements. It requests a formal, binding response in a predefined format that facilitates the customer's comparison of the responses it receives. Generally, an RFP is only sent to a relatively few organizations, those that have been qualified through a prequalification letter, an RFI, or some other process.

The content and format of RFPs have been documented in so many books as to not be worth repeating here. In fact, every organization that uses RFPs as part of its process, as well as every consulting group that advises companies on outsourcing transactions, tends to have their own preferred document format and techniques for obtaining the most pertinent information in the most revealing way from the responding companies.

There are, however, a few critical principles that can get lost between the lines of a company's or a consultant's template for a request for proposals that are worth discussing.

The first is the need to *focus on objectives and results, not resources and methodologies*. The purpose of the RFP is not to document what your company is currently doing and to ask the provider how much it will cost to have them do the same things for you basically the same way. The purpose is to describe your company's business objectives and the results it is seeking from the process to be outsourced. This is a key difference. As organizations outsource, they are shifting the focus of their internal managers away from managing resources—that becomes the provider's job—toward managing results. The provider produces those results for the customer, and it is the provider that is responsible for the resources—people, processes, and technologies—used to produce them.

The second principle is to define those desired results in *clear, complete, and measurable terms.* The RFP essentially answers two questions: What results does the organization seek? How will the organization determine whether or not those results are being achieved? The scorecard that the organization plans to use to measure these results is the centerpiece of a good request for proposals and the development of that scorecard is discussed later.

One of the most powerful effects an outsourcing analysis can have, even if a contract is never signed, is that it forces the organization to define in detail the scope, activities, resources, and information that make up one of its business processes and to capture in objective, measurable terms the results expected. This analysis alone, which the organization has to do before it can successfully engage the marketplace, has tremendous value.

The third key principle of an effective request for proposals is that it describe all of the *factors that will go into evaluating the providers' proposals,* and even the relative weight that will be applied to each. Certainly the financials of the proposal will be important, but, so will a number of other factors: the organization's confidence that the approach being proposed will deliver the intended results both today and in the future; the level of risk involved and how those risks are mitigated and shared; the proposed terms and conditions of the contract, especially acceptance of any specific contract terms the organization defined in its RFP; the proposed transition plan, especially its human resources elements; and how the provider will manage the relationship over time.

The fourth principle is to *specify the information and format required* so that the proposals can be readily compared to each other. This means identifying the frequencies and volume drivers of the business activities that make up the process so that all proposals are based on a similar set of base workload assumptions. It also means specifying the actual information requested from organizations responding to the RFP and the format in which it is to be presented.

Two additional principles for a good RFP are to *define the current problems and costs* associated with the existing process, and for the organization to use the RFP to *position itself as a good prospective customer.* The former reflects the simple reality that in most cases the customer is outsourcing to solve a problem, and it makes perfect sense to explain to a prospective partner or partners exactly what those problems are. Similarly, even though some may reject the idea from a negotiation standpoint, sharing current costs provides valuable insight into how the process operates today and what its underlying cost drivers are. Both of these pieces of information are critical to providers, who will ultimately be long-term partners in crafting the right solution. If an organization believes a good "deal" can only be won by withholding this information, then an argument can also be made that the result is likely to be a deal that's fundamentally flawed, not likely to produce the value expected in the long run, and not worth doing in the first place.

Using the RFP to position the organization as a good customer for the provider is important, as well. Service providers know that the only way they can be successful is by establishing long-term, growing relationships with high-quality customers. In today's market good service providers are inundated by requests for proposals. "No bid" responses to these unsolicited RFPs are commonplace. Top providers put as much effort into evaluating and selecting the right potential customers as their customers do in evaluating and selecting them. Providers cannot afford to invest time and money responding to every request for proposals they receive. On the other hand, service providers will put an exceptional level of effort into developing a high-quality response to organizations they see as potentially great long-term customers.

Moving Beyond the RFP

Although the request for proposals is the most common vehicle for capturing and communicating requirements to the marketplace, it is certainly not the only one, nor is it best for every situation. Other approaches can yield even better results, especially when the number of potential providers is limited, when it's believed that real breakthroughs are possible if the providers are involved early in the redesign of the process, and when the customer is creating a new process.

In these cases, a more collaborative approach works better. Also, as outsourcing becomes a greater part of strategic planning—as opposed to an operational decision—the need for collaborative approaches is growing; having more than just the request for proposals as a tool for developing outsourcing relationships is a real advantage.

One great vehicle for capturing and communicating requirements in a less formal more collaborative way is the case study. Here, instead of an RFP, the organization produces a two- to four-page business case document, explaining its current environment, what the organization believes is likely to occur in its industry and business over the next few years, the challenges and opportunities these changes will create, and the types of approaches to addressing and leveraging those changes that are currently under consideration. This case study is then provided, under nondisclosure agreements as appropriate, to a carefully selected small group of potential providers. These providers respond to the case study through both a written management brief and an executive presentation, describing how they would approach solving the challenges the organization faces. The resulting dialogue leads to the selection of a preferred approach and a preferred provider. This, in turn, kicks off a collaborative process involving the two companies in the joint design, development, and implementation of the ultimate solution. The final design, essentially covering everything that would have been in the response to an RFP anyway and more, develops out of this process.

Another collaborative approach is to separate the qualification of potential providers from the design of the solution. This can be done by having providers go through an independent qualification process with a central group, such as purchasing, to get onto a preferred supplier list for a range of processes or business functions. Once on that list, providers can then be brought in by any of the organization's project teams to work with them in the design and prototyping of solutions for specific outsourcing opportunities. The final contract is awarded to the provider whose solution is selected by the project team through the design and prototype process. This is a well-tested supplier-management strategy in manufacturing, and it can work just as well for other business processes.

Whether using a formal process involving prequalification letters, requests for information, and requests for proposals or a more collaborative process, such as the case study approach, keep in mind that the process is simultaneously serving more than one purpose. The obvious purpose is that it communicates the organization's requirements to the marketplace. The less obvious but just as important purpose is that it helps the organization define its own needs in clear, complete, and measurable terms; it develops agreement across the organization on those requirements; and it ensures continuity of that understanding across a selection process that can last for a number of months and involve different individuals, in different roles, at different points in time.

Creating the Scorecard

Defining desired results in clear, complete, and measurable terms is key to managing any business process, whether it's outsourced or not. It remains the essential, unchanging responsibility of customer management before, during, and after outsourcing. In many ways it's both the true art and science of management in today's world. When organizations outsource, they are asking the provider to assume responsibility for "how" results are achieved, but the company's manager is still the one with responsibility for understanding and defining "what" needs to be accomplished.

Although the term *service level agreement,* or SLA, is commonly used with outsourcing, it can carry a connotation that actually moves an organization away from a focus on results toward a focus on the internal workings of the process—which is the wrong direction. The service provider will certainly want to track and report for itself, and possibly to the customer, many of these internal service level measures—they can be important indicators of what's happening within the process, and they are irreplaceable as a diagnostic tool when a problem develops or as an early warning sign of potential problems. However, because the customer needs to be focused on the results of the process, not its inner workings, the techniques of scorecards, business scorecards, or balanced scorecards are more powerful and effective.

The scorecard essentially defines what's important. This definition has to take place before and throughout the period the relationship is being crafted and managed. Any outsourcing contract that does not connect to an agreed upon scorecard has not yet been fully defined and negotiated, and cannot really be implemented. It's the scorecard that makes what's important measurable. The scorecard describes what both organizations are trying to accomplish, the objective means by which results will be tracked and reported and the cornerstone of any effective system of motivation and continuous performance improvement. The scorecard lets everyone involved know what's important and how the information needed to determine if it's being accomplished will be collected and reported.

If a scorecard for the process does not already exist, then the organization, as part of mapping the process and developing its own business requirements, creates it. Since the scorecard describes what's important, it's essentially the same whether or not the process is outsourced. As Figure 8.1 depicts, there are five layers to a scorecard: categories, attributes, metrics, tools, and ratings.

Categories are the highest level characteristics used to measure the process. They define its essential purpose and value—what's most critical to achieving the organization's business objectives. The categories address such characteristics as quality, customer satisfaction, timeliness, financial performance (i.e., costs, revenue), conformance to requirements (i.e., regulations, audit requirements), speed, flexibility, and innovation.

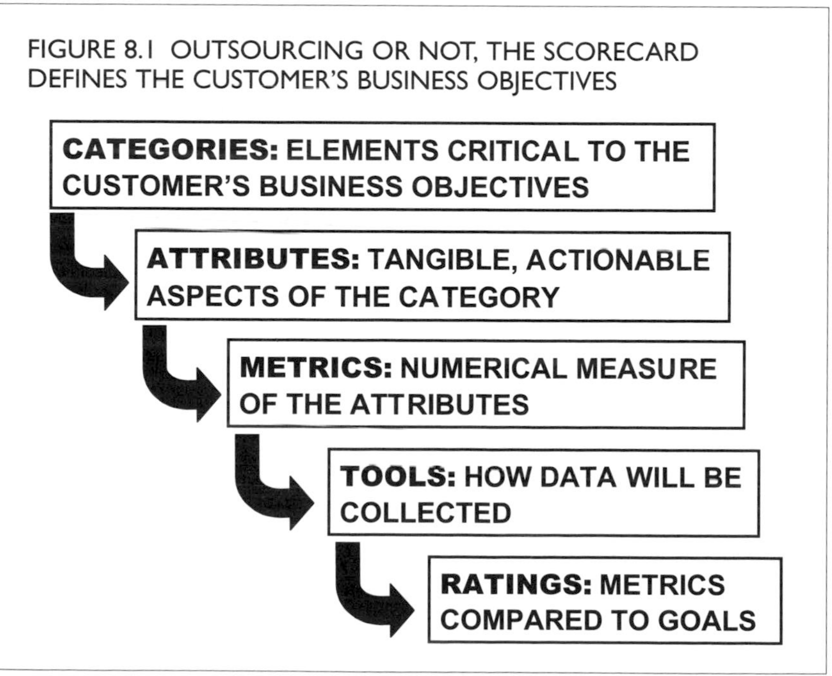

For each category, one or more *attributes* are then defined. These attributes are unique to the process and to the customer's business objectives. They are the tangible and actionable elements of each category. The difference between categories and attributes is easily illustrated with, for example, food. It's easy to say that high-quality food is a critical characteristic. Therefore, quality is a category in which food services would be measured. But what are the attributes by which the quality of the food will be determined? Are they taste, temperature, freshness, appearance, or a combination of all of these? It's in choosing the right set of attributes that a specific customer defines quality within the context of its business.

Next, each attribute requires a *metric* by which it can be measured. The metric must be supported by one or more *tools* that will be used for collecting the data. Continuing with the food services example, if taste is selected as an attribute, how will it be measured and reported objectively? One approach might be customer evaluation forms, where the customer is asked to rate the food's taste, possibly in comparison to similarly priced meals at other outlets. The tool in this case could be a survey instrument with a ten-point scale. An alternative approach might be audit-oriented, where mystery shoppers evaluate and report on the food's taste using a specific scoring system.

Finally, the results of the metric for each attribute and collectively for each category must be *rated* against the desired outcomes. That is, what was the score and does it meet, fail to meet, or exceed the desired result?

A two-phase process works best for developing the scorecard. Phase I is one-on-one interviews with the key stakeholders in the process. These stakeholders include the executives responsible for the process; management-level individuals who oversee the process; the end-users and customers of the process; and individuals who contribute to the process, including suppliers and vendors. The purpose of these one-on-one sessions is not to collect current performance data but to learn their wants and needs from the process itself. The goal is to uncover and clarify what attributes define, for that individual, a good result from the process. What does superior performance mean to them? The person or team conducting these interviews should work from a prepared set of questions—a set that explores each element of the process and its deliverables—but should also be prepared to ask follow-up questions, such as: Why? What do you mean by that? How is that answer related to what you said before?

All of the attributes identified are then grouped into categories based on their affinity to each other. The result is a preliminary list of categories and attributes. A preliminary list of possible metrics for measuring each attribute can be prepared at this time, as well.

Phase II is to assemble a group of stakeholders, including many of the individuals interviewed during Phase I, and to present to the group the preliminary list of categories, attributes, and potential metrics. The discussion begins with a development of a common definition of the categories and then of the individual attributes and metrics. The goal is to reach consensus, to assign a weight and priority to each category and to each attribute within it, to gain common agreement to the metrics and the tools to be used to collect the data, and to develop the ratings for each.

As an example, the scorecard developed through this process for a call center operation might have the categories quality, timeliness, financials, and productivity.

The attributes and metrics for quality might be customer satisfaction measured as the percent of customers rating overall call processing as excellent or very good, effectiveness measured as the percent of customers rating the representative's performance as excellent or very good, and compliance measured as the percent of calls handled in compliance with federal and state regulations and company policy. Note that two of these attributes are customer-focused while the third is focused on a critical internal business measure of quality.

The attributes and metrics for timeliness might be cycle time measured as the percent of calls answered within a certain number of seconds and abandon rate measured as the percent of calls abandoned by a caller prior to a response.

The attribute and metric of financials might be unit costs measured as the total operating expenses divided by call volume. The attribute and metric of productivity might be average handling time measured as the total time spent on calls divided by total calls.

Note that in this example, each of the categories, attributes, and metrics are specific to the individual customer and how it connects the process outcomes to the business objectives it is trying to accomplish. Also note that the number of attributes that make up the scorecard are fairly limited. Six to 12 well-selected attributes works best; fewer and the overall performance may not be reflected accurately, many more will distract from the goal of focusing attention on what's most important.

Considering Providers

Throughout the process, whether it's more formal or collaborative, the customer is evaluating the service providers in terms of their overall capabilities and fit. In making this assessment there are a wide range of provider characteristics to be considered. Every customer organization needs to create its unique list of key characteristics for each outsourcing opportunity. It also needs to assign a relative weight to each characteristic, involve multiple individuals in the evaluation process, and then score and compare providers as objectively as possible. Although the selection of a provider should never be made truly scientific any more than the selection of an executive should be, it helps to use a scoring technique and a template to bring as much objectivity to the process as possible.

Certainly the competitiveness of the solution itself is a major factor. However, the competitiveness of the solution is only one factor to be considered. Other factors, including the organization's demonstrated competencies, its total capabilities, and the likely relationship dynamics between the two companies are of just as great, if not greater, importance over the life of the relationship.

Competencies

Organizations outsource to tap the competencies, including the scale and the scope, of the provider's operations. These competencies are reflected in the provider's people, its processes, and its technologies. A track record of ongoing investment in each of these is essential to the provider's ability to deliver. Since this is the provider's business, the benchmark is simple: best-in-world. In selecting providers, an organization should be seeking those whose competencies are as close as possible to best-in-world.

They should also be evaluating the provider's competencies through their track record of innovation. Innovation is a powerful reflection of the organization's competency and ongoing investments in its field. How many innovations—new methods, technologies, advances in the field—has the company created and brought into operation over the past year, two years, or another appropriate time frame? How does that compare to other firms in the field?

Another dimension of competency is proven performance and industry experience. What other organizations in your industry does the provider currently work for? What is its record of success with those firms? When seeking a unique competitive advantage, an organization may not want the provider to be delivering similar services to direct competitors. On the other hand, for competitively sourced operational activities this can be of little if any consequence. In fact, a provider delivering best-in-world services across the industry for a commodity type of activity can quickly create a situation where any competitor not using its services is at a disadvantage. For example, at one time all of the major office supply superstores used the same provider for credit application processing precisely because the firm was excellent at it and had reached a level of scale and quality no one else could match.

Process competency should be demonstrable both from a historical and ongoing record of continuous improvement. Top service providers should already be operating at performance levels well beyond where the customer is and should be able to demonstrate the track record of continuous improvement that got them there. Even more important, they should be able to identify the next levels of improvement they already have in design and when they will be ready for roll-out.

Capabilities

Paying careful attention to the provider's total capabilities is critical because the customer organization is making a significant investment in entering into the relationship—a relationship that, going forward, is essentially an asset of the company. The first of these capabilities is financial strength on both a cash flow and a balance sheet basis. Providers that are financially strong and have developed that strength through a record of performance are better long-term partners. The organization's overall infrastructure and its total resources are important as well. Another important dimension of total capabilities is an organization's management systems, such as recruitment and training programs, management and executive development, risk management, and financial management systems. It's very fair to ask about these and to assess their strength.

Another aspect of total capabilities is the provider's complete suite of services. The organization may be engaging the provider for a particular solution today, but in the future its needs will change and evolve, and it will likely find itself looking for providers for related processes. Does this provider have the depth and breadth of services to grow as the business changes?

Relationship Dynamics

Finally, a number of factors that can have a powerful influence on the overall dynamics of the relationship over time should be evaluated and rated. One such dynamic is culture and values. Every organization has a unique culture and value system—how it makes decisions, manages people, rewards or penalizes certain types of behavior. When organizations enter into outsourcing contracts, those culture and value systems become very important. How well will they fit with each other? What aspects will complement and even enhance each of the organizations? Are there other aspects that will grate on the nerves of the separate organizations?

Another factor that will profoundly influence the overall relationship dynamics is the provider's mission and strategy. Where is it going with its business? Is the process under consideration for outsourcing viewed as key to the provider's future or might it in fact be a cash cow providing a launching pad for a new strategic direction? Flexibility is important, as well. What is the provider's track record in responding to changes from its current customers? How easy or how difficult is it to get the provider to adjust to changes in its customer's business? Is the provider flexible in some areas but rigid in others? How important is flexibility now and in the future?

The provider's management system for overseeing its relationships with its customers also needs to be considered. How does it do it? Is it people-based, technology-based, or both? How much does the provider invest in relationship management? How comprehensive, repeatable, and proven is its process? Is it leading or lagging in this aspect of outsourcing?

Finally, consider relative size and relative importance as a customer. The relative size of the two companies certainly influences the dynamics of the relationship. A large customer working with a smaller provider may feel empowered in the relationship, but that position of power can backfire if the provider becomes too dependent upon the one large customer. Tension, leading to continuous improvement, can be lost, as can economies of scale and scope that might have come from a large provider working with other large customers. On the other hand, a provider that is many times larger than the customer may eventually become inflexible and nonresponsive to the needs of a relatively small part of its business. Overlaying the size consideration is the relative importance factor. Marquee names or strategically well-positioned customers may be far more important to the provider than size alone would suggest. How important do you want to be to the provider's business?

In all of these cases, the key principles in selecting a provider are to develop a comprehensive list of factors to consider, to view the relative impact and importance of each, and to develop a repeatable, as objective as possible, process for evaluation, analysis, scoring, and decision making.

Summary

Outsourcing relationships are best developed within the framework of a strategic analysis. The goal is to achieve a sustainable fit between the customer's needs and the provider's capabilities. Done well, both organizations deal up front with many of the issues that might otherwise erode the relationship over time. A well-crafted relationship looks ahead to the business environment, markets, competitors, technologies, and societal changes of the future, and considers how the organizations will work together to meet these challenges. It requires that the customer understand and communicate its needs in clear, complete, and measurable terms. It also requires that providers be selected based upon overall fit, not just the lowest bid.

Techniques for making this happen are: (1) traditional requests for information and requests for proposals; (2) the use of case study analysis to build the relationship through jointly developed solutions to a set of current and emerging problems; and (3) joint design and strategic planning sessions with prequalified organizations.

Which approach an organization selects for a specific project depends upon a number of factors, including organizational norms and experiences; the scope, complexity, size, and risk of the project; the number of available providers; the maturity of the marketplace; whether it is an existing or new process; the resources required and available for the task; and the customer's timeline.

Quick Reference Guide

The following is a quick reference guide for use when engaging the marketplace for outsourcing.

Developing and Communicating Requirements

- Does the team developing the requirements document have representation from functional management, process experts, customers/users, procurement, finance, human resources, and legal?
- Has the current process been diagramed, including clear distinction and rationale for in-scope and out-of-scope activities?
- Have current costs been captured for each activity, including people, supplies, equipment, overheads, and capital costs? (See Chapter 9.)
- Has a scorecard for the current process's quality, customer satisfaction, timeliness, financial performance, conformance to requirements, speed, flexibility, and innovation been documented and measured?
- Have future process requirements, based on reasonable potential scenarios, been identified and documented?

Does the requirements document describe:

- Objectives and desired results, while allowing providers to propose specific resources and methodologies to be employed?
- Current and future volumes in sufficient detail for providers to forecast workload levels?
- The number and location of recipients of the services?
- The desired relationship between the companies, including such considerations as transfer of assets, people, exclusivity, sharing of risks and rewards, and pricing?
- How the relationship will be managed over time? (See Chapter 12.)
- Current problems and costs; projects currently underway, status, and expectations for the provider to assume and complete?
- Key contract considerations, such as intellectual properties, length, termination options, liabilities, and warranties? (See Chapter 11.)
- Why your company will be a good customer for the provider?

Managing the Requirements Process

Has the management of the requirements process included:

- A defined process for identifying the firms to receive the document?
- Compilation of the appropriate contact information for the individuals at the companies to receive the document?
- Definition of the key activities and dates for the distribution, response, review, and selection process?
- Sufficient guidance on response structure; the evaluation criteria; what constitutes a valid response?
- A definition of the internal review process, including roles, responsibilities, and timelines?
- A weighted evaluation criteria; a standardized format for documenting reviewer notes and positions?
- Completion of all required internal reviews and approvals before any providers are contacted?
- When and by whom responders are advised; the next steps to be followed with the selected provider(s)?

Have the following criteria been included in the evaluation criteria:

- Demonstrated competencies (people, methodologies, technologies, benchmark of best-in-world, innovation, industry experience, proven performance, continuous improvement)?
- Total capabilities (financial strength, infrastructure and resources, management systems, complete suite of services)?
- Relationship dynamics (culture, mission and strategy, flexibility, relationship management, relative size, relative importance as a client)?
- Competitiveness of the solution (solution itself, fit to requirements, innovation, risk and risk sharing, financial proposal, terms and conditions, human resources requirements)?
- Past achievement?
- Internal agreement as to the relative weight of these and other evaluation criteria?

Chapter

9

OUTSOURCING ECONOMICS

Building the Business Case

Building the business case for outsourcing can be both deceptively simple and nerve-rackingly complex. It is simple in that it is basically just a matter of comparing the financials for the current, "as is" operation to those for the proposed outsourced operation. It is complex in that organizations seldom have a very good understanding of their current costs; they often find it difficult to forecast the future with confidence; and they have a lot of different financial models to choose from when it comes to analyzing the numbers, each of which can paint a very different picture. Add to this the fact that Chapter 4 already made the case that today's value models for outsourcing are too limiting in their ability to truly project outsourcing's full impact, and the complexity becomes painfully clear.

So, what do organizations do? First, the organization needs to establish an agreed to methodology for capturing current costs and for doing so at the level of its business processes. Similarly, it needs a method for forecasting, with as much confidence as possible, what those volume drivers and costs will be in the future. Next, it needs an approach for taking as many intangible benefits, the "soft side" of the decision, and turning them into measurable outcomes that can be included in the business case and achieved in reality. Finally, it needs to decide which financial analysis technique or techniques it wants to use to create an overall picture of the decision at hand.

Because outsourcing represents a significant change for the business—one that may have as many detractors as supporters—the financial analysis approach cannot be left to chance or to each individual project team to decide on its own. Instead, the approach needs to be established up front by the policy and strategic business unit leaders who are both commissioning and endorsing the analysis.

At the same time, since every organization is different and every outsourcing decision is unique, to suggest that there is a single approach that will serve everyone equally well would be misleading. There are, however, a few basic principles that, when adhered to, lead to a clearer financial picture and better decision making.

Capturing Current Costs

On the surface, capturing current costs would seem to be easy. After all, what business doesn't know how much it is spending? In reality, however, although businesses certainly know how much they are spending in total and by major department, they seldom know how much they are spending to perform a particular business process.

The reason for this is that a business process is made up of discrete activities. These activities are taking place not within a single department, but across many departments—sometimes even in departments outside the organization. Each activity's costs amount to the sum of the actual resources it consumes, such as people, supplies, and equipment. Further, the business process's costs are the sum of all of the activities that comprise it. Unless the organization knows its costs at the activity level, it is difficult to know its costs at the business process level.

Very few organizations know their costs at the activity level. Most only know their costs at the department level, and even that knowledge is somewhat limited. Organizations may know a department's total direct costs, such as salaries, supplies, and equipment maintenance, but they seldom know the costs incurred in performing each activity within the department. Similarly, the relationship between any overhead costs that have been spread to the department and its activities is seldom known. Finally, many overheads, such as finance and human resources, as well as capital costs, are often not even included in a department's budget, so these can get missed entirely.

As a result, capturing the current costs of a business process requires some work. That work begins with the process diagram introduced in Chapter 6. The process diagram is needed because it shows what activities make up the business process, as well as their relationship to each other. It also shows the resources required to perform each activity, including employee time, supervisory time, materials and supplies, technology, equipment, and facilities. The process diagram is the essential starting point for establishing the baseline costs for the business process.

To get to activity costs, the costs of the resources consumed by the activity need to understood. Existing accounting and financial data that reports labor costs, supplies, equipment utilization, and overheads are a starting point. The people involved in performing the activity are the key source, however, for taking that information and restating the costs at the activity level. Once restated in this way, it is then possible to aggregate the costs of each activity and establish the baseline cost for the entire business process.

It's important that all overhead costs, even those not normally included in the department's budget, be traced to the activities they support. Costs that might otherwise be missed if this is not done include occupancy costs for the people and equipment used in the activity, training costs, employee benefit costs, and capital costs.

Finally, the activities and their costs need to be matched to the current process's outcomes as reflected in the scorecard discussed in Chapter 8. This connection between how the activities are performed, their costs, and the results being achieved needs to be clear. In total, the organization's understanding of its current process and costs is only complete when

- the activities that make up the process are fully documented,
- the costs of the resources used in each activity are known,
- all relevant overheads have been traced to the activities they support,
- the current performance of the process is reflected in a scorecard, and
- the volume drivers of the process and the effect of volume on costs is understood.

From Budgeted Costs to Full Costs

These baseline costs and their drivers are essential to any business process improvement program. But, they are particularly important when outsourcing since the organization will be comparing its existing process to the proposals it receives from potential service providers. Service providers naturally present their proposals in terms of the services they will perform, the performance standards they will achieve, the costs for those services, and any volume-dependent considerations. Provider proposals are fully burdened—that is, based upon a clear understanding and reflection of total costs. After all, it's the provider's business. For the customer to meaningfully compare its business process to the provider's proposal requires an equally good understanding of its own operation in similar terms.

In addition to understanding current costs for the business process, the organization has to also be able to make reasonable projections for those costs and volumes over the time frame to be used for the financial analysis. This time frame may be as short as a year or two, but it may be as long as ten years, especially if a longer contract is needed because a great deal of capital equipment is going to be transferred to the provider or the provider is going to be asked to make a large up-front investment that will take several years to recoup.

The challenge this creates for most customers is that the data available for forecasting purposes from their normal budgeting system probably only extends to a year or two, at best. This means that a series of assumptions need to be made to extend that data to cover the planning horizon. These assumptions have to consider probable changes in the business's operations, in the underlying volume drivers, in performance requirements that would be reflected in the scorecard in future years, as well as in technology and other factors that might impact the way the process is performed and its costs.

These assumptions also need to be reasonable. They need to be based on what the organization has historically spent to enhance the process, not what it might spend if all of the needed capital and resources were suddenly made available. The goal is to create a reasonable forecast for the future, assuming continued internal operation of the business process—one that can be fairly compared to the proposals received from the potential providers. Assumptions that are either too optimistic or too conservative yield a poor base for comparison purposes and, ultimately, poor decisions.

Examining the provider's proposal is a matter of comparing the scope of services being proposed, the performance levels being committed to relative to the scorecard, along with the volume assumptions and price compared to the company's internal baseline. This comparison of services, outcomes, prices, and assumptions forms the basis of the financial analysis.

There are additional factors to consider, as well. Are there one-time or start-up costs? Are there expenses not included in the proposal that may be passed along to the organization? Are there costs associated with the current process that will be retained by the organization and are therefore not reflected in the provider's proposal? It is the total of the provider's proposal over the projected period, plus these other factors, that is then compared to the customer's current and projected operations.

In addition, there are investments required for the outsourcing project and ongoing management costs that need to be included. Examples of these are:

Planning costs. These include staff time, travel, and other expenses for documenting the process, establishing the internal baseline, engaging the marketplace, and negotiating and contracting with the provider. If consultants, lawyers, or other outside experts are used, then these costs need to be captured as well.

Transition costs. Transition costs include staff time, travel, and other expenses, both internal and external, for switching to the provider's process. Moving to the new environment may require one-time investments in new systems and technologies. These investments may be within the business process or in other processes that connect to it. They may also be in support areas, such as security, quality control, and scorecard data gathering. They may also include costs associated with overlapping the old and the new operations during an initial period of time.

There are a number of other transition costs to consider. These include termination fees for any products and services to be discontinued; fees for transferring licensed materials and existing services contracts to the provider; relocation costs for moving people and equipment; any tax liabilities that may be created through the sale of existing equipment to the provider; and any one-time stay bonuses, incentives, or severance packages for current employees and managers.

Oversight costs. The new relationship, as is discussed in detail in Chapter 12, has to be managed, and there are up-front and ongoing costs associated with this. These costs can range anywhere from about 1 or 2 percent to perhaps as much as 10 percent of the contract's annual direct costs. Some of these costs will, again, be internal, and others may be associated with training, outside services, or tools.

Forecasting Outsourcing's Benefits

What has been described so far is the base business case for outsourcing. It's a comparison of the direct financial impact of the "as is" option to the outsourcing option. Net present value, return on investment, or internal rate of return techniques will probably be used to account for the time value of money and to reduce the business case to a single dollar figure that can be used to readily compare various options.

But, as discussed in Chapter 4, basing the outsourcing decision strictly on a comparison of the base businesses case leaves a great deal to be desired. First, although cost is always an important factor, in more than half the cases of outsourcing, executives indicate that the top driver of outsourcing is something other than direct cost savings. Speed, flexibility, quality, skills, capital savings, and innovation are important parts of the value equation. These can easily be missed when too narrow a definition of outsourcing's financial benefits is used.

Making Intangibles Tangible

The challenge that organizations face as they begin to expand the business case to include these other factors is the difficulty that comes with trying to take what might be generally seen as "intangible" benefits and making them "tangible." Although challenging and certainly subject to debate and discussion, these intangible benefits often overshadow the tangible ones in the final analysis. In fact, when you consider the fact that

25 percent of the value of most businesses is now "intangibles," such things as brand and market share, everyone in business needs to get more comfortable developing the intangible side of the business case.[1] This can be particularly true for outsourcing.

One approach for turning intangibles into tangibles is the following two-step process. The first step is to determine the likely economic impact in terms of one or more dimensions of shareholder value—that is, costs, assets, and revenue. The second step is to develop a reasonable economic calculation for the size of this impact.

As a simple example, consider a change that would improve the productivity of a manufacturing operation. Improved productivity has to be stated as a measurable benefit, and that measurable benefit needs to be in one or more of the dimensions of shareholder value. In this case, productivity as an operational benefit translates into the measurable benefit of increased production volume. In turn, increased production volume results in increased revenue as long as the units can be sold.

Step two is to develop the economic calculation. In this simple case, it's a pretty straightforward one—the number of additional units that can be produced multiplied by the price per unit. The initially intangible benefit of productivity has now been translated into the very tangible benefit of revenue. Taking this a step further, this increase in revenue can be restated in profit using a pro forma income statement and that profit can be further translated into increased shareholder value based on the company's historical price-earnings ratio.

A hierarchy of outsourcing's benefits, as reported by the executives involved in the decision process, was introduced in Chapter 1. In addition to reduced operating costs—the classic tangible benefit—the other benefits cited in order of frequency are improved focus, increased flexibility (variable costs), access to skills, revenue growth, improved quality, capital conservation, and innovation.

Improved focus, redirecting the organization's resources toward higher-value activities, is almost always cited as one of the top reasons for outsourcing. However, few organizations adequately factor the economic benefit of this into the outsourcing business. It's an intangible. To make improved focus tangible, the operational benefit needs to be identified, as does the element of shareholder value that operational benefit impacts. The same can be said for all of the other benefits cited.

Putting It into Practice

Let's take the example of a company that is currently processing its own customer invoices; producing, printing, and distributing them from a company-owned and -operated facility. If an outsourcing partner were to be brought in, some highly-skilled and experienced individuals could be freed up for other activities. Instead of spending their time overseeing current operations, they can be redeployed into product or process analysis work, sales, marketing, or other areas of the business. What work will they be transitioned to and what will the operational benefits, measurable benefits, and impact on shareholder value be? What economic factors can be used to translate this into a tangible dollar figure?

Another dimension is flexibility. How will the relationship improve the business's overall flexibility, and how can that be translated into financial terms? For example, will the unit costs for an invoice be reduced because reserve capacity no longer needs to be maintained across non-peak times? Will cash flow be improved because the processing time for invoices is now stable throughout the year even as volumes fluctuate? If average days outstanding is reduced, how does this operational benefit translate into a measurable benefit? As the average days outstanding are reduced, will the company's interest costs go down, thereby increasing profitability and shareholder value? Or, will that freed cash be reinvested elsewhere, and if so, what will be the impact? Examining each of these scenarios and translating the operational benefits into financial benefits is central to developing a robust business case for outsourcing.

This takes a little digging. For example, what costs are hidden in the company's operations because of the slow movement of information? What markets is the company not entering because it doesn't have the information or resources to move forward quickly? If the anticipated benefit is improved quality, how does that translate into a financial benefit? It may be difficult to put it into terms of new customers, but perhaps savings based on a reduction in customer turnover, using a figure for the average cost of acquiring a new customer, would enable this operational benefit to be properly reflected as a financial one.

Finally, as discussed in Chapter 4, when making acceleration, flexibility, and innovation tangible, look at both the impact on day one, but also the impact of these three factors over time. Back to the example, what process is in place for rapidly changing, adding, or deleting types of bills or new billing techniques, such as online bill payment? What innovations will be introduced on day one, and what is the system to be used to ensure ongoing dialogue between the organizations that will lead to new ideas being identified at a sustained rate? Techniques for creating these types of opportunities for breakthrough improvements are discussed in detail in the chapter on managing the relationship. Both the costs of these programs and their projected values can be developed into tangible parts of the outsourcing business case.

Summary

Assessing the value of outsourcing, capturing it into a business case, and then using that business case as the signpost for the road forward is a critical step in the outsourcing revolution. A complete assessment of the opportunity includes not only this financial analysis, but also an assessment of the decision's consistency with the organization's overall strategy, risks, and the entire spectrum of potential benefits.[2]

The value is multidimensional. Value assessment is all about identifying the business impact and then framing it in a way that supports executive decision making. It's not just the base case, typically tied to direct costs savings, but all of the benefits—from focus on the core of the business to innovation matter. Translating these benefits that appear on the surface to be intangible into a tangible business case enables a better prioritization of the opportunities available to the organization.

At the same time, capturing all of the organization's current costs as well as the total costs of both implementing and managing the new environment is important. The work required to put together a complete outsourcing business case is significant but well worth the effort.

Case Study: Sabre

In July 2001, Sabre, the Dallas-based provider of technology, distribution, and marketing services for the travel industry, entered into a ten-year, $2.2 billion contract with EDS for management of its data center, network, midrange, desktop, and application development operations.[3] This relationship demonstrated not only the breadth of opportunity that exists for creating value through outsourcing, but the multiplying effect that flexibility can have in the overall value equation and how to capture it.

In addition to the traditional technology aspects of the relationship, Sabre sold its infrastructure outsourcing business unit to EDS. The companies also entered into a number of complementary joint marketing agreements. Favorable analyst and market reaction to this deal created a substantial market cap improvement for Sabre—an improvement that continued throughout the subsequent two years, even with the turmoil and challenges faced by the travel industry.

A key contributor to getting this result was Sabre's focus on designing flexibility into the relationship and the contract. Specifically, four contract provisions that contributed to this were:

1. Additional Resource Charge and Reduced Resource Charge

The question was: How would total costs move as volumes went up and down over time? In Sabre's case, not only does its total cost vary with the number of units of service it consumes, but there is also a price-per-unit adjustment of about 30 percent from the low end to high end of its volume ranges.

2. Termination Rights

Termination clauses in the contract allow for both full termination of the contract and for termination of individual service towers. (Service towers are discussed in more detail in Chapter 10.)

Within each of these towers there are clauses for termination for convenience and termination for cause, providing separate levers with enormous flexibility. Although termination for convenience naturally caries penalties, these penalties were established as a percentage of the net present value of the provider's expected profit over the remaining term of the agreement. The competitive bidding process was then used to ensure that both the percentage and profit amounts and timings were reasonable.

3. Exclusivity

The service provider will always seek exclusivity in providing new or expanded services within the scope of the contract. Sabre did not agree to exclusivity, adding another dimension to the relationship's flexibility.

4. Benchmark Rights

Sabre negotiated the right to benchmark the provider's service quality and prices against the market. Although the intention was to use this clause as infrequently as possible, it was an important part of the company's overall design for flexibility.

The full measure of the value of the flexibility Sabre built into its relationship with EDS was seen following September 11, 2001 and the resulting dramatic impact on business volumes, which fell by about 35 percent in one day. The company not only survived that devastating change in its business climate, but continues to outperform its industry and to beat profit estimates.

Recognizing the volatility of its industry, Sabre's leadership knew that flexibility would be key to the value of this relationship and built provisions for it into its agreement. None of this suggests, however, that the contract is inherently one-sided. Quite the opposite, EDS negotiated favorable terms in aspects of the contract that were the most critical to its business goals.

Chapter

10

PRICING, CONTRACTING, AND NEGOTIATING

Pricing, contracting, and negotiating are at the heart of outsourcing, but not in the way many might think. The popular belief is that the customer maximizes the value of outsourcing by negotiating for itself the best possible deal—with "best" being defined as the lowest price and the most favorable commercial terms.

While getting a great deal is certainly a goal, too narrow a definition of "great" is a fundamentally flawed approach. There are a couple of reasons for this. The first is that in any long-term business relationship both parties have to benefit. If the provider is unable to successfully deliver against the contract at a reasonable profit, it will either find ways to adjust its costs and services to reach "reasonable" or it will end the relationship as soon as it is practical. Similarly, if the organization is not getting the expected benefits or if its needs change—as they always do—it too will begin to reposition the deal in subtle but very effective ways. So, for either organization to be successful, the entire relationship has to be able to adjust and evolve with the changing business needs of both. A good deal is not set in stone; it's a framework for an ongoing work in progress.

Pricing, contracting, and negotiating are really more about establishing a working framework for the relationship than they are about locking in a narrowly defined great deal. There are pricing models, contract structures, and commercial terms that can help make this happen. There is certainly a legal document that has to be created that captures the terms of the agreement that the two parties have entered into. Both are covered in this chapter. But it is just as important, maybe even more important, for executives to understand how to structure a relationship that balances the interests of the two companies, properly allocates risks and rewards, and fairly compensates the provider for the services delivered while ensuring that the organization gets all that it is paying for.

Every deal is different. Every company is different. What this chapter does is show how to use the pricing, contracting, and negotiating of an outsourcing relationship as an essential step leading toward long-term success.

The Relationship Continuum

There is no such thing as a "standard" outsourcing contract, terms, pricing, etcetera. Essentially, one size fits one. However, some popular contract structures do exist, certain commercial terms are almost always addressed, and some consultants and lawyers have their favorites of each. Yet, in the end, each contract and each business relationship is one of a kind. It's a unique blend of the interests of the parties involved, captured at a moment in time.

What there is, is a continuum along which all good outsourcing relationships tend to fall. Understanding this continuum is essential to understanding how to price, contract, and negotiate the deal. In fact, most of the discussions between the parties should really be about where along this continuum the companies want the relationship to operate; once that positioning and its implications are understood and agreed to, price and contract terms become much more straightforward things to negotiate. Too often, companies find themselves negotiating price and terms, when in fact what they are really negotiating is the basic nature of the relationship they are trying to create.

Figure 10.1 shows the outsourcing continuum. The two axes that define the continuum are ownership and risk. Ownership refers to the level of ownership of the people, processes, and technologies used to do the work. Level of risk refers to who has the risk associated with achieving the intended outcomes—conformance, operational, or business. Effective outsourcing relationships are positioned along this continuum, in a way that balances ownership and risks, and reflects how the parties have

FIGURE 10.1 USE OUTSOURCING'S RELATIONSHIP CONTINUUM TO GET THE RIGHT DEAL

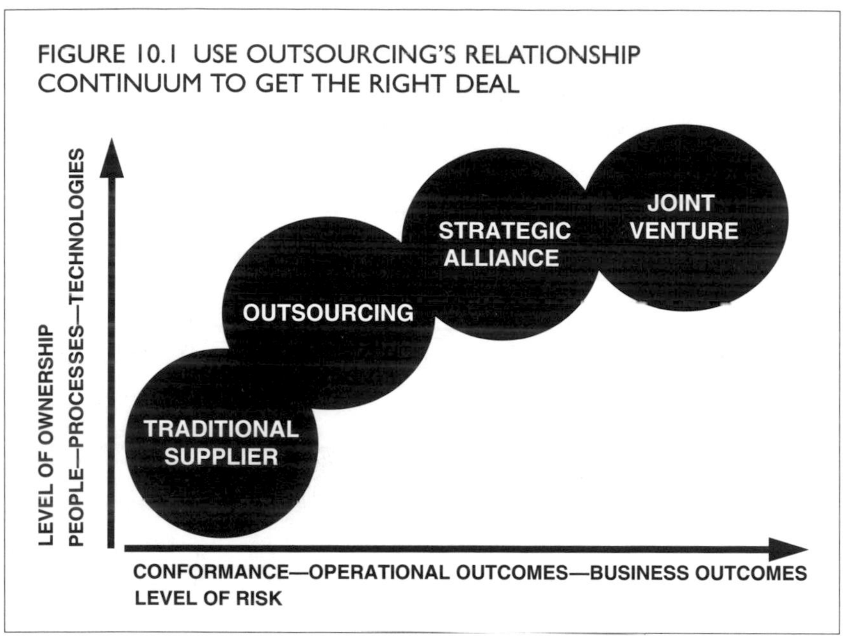

decided to allocate these two dimensions in their specific relationship. Pricing and the contract terms then reflect this decision.

At the low end of the continuum, what some call outsourcing is really not much more than a traditional supplier relationship. In a supplier relationship, the supplier typically provides the people (think staffing), the process expertise (think consulting), or the technology (think product) needed to do the work; but not all three. If all three are supplied, then it's probably for a very narrow and very tightly defined set of activities. As for risk, a traditional supplier can certainly assume risks associated with ensuring that what they supply conforms to the agreed-to requirements, but cannot really take on risk associated with whether the customer achieves its operational outcomes through their use, let alone its sought after business outcomes.

As the two parties move along the continuum, away from this traditional supplier relationship and toward a more interdependent relationship, the situation changes. Now the provider owns most, if not all, of the people, processes, and technologies needed to deliver the business process. The provider can also assume much more of the risk associated with meeting the operational outcomes—the kind of outcomes reflected in a scorecard.

As the relationship moves further along the continuum, the provider takes over ownership of a larger group of people, processes, and technologies. As this happens, it can also take on more risks, possibly even some of risks associated with achieving the customer's desired business outcomes. To do this, the relationship has to evolve toward more of a strategic alliance or even a joint venture between the organizations. Some outsourcing deals have multiple service elements, and in that case each may find that it needs to be positioned separately along the continuum.

Most outsourcing relationships sit somewhere in the middle of this continuum. The provider owns most of the people, processes, and technologies needed to do the work and takes on many of the risks associated with achieving the operational outcomes. If, however, the provider assumes too much or too little risk for the level of ownership it has taken on, then the relationship is fundamentally flawed. This is true regardless of how the deal is ultimately priced or the contract terms massaged.

Consider an outsourcing agreement around a company's receivables. At the low end of the continuum, a supplier's employees could do the work of processing invoices, monitoring overall receivables status, and placing follow-up calls. This work could be done by the supplier following a customer-defined process and using customer-owned technology. Here, the supplier could certainly be expected to assume the risks associated with ensuring that its employees meet agreed-to standards in terms of skills, training, experience, and personal productivity. An appropriate pricing model for this relationship might then be based on hours worked or some other time-driven formula. The appropriate price for that time would take into account the customer's historical total costs for its own employees with equivalent skills and prevailing market prices for these skills on a contract basis. Although some incentives based on achieving the customer's operational and business outcomes might be added, the supplier has limited ownership of the factors that contribute to achieving these outcomes, and so assuming much risk beyond ensuring that the people supplied conform to the agreed-to standards would be ineffective and possibly even self-defeating.

To position the relationship further along the continuum, in the outsourcing range, would mean that the provider has to assume both a greater level of ownership and a greater level of risk. Now the provider might design, own, and manage the entire receivables process as well as most or even all of the technologies supporting it. This is a typical BPO relationship. The provider can, and in fact should, assume an equivalently greater level of risk. The negotiations would focus on the customer's desired operational outcomes as reflected in the scorecard. This scorecard might include metrics for the average time to prepare and send an invoice, for following up on outstanding invoices, for the timeliness and accuracy of data flowing into the customer's financial systems, and for internal and external customer satisfaction with the way the receivables are handled. Risk might be reflected in scorecard-based incentives and penalties. Pricing would probably also shift from being resource-based to being volume-based, such as the number of invoices processed.

Taking this relationship further along the continuum, the provider might agree to integrate its planning process with that of its customer so that the provider is able to anticipate the changes in the organization's business that create peaks and valleys in its receivables volume. In essence, the provider is now becoming a seamless extension of its customer's operations. It can also be expected to take on greater risks and rewards as well, possibly adding average days outstanding to the scorecard, as well as a shared incentive for continuous process improvement. These are still operational outcomes, but they are more closely tied to the customer's desired business outcomes.

Finally, the relationship could be positioned further along the continuum with the BPO provider taking on ownership of the organization's entire revenue cycle process, for example, adding on determining appropriate payment terms based on creditworthiness and handling the actual cash flow. If enough ownership is assumed by the provider, it can and should assume some of the direct business risks as well, perhaps basing some or all of its compensation on the cash collected. The relationship has now become at least a strategic alliance if not a joint venture between the two companies. There is a shared investment in the operation's success, and there are shared risks and rewards for the business results.

As this example illustrates, positioning the relationship along the continuum and then negotiating a reasonable price, pricing model, and terms based on the ownership and risks being assumed by the two parties, is key to the success of the relationship for both parties. If the relationship is positioned too far off the continuum—where the provider assumes either too much or too little risk in relationship to the resources it's controlling—then the organization, the provider, or both suffer.

Successful outsourcing relationships are also structured with the idea that there is a shared commitment to creating an ongoing, expanding relationship between the companies. There's an "evergreen" spirit, as well as an intention to gradually expand the provider's scope of services and level of ownership, balanced with the assumption that higher levels of compensation carry greater risks but greater profit potential. Properly positioning the relationship on the continuum at the start and then gradually moving successful relationships out along the continuum is how real benefits accrue over time to both organizations.

This shared commitment creates the most powerful incentive of all for the organizations to identify and capitalize on new, emerging opportunities and to identify and resolve problems quickly. To both organizations, the relationship becomes something worth investing in.

Failing to structure the relationship for growth along the continuum has the opposite effect. It encourages a short-term, transactional mindset with both parties looking to maximize their individual benefits as quickly as possible. The key is to move away from thinking of the relationship as an engagement—something with a beginning, middle, and an end. Instead, outsourcing contracts should be approached as an alignment of the needs and interests of both companies that is intended to lead to greater synergies and more value over time.

The Modular Contract

Moving from the continuum to the contract is then a matter of capturing

- the intent of the relationship,
- how it will be managed,
- the scope of services to be performed,
- the responsibilities of the parties,
- how the results will be measured, and
- how the provider will be compensated.

All outsourcing service providers will be able to present a standard contract covering these items; one that they have used with other clients in the past. The contract has been refined over time and represents the provider's current preferences. It contains all of the terms of importance to the provider, with each term stated in the most favorable way. For this reason, some organizations refuse to work from the provider's standard contract, choosing instead to begin with their own. This puts the burden on the provider to identify and negotiate for inclusion terms of greatest interest to it. On the other hand, if the contract that the organization presents fails to include all of the relevant terms and conditions, then a great deal of additional work is created for both parties.

Regardless of the approach used, in the end, most good outsourcing contracts have three distinct sections: a terms section, a scope of services section, and a pricing section. This modular structure offers the advantage of enabling the parties to create a "master framework agreement" in the terms section that covers the overall relationship and to then add and subtract sets of services and pricing models for each element of the relationship. The result is a more flexible structure that is easier to change and evolve over time.[1]

The modular contract makes it easier to write agreements that include very different types of services, such as strategic planning versus operational services, where each really needs to be defined and paid for differently. Another advantage is that the modular contract allows for each set of services to be negotiated as a service tower—each tower can then be added, changed, and deleted without directly affecting the other services or the overall relationship.

Terms Section

The terms section defines the intent of the relationship and how it will be managed. It also contains the contract terms that govern the overall agreement. Some common contract terms are listed and defined in the Quick Reference Guide at the end of this chapter.

Be specific in describing the intent of the relationship, its goals and objectives, and how it will be managed. Avoid using terms that suggest a common understanding but are not well enough defined in the document to carry any specific meaning. For example, describing the relationship as a strategic alliance may capture the spirit of the parties, but what does that really mean? If the relationship is truly a strategic alliance, the terms section should talk about the shared strategic planning process to be followed, the type of information to be exchanged, and the resources being committed by the parties to this shared effort.

Another important part of the terms section of the contract covers the initial transition from the customer's operation to the provider's. Common elements of this transition are covered in the terms section, while elements unique to a particular set of services can be covered in the scope of services and the pricing sections for that service.

The transition section describes the plan for converting the customer's current operation to the provider's, including responsibilities, cost allocations, timelines, and operational certification. What equipment and facilities will be transferred to the service provider, including their valuation, responsibilities for warranties, liability for repair to bring the equipment to proper working order, taxes, and any environmental issues? Similar considerations apply if the equipment or facilities are leased and the organization wishes to either assign the lease to the provider or exercise a purchase option and then resell it to the provider. If there are lease transfer charges, whose responsibility are they? What are the organization's obligations, such as providing access to information, resources, and personnel?

If customer equipment or facilities are to be made available for use by the provider but not transferred, the terms section should specify the terms of their use, including who bears the costs of changes, repairs, and future upgrades. Other considerations might include access to customer facilities and required customer approvals for changes to equipment and facilities. Third-party services, equipment, and facilities may also be involved and need to be transferred. These third-party agreements may be assigned to the provider, terminated, or continue and be managed by the organization. Responsibilities and cost should be stated, as well as the parties' rights to change and replace these third-party agreements.

To the extent that this transition will involve the transfer of personnel from the organization to the service provider, the terms section should specify the particulars around the offers of employment, including salaries, benefits, and any guarantees of employment for a specified period of time. It should also specify how the transfers are to be managed, including the organization's and provider's respective roles and responsibilities, allocation of costs, and any indemnities and allocation of risks from employee lawsuits that might arise. Another personnel consideration is training. The terms section should specify who is responsible for training the personnel on new skills or processes needed to support the new operation, how that training is to be provided, and who bears the costs. Additional personnel considerations are covered in detail in the next chapter.

The agreement should specify the parties' responsibilities and cost allocation in relation to projects underway at the time of the transfer.

The terms section should also specify how the relationship will be managed, including project managers at the organization and provider companies, oversight and senior management committees, and operational teams. Roles and responsibilities should be clearly defined, as well as frequency and types of meetings, and how any related costs will be allocated. If formal management techniques are to be used, such as jointly developed annual business plans and formal risk-assessment programs, they should be specified. The process, authorities, and responsibilities for negotiating and agreeing to additions or changes to the agreement should be described, as well. These and other management considerations are discussed in greater detail in Chapter 12.

Scope of Services

One or more scope of services sections are used to describe the type, scope, and nature of all the services to be provided, as well as where and when those services will be made available. Hand-in-hand with a description of the services is the standard of performance, as defined by the scorecard and based on the relationship's positioning along the outsourcing continuum.

Services should be described in as much detail as possible. Include a description of the service and of the responsibilities and duties associated with it. The goal is to make this section specific enough that an independent third party could determine what each party's obligations are from reading it. This is key to preventing later problems that can result from different interpretations as to what services were or were not included within the scope of services.

The scorecard, as has already been discussed, typically reflects, at a minimum, measures of volume, availability, timeliness, milestones, quality, safety and regulatory compliance, and customer satisfaction. Even more business outcome-based metrics will be included in relationships positioned further out on the continuum.

Additional questions to be addressed here include: How will the information be collected? Who owns the measurement system? How are the costs borne? How will the integrity of the data be ensured?

Pricing Section

As far as price itself, getting the services at a fair price is not terribly difficult as long as a few basic things are done, and done well.

What are they? The first is to understand and reasonably forecast the costs of the internal business process—as it exists today and as it is likely to evolve over the term of the agreement. Any deal that produces greater value for the organization at the same or lower cost is a good deal. If, in addition, relevant cost data is collected from independent sources—such as other organizations, benchmark data sources, and comparable proposals from more than one provider—then a fair market price can be established. A price that is better than current operations and reasonable from a market standpoint is certainly a good price; and if a little tough negotiating can get the provider to sharpen its pencil, then that's great. Beyond this, negotiating for the very lowest possible price will ultimately work against the organization's own interests. The working model here, once again, is more that of hiring than it is one of purchasing.

The pricing section of the contract, then, specifies when the fees are to be paid to the provider and, more importantly, how these fees are calculated. There are a number of ways to structure the pricing of an outsourcing contract, and these should align with where the relationship is positioned on the outsourcing continuum. For example, moving from the lower end to the higher end of the continuum, one might find:

Cost plus. This pays the provider for its actual costs, plus a predetermined profit percentage. This approach enables the customer to fix the profit level for the provider and gives the customer direct visibility into the fees it is paying. However, it offers little incentive for the supplier to improve the way the service is performed or to reduce the actual costs.

Unit pricing. This is an approach where a rate is negotiated for each service, and the organization pays based on usage. The rate may be fixed across all volumes, or an additional or reduced resource charge may apply for utilization above or below specified bands. Here, the service provider may be motivated to find ways to increase the customer's utilization of its services, while looking to reduce its internal per unit costs. This can be in direct conflict with the customer's desire to drive down its utilization rate and to share in the benefits of future efficiencies.

Fixed price. With a fixed price, the provider's fee is the same regardless of the volume of services provided. The advantage for the organization is easy budgeting. The problem can be that the provider is motivated to ensure it achieves a consistent profit level, causing it to seek ways of reducing the scope, volume, or quality of services when service demands are at their peak.

Incentive-based. With incentive-based pricing, the organization uses direct incentives to encourage the provider to perform the services at higher levels. Penalties are, of course, the flip side of this. The challenge is to ensure that the incentives and penalties directly correlate to the business value the organization is realizing. Higher levels of service may not, actually, translate into greater value, making the higher payment unjustified. On the other hand, the organization doesn't really want poorer service for which it is paying less; it wants the right level of service at a fair price.

Incentives can be a powerful way of encouraging positive behavior. Carefully structured incentives help both parties perform as intended. It takes effort to devise an incentive program that is fair and produces the desired effect. Recognize that incentives add another dynamic to the negotiations, can work against the relationship if they are not well crafted, and that any penalties should be set high enough to be meaningful but not so high as to be punitive—the goal is to promote the right behavior, not to save money in exchange for poor performance.

Gainsharing. Here, the provider receives a portion of any additional savings it can generate for its customer through its efforts. These savings might come from driving down the costs of raw materials, implementing new technologies, or making suggestions for improvement in the organization's operations. Gainsharing splits typically range from 50-50 to 75-25, in favor of the customer.

Achievement bonuses. These are typically one-time payments for reaching certain milestones. These milestones may be tied to earlier-than-expected completion dates, higher-than-committed service levels, or better-than-expected throughput. Another example, particularly useful when multiple providers for the same services are involved, is achievement bonuses based upon comparative rankings—where top-performing providers receive bonus payments, encouraging continuous improvement and innovation by all.

Risk/reward sharing. This implies that both the organization and the provider have money at risk, and each stand to gain a percentage of the additional value created by their collaborative efforts. For example, if the provider and organization are able to drive down certain costs or drive up revenues, then they share them. Similarly, if costs run higher or revenues run lower than expected, they each share the downside as well.

With a modular contract structure, different structures can be used for different services, and each can be consistent with where on the outsourcing continuum the relationship is intended to operate.

Negotiation Principles

Negotiating is a management discipline in its own right, and there is a wealth of information on the topic for executives and managers to tap. In preparing to negotiate an outsourcing relationship, the following checklist can be particularly helpful:

- Have the negotiating team members and roles been defined?
- Have the organization's key interests been defined?
- Are individuals with all relevant discipline knowledge included, such as legal, human resources, procurement, and functional management?
- Are individuals with sufficient decision-making authority on the negotiating team for both parties?
- Are multiple vendors to be negotiated with at the same time, and if so, have dates for "best and final" offers been established?
- Have sources of objective information for evaluating proposed terms been identified?

- Have all relevant issues been reviewed and negotiated internally prior to negotiation with the provider?
- Has the best alternative to a negotiated agreement for each of these items been determined? (In other words, what is the fall-back position?)
- Has sufficient time been allocated for planning, preparation, and negotiation?
- Have the interests of the provider been considered?
- Have areas of potential value to either or both organizations, beyond the specific services being contracted for, been identified?
- Have a meeting schedule and road map for the negotiations been agreed to by both organizations?
- Has a comprehensive list of items to be negotiated been developed and agreed to?

Keep in mind that introducing all relevant considerations as early in the discussions as possible and making sure they are fully understood by both parties before negotiating any individual term focuses attention on the outcomes sought not the positions of the parties. Also, once the contract negotiation is complete, the customer and the provider will be in a long-term business relationship where both must succeed. Therefore, the final terms must be reasonable for both parties in light of the responsibilities and risks involved. Finally, keep in mind that the negotiations do not end when the contract is signed; the customer and provider will be negotiating throughout the life of their relationship.

Summary

It's through pricing, contracting, and negotiating that the organizations involved define their outsourcing relationship. There are no standard terms, prices, or negotiating techniques for companies to use. There are, however, a few key principles and a common list of topics that can and should be discussed and decided.

Recognize that every well-structured outsourcing relationship sits along a continuum that represents a balance in how the responsibilities and risks are assigned to both organizations. Service providers cannot meaningfully assume risks beyond their level of ownership of the people, processes, and technologies needed to deliver the expected results. Similarly, if the provider is not assuming a reasonable level of risk given the ownership it has of the factors of production, then its interests and the interests of its customer will quickly fall out of alignment.

Once the parties have decided where along the continuum they want to position the particular relationship, the contracting and pricing discussions can become much more about how to capture this understanding in operational terms rather than one of trying to "win" the negotiations. Price becomes a matter of determining what's fair given the responsibilities and risks being assumed. Creative pricing models can be discussed and agreed to—common contract terms can be negotiated as a whole as opposed to having a tug-of-war on a point-by-point basis.

The most important lesson that others have learned is that outsourcing relationships evolve every day of their existence, and only those that are set on a strong foundation of common understanding and shared goals will ever produce the value sought—for either party.

Case Studies

The following examples illustrate some of the ways that pricing can be used to align the interests of the organization and the service provider along the outsourcing continuum:

- One of the world's largest automobile manufacturers entered into a multiyear contract for information technology outsourcing at a newly built U.S. plant. Under the agreement, the provider owned the people, processes, and technologies required to deliver the needed IT and would do so under a fix-priced contract. However, to better align the provider with the plant's overall operational outcomes, a certain percent of the provider's profit was tied to whether or not the plant made its production quota.
- A major hospital and medical supplies company entered into a long-term BPO relationship for materials management (purchasing and fulfillment). They jointly established cost targets and agreed to share any cost underruns or overruns on a 50-50 basis.
- Another hospital outsourced its information technology operation by creating a joint venture with its service provider. The hospital became both the

customer and part owner of this new company. In another case, a major Canadian hospital received revenue credits for being a showcase account for some of its providers.

- A large human resources BPO contract included not only various services on fixed- and variable-term bases, but revenue sharing on new technologies jointly developed by the companies, joint marketing agreements to offer each others' services to clients, and stock ownership in the service provider company.
- A large petrochemical company priced one of its outsourcing contracts on a percent-of-dollars-saved basis.
- An oil well operator entered into a contract with a well pump manufacturer for the manufacturer to own and maintain the pumps itself. Compensation was then based on a percentage of the per-barrel price at which the pumped oil was sold. This ensured that the pump manufacturer not only kept the pumps operating at high levels of availability, but managed this with sensitivity to prevailing market prices. Similarly, a large provider of mining equipment has agreements where it owns and maintains the equipment and is paid on a per-ton-of-materials-mined basis. In another example, an aircraft engine manufacturer has overall engine maintenance responsibility for one of its airline customers. It is paid on a per-flight-hour basis, not a per-maintenance-hour basis, aligning the interests of the customer and provider.

Quick Reference Guide

The following is a quick reference guide to common terms and considerations for an outsourcing contract:

Assignment is the ability of a company to subcontract or assign its obligations to a third party with or without consent. The contract should specify when, where, and under what circumstances and with what preapprovals subcontractors can be used.

Audit is the ability of a company to review the financial records and performance information as they relate to an agreement.

Change of character clauses give one or both of the parties the right to change other aspects of the contract, including services and prices, if there are significant changes in where or how the services are delivered.

Compliance with laws states that both parties will be compliant with all federal, state, and local laws and regulations. If there is a law or regulation that governs the particular relationship, it can be specifically stated.

Confidentiality describes what information is confidential and the party's rights and restrictions in the use of any confidential information.

A great deal of *customer data* may be used and generated in the delivery of the services. Issues such as the provider's rights to access that data, its security, backup, and accessibility should be addressed.

Definition of the relationship describes the parties, their business interests, and their goals and objectives in entering into the relationship.

The contract should specify how *disputes* are to be resolved, including under what conditions and in what manner they are escalated within and between the organizations. For issues that cannot be resolved between the two parties, alternative dispute resolution methods may be agreed to.

Outsourcing providers will frequently seek to be the *exclusive* provider of services within the agreement's scope. If granted, the organization typically seeks protections, which recognize its loss of control.

Force majeure limits performance and delivery in the case of uncontrollable events, such as acts of God or government actions. Responsibilities for maintaining adequate backup, recovery, and business continuity plans should be described, including how any costs are allocated.

The contract typically restricts the parties from *hiring each others' employees* for specified periods of time. Alternately, it may establish a payment structure for compensating the current employer if its employees are hired by the other party.

Indemnity is a promise by one party to hold the other party harmless from loss or damage of some kind, irrespective of the liability of any third person. The liability for a loss is shifted from one party held legally responsible to another party.

The agreement should state that the provider is an *independent contractor* excluding any rights or privileges associated with being an employee of the organization not specifically granted in the agreement.

Insurance requirements vary depending on the type of activity and risk involved. It's important to understand which party's insurance covers what risks and to specify the requirements of each party to maintain appropriate coverage as well as how these costs are allocated.

When organizations outsource, they are combining their existing *intellectual properties,* the intellectual properties of other outside organizations, those of the service provider, and new intellectual properties that may be generated. Questions around the use and ownership rights of these assets should be addressed.

Limitation of liability clauses are standard in most contracts. Typically, certain types of consequential or special damages (punitive, indirect, and incidental) are excluded.

Liquidated damages is the sum that a party to a contract agrees to pay if it breaches the contract. It is determined by a good faith effort to estimate the amount of actual damage that would result.

Most favored customer clauses are used to assure the customer that the level of service and prices they are receiving now and in the future are the provider's best for customers of similar services and volumes.

Multivendor considerations apply when more than one provider will need to work in concert to deliver the desired services. The responsibilities to coordinate these activities and how any costs will be allocated across the parties are specified.

Personnel requirements, such as skills, experience and training of personnel, where the work is performed, provider's right to change personnel, the organization's right to review and approve personnel changes, and any specific obligations of the vendor regarding screening, security, confidentiality, noncompete clauses, and succession planning should be specified.

Safe harbors protect certain payment and business practices that are implicated by the anti-kickback statute from criminal and civil prosecution.

In some cases, the service provider may seek to serve other clients from the organization's premises or from an offsite location that is primarily serving this customer. Any rights, restrictions, liabilities and indemnifications for *sharing resources* by either the provider or the customer should be addressed.

Outsourcing relationships are entered into with the general intent of being long-term, strategic relationships that will continue into the foreseeable future. For practical purposes, however, most contracts have a specified *term,* or period of time, for which they are in force.

Outsourcing contracts specify *termination* for cause, for convenience, as a result of other qualifying events, and at the end of the planned term. There are two key considerations: the definition of the types of termination and their trigger events, and the specification of the responsibilities of the parties and the allocation of costs in each situation.

Venue or governing law designates which state and possibly county will govern and interpret the contract.

A *warranty* is essentially a guarantee that a product will perform as promised for a limited amount of time.

Chapter

11

MANAGING OUTSOURCING'S PEOPLE IMPACTS

There is no denying the facts. Outsourcing affects people and communities. In fact, in early 2004, 80 percent of executives stated that their employees were more concerned about outsourcing and its potential effect on their jobs than they had been just a year earlier.[1]

For in-scope employees the impact can be immediate. They may be offered a different job within their current company; they may be offered a new job with the service provider; or they may be told they no longer have a job. For out-of-scope employees the impact may not be as dramatic and immediate, but it may be no less profound. Their company and the way they do their jobs will change. Just as important, they are likely to begin to wonder: "Am I next?"—with all of the productivity and morale implications that can have.

All too frequently, the benefits of outsourcing are seen as coming at the expense of employees. This is certainly not the case. For the business, outsourcing drives not just cost savings, but improvements in focus, flexibility, quality, skills, capital utilization, revenue, and even innovation. It's a natural response to today's hyper-competitive, global economy, and few, if any, organizations can successfully compete without it.

Although achieving greater economies of scale and scope, which often translates into needing fewer employees to do the same work, is certainly a natural part of the process, outsourcing can create new opportunities for employees as well. If they move into a new job with their current company, it may offer better opportunities for growth than the job they left. Similarly, if they join the service provider, they are now in a revenue-producing activity. They've gone from working in a cost center to working in a profit center, with all of the potential that suggests. Even if they haven't been offered a job with either company, the retraining and other benefits provided may launch their career in an entirely new direction. (Author's note: I finished my MBA and started my current company using a severance package from IBM in the late 1980s.)

We can't avoid change, but we can anticipate and manage it. In considering outsourcing's impact on employees and communities, the overriding principle that should guide management's action throughout the process is amazingly simple: *The impact that outsourcing has on employees is the impact that management chooses for it to have.* It's that simple.

The organization's leadership crafts the outsourcing relationship. They make thousands of decisions, from the most strategic—such as what to outsource and who to outsource to—to the most tactical—such as the effective date of the agreement. The company can design into the agreement certain guarantees for its employees or choose not to. It can set aside some of its savings for employee-transition programs or not. Each of these decisions affects employees, and it is the cumulative effect of all these decisions that ultimately defines outsourcing's impact on employees.

Communications, Communications, Communications

Outsourcing does not have to be a zero-sum game. For executives who choose to communicate openly and seek creative options, and for employees who choose to embrace change, outsourcing can be positive for all involved. This does not mean that the transition won't be difficult, and it certainly doesn't mean that people won't lose jobs. But it also doesn't mean that the end result can be no more than a trade-off of competing interests with no net gain.

Since the late 1990s, research has found that that there is a direct correlation between employee satisfaction and the way the company manages the outsourcing transition process. Communications and timeliness are integral to employee satisfaction, and the more satisfied employees are with the support provided by their current companies early in the transition process, the more satisfied they ultimately are with the overall process.[2]

This means that well in advance of any discussions about a specific outsourcing initiative or a specific contract, management should already have a clear plan for how it's moving the organization forward. This includes articulating a positive vision for the future of the organization, its people, its communities, and the markets it serves—a vision that shows how everyone will be better off when they've adjusted to the new environment in which businesses operate today.

There are nine specific points that management should be prepared to address in communicating with employees and the community. They are:

1. The compelling need for change. Management must define and explain the compelling need for change. In the absence of this, almost any change runs the risk of appearing capricious. The compelling need for change may involve such factors as: changes in customer needs and demographics; competitive pressures; technology; financial performance and structures; and regulatory changes; as well as other factors specific to the business itself. Every decision that management plans to make should be clearly connected to addressing one or more of these needs for change.

2. Cost of doing nothing. Just because things are changing around the organization doesn't necessarily mean that the organization itself has to change. Articulating the cost of doing nothing—in terms of its likely impact on the business's performance and its ability to serve its customers, employees, and shareholders—makes the need for change much more real and compelling. Employees and the community need help in making this connection, and that is management's responsibility. Managers need to make the future tangible to their constituents. In so doing, they build the case that the only question we get to answer is: Will the future be one of our own making or one imposed on us by others?

3. Change techniques to be employed. Businesses have a wide range of tools available to address the changes demanded of them. Mergers, acquisitions, divestitures, changes to the organization's operating and financial structures, cost-cutting initiatives, technology, process redesign, partnering, sourcing, and outsourcing are just a few. Management needs to provide its assessment of the viability and role of each.

4. Role of outsourcing. Within the overall change agenda, what is the specific role of outsourcing? Where and how does it fit? What is the process that management uses to evaluate outsourcing opportunities? What are the key factors for determining where and when it is the right tool for the job? Management must first answer these questions for itself and then be prepared to answer them for others.

5. Benefits and implications for the organization. What are the benefits and implications for the organization of outsourcing? Will it reduce costs? And how will those dollars be reallocated? How will it impact the speed, innovation, and flexibility of the organization? How will these benefits actually be realized, and when? Employees are far more likely to embrace change when they understand how the change will create a positive outcome for the organization in total.

6. Benefits and implications for the customers. Management must go on to explain how the organization's customers will benefit. How will the quality of the organization's products and services be enhanced by outsourcing? How will its resources be redeployed? Why will customers react favorably to the change? Employees will have specific questions that will test management's ability to articulate its fully formed view of outsourcing's impact. The answers need to be clear and well thought out. If the only apparent reason for outsourcing becomes one of saving money at the expense of employees and customers, then the negative portrayal of outsourcing that is prevalent in the press will simply be confirmed.

7. Benefits and implications for employees and the community. How will outsourcing affect the individuals—both those in-scope and those out-of-scope? What is the organization prepared to do to work with those affected? What is it not prepared to do? These questions are of immediate concern to in-scope employees, but the answers are just as important to those who are out-of-scope and certainly realize that their area may be under consideration for outsourcing in the future.

8. Timelines. When will decisions be made, and once made, what's the timeline for their implementation? Management should establish a framework for how it does its work so that employees have a roadmap to follow going forward. In its absence, individuals are left to their own speculation as to when decisions may be made and how long they will have to react to the changes that may be thrust upon them.

9. How we'll measure success. Finally, how will the organization's management know that the desired outcomes are being realized? How will it capture and share that information with its employees? Management's ability to answer this question is central to its ability to present the outsourcing decision as one that was reached with a full understanding of the implications to the business and how the benefits will be measured and ultimately achieved.

There is simply no substitute for open and honest communications. Management may not always have all the answers, but those that it does have should be shared, and those that it doesn't should be acknowledged with a timeline for developing the answer.

There are a wide range of techniques available to managers for having these conversations with employees. Large formal meetings are just one. Others include smaller, less formal meetings; newsletters; e-mail; voice mail; Web sites and chat facilities; and town-hall style meetings with senior management. It's also very important to communicate first with supervisors and managers. These individuals are the front line communicating directly and continuously with employees.

For Employees, It's Personal

It's important to realize that without effective communication and action on the part of management, outsourcing will be seen by employees as an unanticipated and undesired "choice" that has been imposed upon them. Employees chose to apply for their current jobs with their current employer. They accepted the employer's job offer along with all of the current and anticipated implications of that choice. Once hired, they chose to advance their career in a certain way—to accept certain positions, responsibilities, and challenges, and to decline others. They shaped their jobs and careers to their desires within the framework of the opportunities and options that their job and employer permitted. Employees did not "choose" to be outsourced. Keep in mind that to the employee, it is they and their jobs that are being "outsourced," not the function or business process.

Not only did the employee not choose to be outsourced, but the resulting impact on the individual is significant both personally and financially. Even if offered a new job, every aspect of an employee's pay and benefits may be affected. Their pay rate and structure, the dates and intervals at which they are paid, sick time, vacation time and scheduling, health benefits, retirement savings plans—all may change to one extent or another.

Then there's the future. How will they be measured and rewarded for their performance? How well will they be able to compete for bonuses, awards, and promotions? What is their future security and stability? These are all very real considerations for employees.

Outsourcing also affects the "job" itself and all of the tangible and intangible aspects that shape an employee's view of his or her job; the location where the work is performed and the work itself; the tools and training that the employee receives and expects to receive to help him or her be successful; the organization he or she will be working for, its image, and what it's believed to stand for; the senior management; and most important, the employee's direct supervisor—his or her boss.

Another very important factor in how employees view their jobs is their peer group. One of the most important factors to employees in evaluating their jobs and in making the decision to stay with a new outsourcing company is the peer group. When their peer network is broken up, there can be a period of mourning, making employees more likely to leave.[3]

Creating Positive Employee Outcomes

The challenge, and responsibility, for managers is to demonstrate through word and action that, far from meaning the loss of choice and other negative consequences, outsourcing can and does produce very positive results for employees.

For those employees taking on new jobs within their current company, the new business structure creates new opportunities for them. New jobs in managing and integrating the work of the two companies are created. Opportunities for job rotation between the companies can help employees build their skills and experiences. Training based on the unique competencies of the provider's organization can help develop new skills. Participation in joint management and quality improvement teams provides additional opportunities.

New career opportunities are created for employees going to work for the provider as well. These individuals are going from back-office jobs to front-office jobs. They now work for a company that views their skills as revenue-producing, not as revenue-supporting. As a result, the training they'll receive is a real opportunity for personal growth and development. Often, it's training that was simply not available to them while they were doing that same work for their former company.

Although some job loss occurs before, during, and after outsourcing, service providers generally need many of the client's current employees and often work hard to attract and keep them. For example, CSC, a technology outsourcing provider, has a one-year, 95 percent retention rate for employees who come into the company through new outsourcing contracts. Morrison Management Specialists, a provider of food and nutrition services for the health care industry, seeks similar results in its new engagements. Morrison not only uses a national network of human resources professionals to aid in employee transition, but has made significant investments to support that effort. The company developed its own interactive CD-ROM to guide employees through the transition process and operates a state-of-the-art training center at its Atlanta headquarters to help bring new supervisors on board quickly.[4] Providers like these invest in recruiting, developing, and training new employees specifically because they know these individuals are essential to the future success of their businesses.

The result can be greater opportunity for career advancement. A classic example is a large hospital maintenance company in which some of the women who started 12 or 15 years ago pushing vacuum cleaners are now division heads or vice presidents owning substantial blocks of company stock. As hospital employees, most of them would still be pushing vacuum cleaners.[5] In 2001, 6 of CSC's 16 most senior management positions were held by individuals who joined the company through outsourcing contracts.[6]

Even when employees lose their current jobs and don't go to work for the provider, management can still do a lot to create a positive result for these individuals. They can fund retraining and other transition services leading to new and perhaps better opportunities for these former employees—whether they stay in their current field or move into new ones. In one large information technology transaction, a local university was brought in as a partner specifically to lead this retraining effort for employees.

Outsourcing can also be a catalyst for entrepreneurs. As hospitals have been creating same-day surgery centers, many of the services of those centers—transcription, staffing, billing, and accounting—have been outsourced to entrepreneurial start-ups run by former employees. One example is Earnhart & Associates, Ltd., a Dallas-based provider founded by a one-time hospital employee. The company has been part of more than one multimillion-dollar start-up providing these services back to former hospital employers.[7]

Other techniques can be used to spur the creation of new companies providing services to the former employers. Employee stock ownership plans (ESOPs) and other approaches have been used to help launch new companies through outsourcing. The Foundation for Enterprise Development (http://www.fed.org) is a nonprofit organization dedicated to advancing the use of entrepreneurial employee ownership. It was started by Dr. J. Robert Beyster, founder of Science Applications International Corporation, itself a leading employee-owned information technology outsourcing service provider.

When unions are involved, the issues are almost always about the immediate and potential loss of union jobs and any proposed changes in a job's wages, benefits, or work rules. Even if the employee has an opportunity to go to work for the service provider, if that new job is not under control of the collective bargaining agreement of the existing union, then it is a "loss" to the union. Often, the changes resulting from outsourcing are taking place within the larger framework of long-term struggles over jobs. Therefore, history and prior actions play a major role in the union response. So does the overall employment climate.

If any employees within the potential scope of an outsourcing project are represented by unions, the earlier the union is involved and brought to the table as a partner, the better. Early discussion and frank dialogue can actually lead to creative approaches. For example, when Bell Canada decided to outsource its residential installation and repair business, its union created a company to take over the work. The result was maintaining the current workforce and creating new opportunities for the union and its members.

A Management Plan for Action

Management's focus has to be on taking specific actions—in words and deeds—with the express purpose of helping its employees work through the change that outsourcing represents in both their lives and their jobs.

Even before evaluating its specific outsourcing plans, management should take stock of overall employee attitudes toward the organization and its management. Outsourcing is not a change taking place in isolation but is, in fact, just one event within the overall tapestry of what's happened in the past and is happening today—both inside and outside of the company. The timeline for preparing employees for change and assisting them through the process begins about 12 months before any actual deal is done and employees are transitioned through about 12 months after that date. (See Figure 11.1.)

Management's initial focus should be on preparing the organization for change and then preparing specific in-scope groups for change.

FIGURE 11.1 HR PLANNING SHOULD BEGIN 12 MONTHS BEFORE THE FIRST DEAL

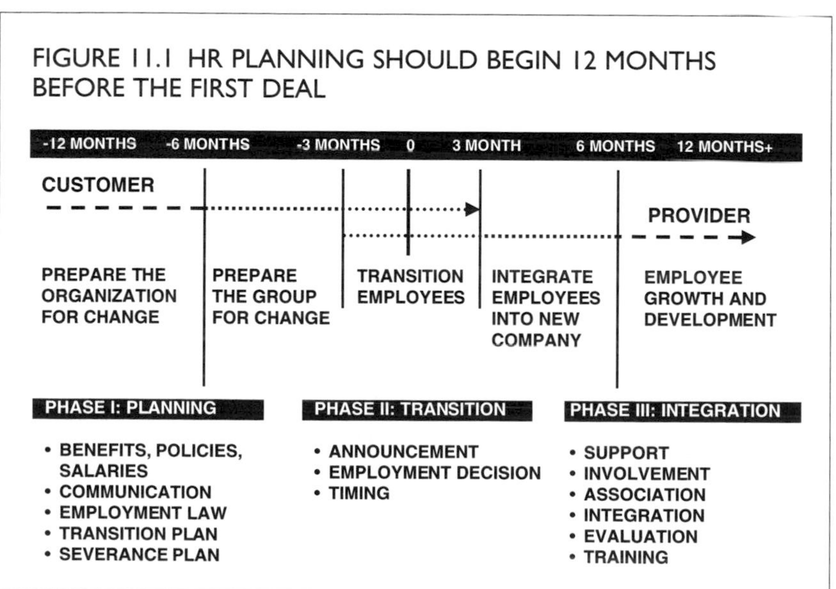

Once the initial announcement is made, employees will quickly begin the process of comparing, very specifically and based on their individual criteria, the immediate and long-term implications at the personal, financial, and job level. Each and every one of these implications must be carefully thought through by management in advance. Once decided, management should then fully and effectively communicate these implications to its employees. There is simply no substitute for management stepping up to its clear responsibility to do its homework and to do it well.

It is also critical to manage the communications coming from both the employee's current company and the new one. These communications must be clear, consistent, and in line with any and all employment laws and precedents, including such considerations as co-employment, protected groups, government-mandated programs, and the WARN Act—not to mention additional legislation that may be enacted in the future.

At transition, the burden then shifts primarily to the new employer—the service provider—who must first focus on integrating the new employees into its organization and then turn its attention to longer-term growth and development efforts.

The best time to advise employees that an outsourcing evaluation is in progress or a decision is pending has long been the subject of debate. One side would argue that sharing information too early can lead to the loss of key employees and an overall decline in morale. The other side would point out that rumors develop no matter what management tries to do, and that the effect of these rumors without clear, factual communication from management leads to even greater disruption.

The organization's human resources professionals, who should be part of the team evaluating outsourcing from the beginning, also play a major role once the announcement is made. A structured meeting between staff members and human resources following the announcement allows employees to express their concerns, frustration, anger, or excitement. In addition, human resources professionals are well equipped to explain in detail the transition process and the options available to the employees.

Employees may have choices to make, and it's important to ask them to make their decisions and choices in a timely manner. For example, at some point in the process, employees may need to make an employment decision—whether to accept or decline a specific job offer. The timelines for making this decision should be clear and not too protracted—about two to three weeks is optimal.

Managing Public Perception of Outsourcing

Outsourcing has increasingly become a hot-button issue. Since the media tends to sensationalize outsourcing's impact on employees and communities, the critical first step in managing public perception of outsourcing is to properly assess the probability of media attention. The characteristics of the deal, the type of organization, the number and types of employees impacted, and the impact on the community at large are the key factors.

In particular, in assessing the probability of media attention, consider the following:

- *Does the company have a history of negative press coverage on outsourcing?* Negative press on outsourcing has a cumulative effect with subsequent deals coming under increasing scrutiny following earlier negative public reactions.
- *Will the deliberations be public?* This is likely to be the case for public companies or organizations with unionized employees.
- *How many people will be affected and what are their levels?* Public reaction to outsourcing is decidedly more negative when large numbers of lower-wage, minority-group employees are impacted or when it involves the offshoring of professional-level positions.
- *Will employees be "kept whole" in terms of pay, benefits, and job security?* This is a critical decision that management must make in formulating its strategy and should be done well in advance of announcing the deal. If employees will be kept whole, then there is often little story for the press to cover.
- *Is outsourcing being driven by financial problems?* Generally, outsourcing announcements by firms in financial difficulty receive more public scrutiny.
- *What is the provider's reputation for dealing with transferred employees?* Often, negative public reactions occur after the fact because of things the provider does or the provider's history of problems leading to greater media scrutiny.
- *Will the executive team be visible and proactive in managing public perception? Does it have experience with outsourcing?* Visibility, when needed, and experience are important in avoiding negative public reactions.

Once the probability of press coverage and a negative public reaction is assessed, management should develop an appropriate action plan, addressing both by how the deal is structured and how it is communicated. In developing that action plan, the following should be kept in mind:

- *The public image is made in the media.* It's clear that the amount and character of the media's coverage of an outsourcing engagement greatly determines the public's perception of the deal.
- *The goal is not to have to manage public opinion.* Outsourcing engagements do not require public opinion management when they don't attract media attention. Either create no public perception through little media coverage or create a positive perception by featuring innovative aspects of the deal.
- *The deal and its perception unfold together.* Many outsourcing deals are created with the public's perception in mind. Aspects of these deals are shaped to make the deal more acceptable to the public and the community.
- *Like politics, all outsourcing is local.* While there is currently a national debate on offshore outsourcing, it is still fundamentally a local issue. It's about local jobs and the impact on the local economy and community. Most negative public perception of outsourcing will center on this. It is important to treat outsourcing as a local issue in each affected community.
- *Shape public opinion by shaping employee opinion.* If the media is the connection to the public and the public's perception, then the employees are the key to the media. Layoffs and other features of the outsourcing deal attract the media, and disgruntled employees nourish negative press.

Summary

As leaders, an organization's management has the responsibility to make certain that employees understand the business, how it operates, and the key measures and drivers of its success. The goal is to help the organization's employees come to see that as changes take place, whatever they are, that they are not gratuitous—that they are sound responses on the part of management to the opportunities and challenges the business faces.

This education process begins by helping individuals better understand the realities of the current and future environment in which the organization operates. In so doing, the organization prepares them for any of a wide range of changes that may be needed. The better informed employees are, the better prepared they will be.

Management must be prepared to work with people to help them deal with the personal and professional ramifications of an outsourcing decision. Management cannot and should not abdicate this responsibility.

Open and honest communications only work when they are matched by action. Executing as planned and in a timely fashion are the keys. Following up on each and every employee commitment is mandatory.

Chapter

12

CREATING AND MANAGING THE NEW

More than half of all organizations spend 2 percent or less of an outsourcing contract's cost managing the relationship. However, more than 60 percent of these same executives say they are *losing 10 percent or more* of the contract's value because of poor working relationships between the organizations. Twenty-one percent say they are losing more than 25 percent of the contract's value.[1] Closing this gap is the single biggest problem outsourcing faces as a management practice. It also suggests that the return on investment from increased spending on managing these relationships would be significant.

Why isn't more being done? There are probably a lot of reasons. One is that because companies often outsource to save money, spending more to manage the relationship can be a tough sale. You can almost hear senior executives asking, "Didn't we outsource this so we didn't have to manage it?" Another reason is that outsourcing management is itself a loosely defined discipline with little empirical data to support its value proposition and operational needs. Another may be that few organizations would know where to spend the money even if it was budgeted. After all, little is known about which practices yield the greatest returns. In many ways, the implementation of outsourcing has well outpaced the development of its management practices.

This doesn't have to be the case, and this chapter provides a cohesive model for identifying where and how to invest in ensuring the continued success of current relationships and gaining even greater value in the future. It looks first at the migration to an outsourced environment and then at its sustained management.

Migrating to Outsourcing

There's nothing like a successful migration to boost the likelihood of success in the ongoing management of an outsourcing relationship. Although the technical aspects of the migration will differ from process to process and from company to company, the critical management elements do not.

The foundation for a successful launch is built in throughout the outsourcing process in selecting the scope of the process to be outsourced; developing the process diagram; selecting the provider; building the scorecard; and pricing, contracting, and negotiating the relationship. How the organizations will manage the collaborative work on "day one" should be an integral part of the decision making throughout.

Building from the process diagram and the scorecard, the operational interfaces between the organization and provider need to be defined in detail—the people and system interfaces, the data flows, the reporting capabilities, and where and when these things will happen. These interfaces then need to be tested, and volume forecasts for the ramp-up to production need to be established and agreed to by all involved.

Risk assessments need to be performed and contingency plans developed for each step in the migration plan. The management structure, communications plans, and human resources plans need to be brought into operation. Once all of these elements are in place, management approval for launch is needed from both organizations, and daily progress needs to be tracked and reported. There is simply no substitute for early identification and resolution of problems. Poor results during the migration can create lasting perceptions that stay with the relationship for years to come.

As the new operational environment is coming online, so is the new management system. The following ten principles should be used to shape that management system.

Principle #1: Keep the Strategic Responsibility Close to the Top

Operational and management issues are dealt with at multiple levels within the organization, but the strategic responsibility—the responsibility to ensure an ongoing alignment of the interests of both the organization and the provider—is something that cannot be delegated. The functional executive is ultimately responsible for ensuring that the organization realizes the value anticipated from the services outsourced. Therefore, the management structure should be designed to ensure that the overall strategic responsibility for the relationship remains at the highest executive levels.

Some organizations even add a separate executive, reporting to the CEO, COO, or CFO, as the organization-wide coordinator of all of its major outsourcing projects. This executive works with the functional executives to assist them in the identification and implementation of outsourcing initiatives. This executive becomes a focal point for ensuring sustained senior executive focus on outsourcing and on the relationships created.

Organizations such as Bell Canada, Coors, the Toronto Hospital, American Express, and others have adopted this approach. At one New Zealand company, Meridian Energy, the CEO treats the senior executives in the provider organizations for his major outsourcing relationships as if they were his direct reports—they attend every other quarterly leadership meeting right alongside his own executive team. The key is to not allow senior leadership to become disconnected from the strategic importance of the relationship between the organization and the provider.

Principle #2: Create Multilevel Organizational Links

Just as the strategic link between organization and provider must be kept close to the top, there also needs to be links at multiple levels. The complexity of the relationship between the organization and the provider should not be underestimated. Decisions will need to be made on a continual basis that affect day-to-day activities. Other decisions will impact the overall scope of services, as well as the overall tenor of the relationship. The management structure must facilitate and support all of these.

The multilevel management structure should include layers of teams focused on the operational, tactical, and strategic aspects of the relationship. These teams should be comprised of individuals from both organizations representing all the needed disciplines and interests—operations, finance, end users, and others. Figure 12.1 shows this multilayer approach.

Operating committees, made up of individuals directly involved in the operational activities, ensure day-to-day communications between organization and provider, resolve issues as they occur, and report issues that cannot be resolved at their level.

A management committee, with overall responsibility for the contract and its deliverables, ensures that both organization and provider understand how performance compares to expectations, as reflected in the scorecard. They are also the focal point for approving changes in scope or deliverables and the arbitrator for unresolved operational issues.

Finally, the executive steering committee should be led by the executive with overall strategic relationship responsibility. This team is tasked with the ultimate responsibility of ensuring the ongoing health of the relationship and resolving any major issues that develop.

There is often a tendency to make relationship management the responsibility of one key person in each organization. This is a mistake. Relationships of this complexity require links up, down, and across the

FIGURE 12.1 USE A MULTILAYER MANAGEMENT APPROACH FOR OUTSOURCING SUCCESS

EXECUTIVE COMMITTEE	• Monitor Health of Relationship • Review Strategic Plans • Resolve Major Issues
MANAGEMENT COMMITTEE	• Review/Approve Key Contract Deliverables and Changes • Review Functional and Operating Plans • Approve New Service Levels • Approve New Customer Requirements • Resolve Issues
OPERATING COMMITTEES	• Day-to-day Management and Operational Activities

businesses. The role of the relationship managers in outsourcing, both on the organization and on the provider side, is not to be the funnel for the communications but, instead, to orchestrate the communications taking place across the businesses.

Principle #3: Conduct Regular, Goal-Oriented Meetings

There is simply no substitute for regular, goal-oriented meetings between the organizations. These meetings should have defined frequency, consistent attendance by the principals involved, continuity from meeting to meeting through formal agendas, assigned action items, and follow-through.

One critical point: Meetings between the responsible people in the organizations are the basic element of the management structure. Their effectiveness is central to the overall success. In fact, the one thing that has to happen when and if problems develop is an increase in the frequency of the meetings. Problems can only be resolved through the ongoing communications of the parties involved.

Principle #4: Use the Latest Communications Technologies

In addition to traditional face-to-face communications, electronic systems are powerful tools for managing the relationship between the organization and the provider. Outsourcing exists in a virtual world. One of its very drivers is the fact that technology has made much of the work of today's modern organization placeless. This same technology opens up a whole range of new communications tools. Use of these tools should be an integral part of the outsourcing management structure.

The Internet, voice mail, teleconferencing, e-mail, discussion groups, instant messaging, and online collaboration tools are all being used. Many companies place their operational dashboard right online for both organizations to see, using industry standard data formats to feed the systems.

Organizational structures and responsibilities, with names, photographs, and biographies, can be included as well to facilitate communications and create a feeling of team. Technology enables outsourcing. It also enables its management.

Principle #5: Define the Escalation Process

Just as problems surface almost daily in any in-house operation, problems have to be expected with outsourcing.

An important element of the management structure is the "escalation" process for problem resolution—the process by which unresolved issues are brought to a higher level. The escalation process is critical to both parties. Define it in advance. Make certain that everyone knows how it works and what his or her role is. Use an objective scoring system to rate the status and severity of issues. Make the escalation process automatically tied to an objective scoring system, such as rating items as "green," "yellow," or "red."

Make certain that all parties realize that the focus is on solving the problem, not assigning blame. Be consistent, quick, and fair.

As mentioned earlier, technology provides new techniques for surveying the positions of impacted parties and keeping everyone informed.

Define a process for establishing working groups to investigate and make recommendations on issue resolution. Define in advance the people who make up these groups and the processes they will follow to make their recommendations.

The bottom line is to make certain that the management structure ensures that issues will be escalated until resolved satisfactorily.

Principle #6: Use the Scorecard to Report Results

Regular communications and performance reviews are the essence of the outsourcing management structure—many of the key principles of which have just been reviewed. In turn, the scorecard is the essential tool for gauging performance. Defined when the relationship is created, the scorecard declares what is important, keeps the organizations focused, enables objective tracking, and is a powerful motivator of achievement. From day one, the scorecard must be the objective basis for understanding what is working, what isn't, and for measuring improvement.

Making sure that the ability to collect and report scorecard data is in place on day one is a critical task of the transition team. The outsourcing relationship simply cannot be managed without an objective scorecard. In its absence, opinions, instead of facts, reign.

Principle #7: Consistently Apply Incentives and Penalties

Incentives and penalties need to be fairly and consistently determined and applied. Failure to apply them uniformly undermines their value and, over time, can undermine the entire relationship. If incentives are earned but not paid, then the effort goes unrewarded and is unlikely to be repeated. By the same token, if penalties are not enforced, then how important can the outcome actually be to the organization?

The entire reason for incentives and penalties is to motivate behavior. As the organization receiving services, you want the provider's account team to be recognized by its management for its achievements. Just as important, you want the account team to be able to marshal resources to correct problems that may be causing penalties. Financial incentives and penalties, if fairly and consistently applied, can have this effect. In the case of penalties, the goal is not to punish. Nor is it to pay less for poor service or to simply attempt to recover costs incurred as a result of problems. The true goal of incentives and penalties is to get changes enacted that fix the problems and increase the probability of repeatable successes.

Principle #8: Reward the Provider's Employees

The next principle of a sound management structure for outsourcing is to extend the incentive system so that it rewards the provider's employees. Just as incentives are powerful motivators for an organization's own people, they are equally powerful for the provider's. One caution, however, is to make certain incentive programs do not flow directly from the organization's management to the provider's employees. If this happens, a coemployment situation can result. Under coemployment, both companies become parties to the employment relationship with the individual. This, in turn, can have specific personnel and legal implications.

There are still a number of ways to recognize the provider's employees. They can indirectly participate in the organization's award or bonus programs. One example is American Airlines, which extended its AAwards program to its provider's employees, with the awards being granted through the provider's management team. Another way is for the provider to tie customer input, such as letters of commendation or customer satisfaction surveys, into its internal recognition program. Still another approach is joint celebrations. These enable both companies to recognize the people who have made their collaborative accomplishments possible.

A final, and somewhat less-recognized, incentive is for the organization to keep in mind that career advancement is often the most powerful incentive available. This is a difficult issue for many organizations. They want the provider's best people assigned to them. On the other, they don't want to lose these people through advancement. In the long-run, it is in the customer's best interest to encourage and support the achievement and advancement of top performers.

Principle #9: Implement the Change Process

Another key element of the management structure for outsourcing is the change process. The system to be used for identifying, negotiating, and implementing change must be defined and mutually agreed to in advance.

Successful organizations position the change process as an integral part of the management structure. Each level of the management structure deals with change—operational, tactical, and strategic. And they do so as part of their regular agenda, continually negotiating and implementing needed changes.

Kodak, in fact, sent managers from both its organization and its provider to joint training programs on principled negotiations. They also agreed, in advance, to the structure of the teams that would develop and recommend changes in the relationship. In effect, the way changes would be handled was locked in as an essential part of the management structure.

As a final point on the change process, consider implementing a 360-degree review process. Encourage the service provider to provide feedback on improvements the organization can make that would advance both of their interests.

Principle #10: Treat the Relationship as a Valuable Asset

The final principle captures the very essence of what has been discussed so far. When developing the management structure, recognize that the relationship required a significant investment of time and resources to create; that the services being contracted are critical to the business's operations and important to your customers. With this in mind, manage the relationship as what it is—a strategic business asset. An asset that is just as important as any traditional asset—people, facilities, technologies, and customer relationships.

Interdependent Management

This leads naturally to the need for both interdependent management systems and interdependent planning systems.

As outsourcing relationships expand and proliferate, new interdependent management systems are routinely developed. One current development is the project management office, another is the collaborative governance board.

Outsourcing relationships include not just operational services that need to be managed on a sustained basis; they also generate a constant stream of discrete projects. These projects are in response to changing requirements and to service enhancements introduced by the provider. The challenge of project definition, estimation, and measurement grows geometrically as the number of organizations working together on a project increases. Without a project management office, project spending can spiral out of control, both in terms of the number of projects that get commissioned and the organization's ability to coordinate the work of its providers. For large organizations with a number of outsourcing relationships, the volume of projects to be coordinated can be significant. In early 2004 Procter & Gamble had more than 170 active projects in its outsourcing project management office.[2]

The focus of the project management office is to ensure that the right projects get done right. To do this, the project management office can be seen as being made up of four major components: project portfolio management; project execution; project tracking and reporting; and project management competency.

Project portfolio management means taking the business objectives and ensuring that the right projects are initiated with the appropriate priority. It also means constantly check-pointing these projects back against the changing business needs to make sure that a project that might have been right a few months ago is still right today. Stopping projects when the business case no longer makes sense can be the most difficult thing to do, but at the same time, it can be the most value-creating. Looking for redundancies and overlaps in the project portfolio and making project sponsors aware of opportunities to use or reuse work already being done and paid for elsewhere is also part of project portfolio management.

Project execution in the outsourcing environment requires a level of rigor akin to the kind that went into defining and crafting the outsourcing relationship to begin with. Previous internal methods typically prove inadequate for projects involving multiple internal organizations and multiple provider organizations. This means both the project definition and workflows, but it also means sharpening cost projection skills, as well. It means having a well-defined and agreed-to system for measuring and reporting project information to the central project tracking system, including standardized feeds based on an information exchange architecture such as XML. Project tracking and reporting also include the ability to compare project data against industry benchmarks. These project tracking systems are just as important for the project elements done internally as they are for the parts performed by the providers.

Project management competency is the fourth element of a good project management office and cannot be taken for granted. Activities here include: the ongoing development of project management standards and supporting tools; maintaining a center of excellence on the discipline of project management; promoting training and certification; and consulting with unit heads on project management.

Another way of managing interdependent operations across one or more outsourcing relationships is with a collaborative governance board. This governance board assumes a shared responsibility for the overall results delivered to the organization—from ongoing strategic planning through enabling of the day-to-day operations. It becomes the central body for connecting the services to the internal or external clients receiving those services. It begins by creating a board of advisors made up of leaders from the organization as well as each of the major service providers. This board overseas the entire program. It meets formally as often as every two weeks, with ongoing communications among board members between meetings. The board's resources are pooled and shared across the members, as is the accountability for the outcomes achieved and the financial benefits produced. This means that, within the framework of the relationship, all resources, information, and practices are shared.

This kind of governance structure focuses the relationship on innovation not initiatives, intimacy not implementation, outcomes not output, and interdependence not simply integration. Trailblazing this approach along with a top-down restructuring and business process–based outsourcing of all their real estate operations, PricewaterhouseCoopers, the world's largest professional services firm, has reduced annual expenses by 34 percent and driven $164 million to the firm's bottom line.[3]

Interdependent Planning

Management tools that integrate the planning of the organization and provider are just as important as ones that integrate management. One of these tools, pioneered at Bell Canada, is the outsourcing business plan.[4]

The outsourcing business plan puts a formal process in place for periodically reviewing and updating all aspects of the relationship between the companies. This shared commitment to its development, as well as the process to be followed, can and should be written right into the contract. Frequency can vary, but annual is the most common—aligned with the customer's annual planning process. The business plan itself is made up of four key sections: strategy, operations, financial, and management.

The strategy section of the business plan realigns the relationship and services to any changes in the organization's corporate direction and objectives, both operational and financial. In addition, it reviews the previous year's performance to identify any gaps that may have developed. It's also an opportunity to identify new initiatives and services that the provider will introduce to support the organization's changing needs. Changes in the business climate that may positively or negatively affect either organization's business or the specific services and the way they are delivered are identified and assessed. Finally, the initiatives and targets in response to all of these considerations are described.

The next section of the business plan operationalizes the initiatives outlined in the strategic section. It describes the specific actions to be taken, along with the deliverables, dates, and responsibilities. The steps in achieving these goals, such as new service launches, process improvement, and cost reduction, are stated. New and revised scorecards are documented, as well as any required changes in the data collection and reporting. Required formal contract updates are laid out.

The financial section updates the outsourcing business case to reflect new investments and changes in costs, pricing, and pricing models. It ensures that the financial impacts of any changes are identified, justified, and agreed to by both parties.

The management section reviews the strengths and weaknesses of the current management process along with any changes to be implemented during the upcoming period. This may include planned personnel changes, training programs, new management tools to be implemented, and so on. Communications is also an important part of the updated management plan. This includes communications in both the organization and provider, upward and downward, to the users of the services, and any other stakeholders that need to be updated on the current status and planned direction of the relationship and the services being provided.

The outsourcing business plan provides for a periodic review and update of all the key elements of the relationship—strategic, operational, financial, and management. It helps ensure that both parties are addressing problems, needed changes, and new opportunities in a regular, planned, and formal way. It also ensures that the result of this review is a deliverable—a document that members of both the organization and the provider can use to understand changes and their role in them as the relationship moves forward.

Another interdependent management tool, developed at Microsoft, is the outsourcing risk assessment, or what the company calls a Comprehensive Outsource Risk Evaluation (C.O.R.E.).[5] The purpose is twofold. First, it recognizes that as effective as scorecards are for managing performance, they are essentially trailing indicators—looking in the rearview mirror at what has happened and only suggesting where things may be headed. Risk assessment, on the other hand, is a forward-looking tool that, when done well, is an early warning system of problems to come. Second, it recognizes that as organizations become increasingly interdependent through outsourcing, the risks any one company faces are risks that all of the companies in the system face. Through careful planning, these risks can be identified early and mitigated.

A company like Microsoft works with outsourcing providers worldwide in many areas that directly affect its ability to get product to market, such as packaging, licensing, fulfillment, and distribution. Identifying the circumstances that could jeopardize a provider's ability to deliver is critical and, when done jointly, becomes a powerful management system.

Outsourcing risk assessment uses a consistent, repeatable methodology to categorize and examine the business risks providers face. These risks can be categorized at the highest level into "risk families," such as infrastructure risks, business control risks, business value risks, and relationship risks. The specific risks within each category can then be identified, ranked for potential impact, and evaluated. By making this a joint review, looking at both the organization's and the provider's environment, the probability of future disruptions can be reduced.

These and other interdependent planning techniques achieve a number of things. First, they reduce the potential for surprises that almost always diminish the value of the relationship. Second, they represent processes for continually moving the relationship and its value to both organizations forward. Third, they deepen the working relationship and understanding of the two organizations.

Summary

Implementation and relationship management is all about taking the contract and turning it into an asset. This means making an investment in what is essentially a newly formed entity so that it increases in value over time and, in turn, increases its value to the organization and the provider, and to the organization's customers.

A key principle for achieving this is the creation of multiple connections between the organization and provider at as many layers as possible—not just the day-to-day operations, but at the management and executive levels. It means linking the organization and provider strategically and tactically. It means putting in place new management systems at the project and the process governance levels. It means using new tools for strategic planning, project planning, operational tracking, and risk management and mitigation.

Most organizations know that they are spending something in the neighborhood of 1 to 2 percent of the annual contract cost in its management. They also know that they are leaving upwards of 20 percent of the relationship's value "on the table" because they lack the level of interdependent planning and management needed to ensure a solid working relationship across the organizational boundaries. Even a small investment here can produce a manyfold return for both organizations and providers alike.

Quick Reference Guide

How do you tell if your current provider is getting into trouble? Most important, how do you tell before their problem becomes yours?

There are two things to look for. The first are negative trends in the provider's current performance. The second are changes in the provider's overall business condition that may lead to performance problems down the road.

The following quick reference guide can help identify these negative trends early:

Current Performance:

- Inconsistency in the level of service provided
- Increase in the noise level about the provider's services
- Problems getting passed around and not solved
- More frequent need to escalate problems to get them fixed
- Increasingly rigid interpretation of scope of service, costs, and other contractual terms
- Unanticipated turnover at the management ranks
- Unanticipated turnover in the employee ranks
- Frequent requests for you to better prioritize your requirements
- Less interest in opportunities to provide new or expanded services to your company
- Increased visibility of problems with the provider's subcontractors
- A perceived change in your importance as a customer
- Less frequent contact with the provider's senior management
- Inconsistent information from people on the provider's team

Overall Business Condition:

- Deteriorating financial condition at the balance sheet, P&L, cash flow, credit, or equity levels
- New marketplace, legal, or public relations issues
- Increase in executive turnover
- Increase in employee turnover
- Declining client retention rate
- Loss of one or more major current customers
- Negative change in financial condition of one or more major customers
- Win of a major new customer
- Entry to or exit from a new line of business, geography
- Problems in the parent company or other large business unit
- Problems with a major subcontractor

Section Three

THE OUTSOURCED ENTERPRISE

Chapter

13

OUTSOURCING'S FUTURE HISTORY

In many ways, the evolution of outsourcing as a management practice mirrors that of information technology (IT). After all, the modern computer first came on the scene in the late 1940s and early 1950s, with limited understanding of the tidal wave of change it would create. As its use grew, it began to fundamentally transform business and our way of life. Entire new career opportunities opened up—everything from keypunch operators to programmers. At the same time, other jobs were eliminated. Clerical jobs in departments from purchasing to accounting were the first ones to go, and over time many other, even higher-skilled jobs, were automated out of existence. There was even popular discussion about how computers depersonalize companies for both their customers and employees. Of course, new jobs were created in an entirely new industry and in the technology departments of the companies; and today information technology allows companies to serve millions of customers in very personalized, very targeted ways.

We have learned to embrace the changes that information technology has thrust upon us. On the whole, few people could imagine their lives without instantaneous access to the global information infrastructure for everything from buying a present to balancing a checkbook. As an industry, information technology has played a pivotal role in the development of the global economy and has been a major contributor to the quality of life we now enjoy. Does this mean that every aspect of information technology is good? That the transition has not been painful for some? Or that every IT project proves to be a success for the company that undertakes it? Of course, not. But most would agree that, as an industry and as a business tool, information technology has an overwhelmingly positive impact. It is certainly an inseparable part of our lives.

In many ways, outsourcing's recent past and probable future are following the same path. Just as technology is driven by an unrelenting desire to improve productivity, and to leverage knowledge and work, outsourcing is driven by just as powerful a set of forces. In fact, all wealth as we know it comes from outsourcing—that is, specialization and trade. Specialization is why few of us cut our own hair; build, renovate, or maintain our own homes; or, for many, even cook many of our own meals. We even outsource much of the education of our children to specialists.

We do these things because someone else has made the investment to get very good at something—to specialize at it. As a result, they can do it better and less expensively for us than we can do it for ourselves. In turn, we develop our own specialties, especially our work and career skills. Specialization is what drives economic activity. We are paid for our specialized abilities, we pay others for theirs, and the difference between the two creates wealth.

Innovation plays an essential role as well. Innovation is often the catalyst for the initial specialization, and once the specialization begins, a constant stream of new innovations fuels its progress. Innovation drives specialization and ensures its sustainable economic value.

So, with 70 to 80 percent of the typical manufacturing operation already outsourced and the other areas of business on a similar trajectory, it's important to start thinking about how outsourcing, both domestically and offshore, is likely to impact all of us. Beginning to understand these changes and where they are taking us will help everyone adjust to the new order of things sooner. It also helps us take advantage of new opportunities being created.

Employees as Craftsmen

Few people realize that work was not always organized into the modern-day "job." The job as we think of it—a defined set of ongoing activities and responsibilities positioned on an organizational chart—was actually a creation of the industrial revolution. It enabled the work of large numbers of people to be organized in ways that had never before been needed.

Prior to the emergence of the job as the most common way of organizing work, the craft model dominated. A person entered a field as an apprentice, working for a craftsman, learned the trade, and, once mastered, began to take on work from customers directly. Certain professions, such as the construction trades, continue to use this as their dominant work model even today.

Although few would suggest that modern societies would ever return fully to the craftsman model, the increased use of outsourcing does suggest that elements of it are returning, or that, at a minimum, employees should be using the craft model as a mental-map for thinking about and managing their careers.

Specialists Will Work for Specialists

Outsourcing is, first and foremost, about specialization. This specialization is taking place at the organizational level and at the job level. For example, almost all net job increases in information technology take place in the services side of the industry.[1] The industry is now dominated by the large, specialized services firms, such as CSC, EDS, IBM, and Unisys. Similarly, electronics manufacturing skills are increasingly concentrated in companies like Solectron, the number one electronic manufacturing services company. Solectron is now larger than many of its more famous technology customers, companies such as Apple Computer, Sun Microsystems, and Lucent Technologies. Even food services expertise is increasingly concentrated in that industry's specialists, firms such as ARAMARK, Compass, and Sodexho.

We can reasonably expect that, as the use of outsourcing continues to grow, every field will develop its own specialty services firms and that a growing percentage of the specialists who work in that field will work for those companies.

From Cost to Profit

As employees move into these specialty firms, one very important change is that they go from working in a cost center to working in a profit center. For the specialized firm, they are not a back-office operation, they are a front-office operation. They are how the company makes its money.

This is double-edged sword. People on the front line have the opportunity for greater rewards, but they also have more responsibilities and greater risks. Their work directly affects the company's customers and its revenue. Winning a new customer opens up immediate opportunities and immediate new demands that have to be met. The individuals doing the work are working with customers and need to be customer-focused in the way they do their jobs. Missed deadlines or failures in execution are no longer just disappointments, they create very real customer problems.

From Content to Context

This also suggests that the level of skills and knowledge expected of specialists will advance at an accelerated pace. The routine aspects of their field, the things that can be done by any competent professional, will get rapidly commoditized. This commoditization will happen in a number of ways. One is offshoring and another is technology.

Offshoring allows well-trained professionals, earning wages that are a fraction of what they are in developed economies, to take on the definable, repeatable parts of the job. Today it's India, the Philippines, Eastern Europe, and China. Tomorrow it will be Afghanistan, Ghana, Thailand, and Vietnam. Now that the world has been wired, we have to assume that smart, hard-working people everywhere will find ways to get the education they need and to somehow plug themselves into the global talent pool. Once plugged in, they'll be put to work.

Another way that the more routine end of the specialty will be commoditized is through technology. Every day more and more knowledge is being captured and put into information systems. These systems are being used to automate work and make the know-how available to customers on a self-service basis. This means that specialists will need to continually move up their field's skill curve if they continue to demand today's salary tomorrow. They will need to move away from this routine work by focusing more on the context of what they do; working at the point where they create value by knowing how to connect their specialty to emerging needs—where the new value opportunities exist.

Everyone Is Self-Employed

Another dimension of employee as craftsman is the self-employment model, whether or not one is currently working for a company.

People who are self-employed approach their careers quite differently than those who hold traditional jobs. They know that they will only have work tomorrow if they satisfy the needs of the client today. Understanding and constantly adjusting to these changing needs becomes a central focus of their workday. When people are self-employed, they also initiate the development and enhancement of their skills. They certainly don't look to their customers to train them. Instead they recognize that in a constantly changing, competitive marketplace, they need to develop skills ahead of customer demand and ahead of the competition.

They also see themselves and their skills as portable, able to be taken from one customer to the next. Their value is not defined by their job description; it's defined by their knowledge and experience. They are also constantly developing and keeping their professional network fresh. They are continually seeking out the next customer, one that will be willing and able to pay them the highest market rate for the work they do.

Executives as Integrators

Outsourcing is also changing the role of managers and executives. Their responsibilities are increasingly shifting toward the kinds of integration skills associated with top general managers, and away from the functional and operational expertise that characterized the past.

Lateral Leadership

Mike Useem, of the Wharton School of the University of Pennsylvania, was one of the first to capture this change in quantifiable terms.[2] He called it *lateral leadership* and went on to identify four capabilities that make for a lateral leader—to be able to think strategically, make deals, govern partnerships, and manage change. His research found that not only were these capabilities recognized as needed, but that companies were increasingly willing to pay a premium for midlevel and senior managers who possessed them.

In a traditional hierarchical structure, where the business owns, manages, and controls most of its factors of production, only the top executives work laterally. As outsourcing continues to expand, every manager, at every level of the organization will be increasingly operating this way. They will be blending a wide array of internal and external resources and competencies to deliver results for their internal and external customers. They will not simply be using general services that the purchasing department contracted for on behalf of the corporation; they will be selecting and crafting outside relationships with the same care and interdependency associated with selecting their employees.

And, of course, outsourcing is just one form of outside relationship increasingly central to the operations of most businesses. Between outsourcing, strategic alliances, joint venture, and other collaborative relationships, the work of the future manager is likely to be far more externally focused than internally.

Project and Process Leadership

Greater use of outsourcing also leads to a greater focus on project leadership and process leadership. Increasingly, the work of the business will be done by bringing together teams of people, from across these multiple outside relationships, for the purpose of delivering a specific result. These teams come together for the project at hand and then disband once it's done.

A parallel for this can be found in the studio model for producing movies and television shows. The studio funds the project and manages the promotion and sales channel, but the actual film is an ensemble cast of producers, writers, directors, actors, costume artists, and many others brought together for that project.

Project leadership requires different skills, tools, and management systems. The ability to blend the competing interests of the team members and keep everyone focused on the task at hand and their role is key. All the other common management systems exist, but in different forms. Budgets, work plans, issue identification and resolution, personnel management, compensation, and others are focused on the completion of the project on time and on budget, not on the sustained operations of a department.

At the same time, outsourcing is creating a greater focus on process-centric skills. This makes the ability to work across the organization, from the customer-in perspective, increasingly important. It requires an understanding of all of the different disciplines and specialties that are woven together to produce the customer result. It requires the ability to communicate effectively with a wide range of professionals, each with very different backgrounds and skill sets. It takes an awareness of both the overall business and how each piece fits.

Global Leadership

As outsourcing increasingly goes global, the ability of managers and executives to work with different people in different countries will become increasingly important, as well. At one time, perhaps only an executive in purchasing and a few other top executives had direct business dealings with suppliers in other countries. With global outsourcing, executives in every area of the business will be doing this. Customer care executives will be overseeing a global network of call center providers. IT executives will be working with development teams in India and Russia. Research managers will be funding projects all around the world.

Each country has its own unique culture that directly affects how information is communicated, negotiations conducted, and decisions made. In the future, most managers, even in small and midsize companies, will need global experience to draw upon to do their jobs well.

Enterprises as Reverse Prisms

Finally, the increased use of outsourcing will change many characteristics of firms themselves. Three that are briefly examined here are innovation, knowledge management, and risk management; all of which are profoundly impacted by the increasingly outsourced enterprise. The net effect of these and many other changes will be to change the organization into a prism—a prism that is successful because it's good at bringing together its internal capabilities with external capabilities and focusing the result, with laser-sharp precision, on the needs of its customers.

Outsourcing for Innovation

In today's information-intensive business environment, constant innovation is the only sustainable competitive advantage. And, as introduced in Chapter 4, using outsourcing to increase the rate of innovation can have an exponential effect on the base business case of any outsourcing contract. According to James Brian Quinn, "Leading companies have lowered innovation costs and risks 60 percent to 90 percent while similarly decreasing cycle times and leveraging the impact of their internal investments by tens to hundreds of times" by outsourcing innovation.[3]

How? By using outsourcing to tap their innovation chain much as they currently tap their supply chain. Drug discovery in the pharmaceutical industry is just one example. By outsourcing to research centers using high throughput screening techniques, where much of the testing process is automated, a pharmaceutical company can leverage its research efforts. These outside centers can test tens of thousands of compounds at the same time and cost that their wet lab would need for just a few compounds. Newer, even more innovative and powerful approaches are emerging in this R&D innovation chain every day. For example, Point Pleasant, New Jersey–based Sunyata Molecular Corporation is designing compounds at the atomic level using advanced nanotechnology to analyze molecular particle flows *in silico*, that is, in the computer. Compound design and evaluation will then take seconds of computer time enabling the company's wet chemistry labs to focus on only the most promising compounds.

Other companies, such as Cisco, Dell, and Intel, have similarly turned their supply chains into innovation chains. Shifting from a supply-chain mindset to an innovation-chain mindset requires creating integrated, interdependent operations focused on goals that excite all partners with both the vision of what they are creating and the potential rewards to be shared if they are successful.

Knowledge Management

Innovation comes from knowledge and so knowledge management, across and throughout the parties to the outsourcing relationship, will become increasingly important as the number and sophistication of these relationships increases.

Most experts characterize knowledge capital into three different types: human capital (the knowledge of the firm's employees); structural capital (the infrastructure used by the firm to organize its knowledge); and customer capital (the franchise an organization has with its customers). The challenge is to create strong connections between the parties to the outsourcing relationship that encourage the sharing of this knowledge capital across the network of companies and individuals involved. This will continue to be a real challenge for businesses as long as the traditional sense of organizational boundaries dominates our thinking.

One emerging technique for shifting this thinking is called the enterprise partnership model.[4] iPSL, discussed later, is an example of this. So is the recently created relationship between Lloyds of London, IUA London Markets, and Xchanging for back-office processing of insurance premiums and claims.

In both of these cases, a new business entity was created and the relevant knowledge capital of the separate parties transferred into it. Some of that knowledge came from transferring key people from each of the separate businesses into the new entity. That knowledge is then put to work by adopting a common framework for understanding and solving business problems. In some cases this framework may be a proprietary model favored by one of the parties. In others it may be an industry standard technique, such as Six Sigma.

At the same time, the new entity is able to begin to implement its own unique techniques for creating structural knowledge capital. This is accomplished by identifying common bodies of knowledge that can be reused across various aspects of the operation, and then developing and deploying tools that help make that knowledge available to people where and when it's needed. In addition, customer knowledge capital is enhanced through formal management systems, as well as through more informal, ongoing communications links between the new entity and its original parent companies.

Given the central role that knowledge management will play in the future world of business, other forms of relationships that encourage the sharing and rewarding of knowledge capital within the framework of outsourcing will emerge.

Networked Risk

As outsourcing increases, organizations become increasingly interdependent. This interdependence means that the risks to the organizations become interconnected as well. The use of outside organizations does not eliminate the responsibility of an organization and its board to ensure that the work done on its behalf is performed in a way that is compliant to all applicable laws and industry regulations. This principle has already been established in the banking industry through regulation, and for health care through HIPAA. Similarly, Sarbanes-Oxley places requirements in the areas of attestation of controls, accountability, and security that need to be met internally but also through the company's network of providers.

The network risk management ideas presented in Chapter 12 represent just a starting point for the changes to come. Outsourcing means interdependence. Interdependence means all organizations in the network are dependent upon each other for their success. This is one of the great organizational changes emerging through outsourcing.

Summary

The outsourced enterprise will transform every aspect of work and organizations as we know them today. It will raise the bar and the reward for specialists. It will force managers at every level of the organization to think like a CEO. It will transform businesses into reverse prisms, taking the spectrum of capabilities available to them from the outside, combining them with their areas of unique capability, and then focusing the result to create solutions for their customers.

Chapter

14

OUTSOURCING IN ACTION

The following case studies illustrate the power of outsourcing to transform organizations as well as the principles and ideas discussed throughout this book.

Transforming Shared Services through Outsourcing: Aetna

Background

Aetna is a 150-year-old company and the second largest provider of health care and health benefits in the United States. In 1996 the company exited its traditional property, casualty, and individual life business to focus exclusively on the health and wealth markets. By 2003 the company had further narrowed its focus to exclusively focus on the health insurance market. At the time, it had 31,963 employees serving more than 140,000 unique customers in all 50 states. Aetna had the largest percentage of the Fortune 500 as its clients in its industry and had 13.9 million health care members, 11.9 million dental members, and 11.7 million group insurance members.[1]

As part of this transformation, the company's new chairman challenged its top leaders to take $100 million in annual costs out of its operations. A difficult challenge in a company steeped in history, especially one with a culture of "Aetna jobs for Aetna people." The company historically did not outsource work and, in fact, had multiple generations of Aetna employees whose jobs would be affected by any outsourcing decision.

However, the stakes were enormous. A $100-million expense reduction was the equivalent, at the company's margins at the time, to almost $1 billion in additional revenue. Seeing this reduction not as cost savings but as a revenue offset put the significance of the opportunity in perspective.

Aetna Business Resources

Corporate shared services at Aetna were known as ABR, or Aetna Business Resources. ABR was responsible for all aspects of corporate real estate as well as many administrative services, such as mail and records, transportation, security, food services, facilities management, telecommunications, design and construction, leasing, employee relocation, and executive travel. These functions represented $170 million of operating expenses to the company with approximately 700 full-time employees—all of whom were Aetna employees.

Prior to the chairman's challenge to reduce costs, ABR had already been through a reengineering and continuous improvement program that had removed significant waste and had brought its practices to performance levels consistent with other similar-sized organizations. ABR had seasoned professionals running each of its service lines. This did not, however, mean that there were not gaps between the actual value being produced by the processes within ABR and what the internal customers of these services needed and expected. To identify and address these gaps as part of an overall effort to streamline the shared service operations, ABR's leaders embarked on an improvement program called "customer-in."

ABR's Customer-In Program

The customer-in improvement program began with more than 200 interviews of ABR's three major stakeholders: its own staff; the company's senior management (the economic buyers of its services—whether paid for on an allocation or a fee-for-service basis); and the actual customers of the services provided—Aetna's 30,000 or so employees.

Gaps were found. The first was the orientation of the internal shared services operation. It was delivering very well at a transaction level—providing the specific service requested in a timely and efficient way—but had little orientation and alignment to the company's overall strategy and little sense of the bigger picture in terms of how its services translated into value for Aetna's customers. Technical skills were high, but customer relationship skills were low; after all, they had always been captive customers of ABR's services. This also meant that any real commercial alignment of performance, risks, and rewards was simply not present—ABR had the franchise for these services and was simply not subject to a competitive environment.

The second gap was in integration. ABR's services were not integrated and not focused on producing the actual value the internal customer sought. There was a perception that ABR, not its customer, was in control of the decisions being made. In essence, ABR's services were seen as necessary, but not as adding real value for its customers.

First Steps

The first step was to add a new "commercial" skill set to ABR in lieu of continuing to add traditional skills in its service areas. This meant repositioning ABR as the ABR Management Company. Skills that were added included: finance and audit, supplier management, process improvement, benchmarking, performance management, and consultants and facilitators. This was an essential step toward ABR seeing itself as a contractor, one that could, in fact, lose its customer's business if it failed to deliver properly and to efficiently manage its internal operations and costs.

The second step was a bundling of all the company's corporate services under a single management structure. This meant adding additional asset management and even energy services to the mix, as well as information technology (IT) services, such as infrastructure and strategic IT planning.

Outsourcing

The second step was to use a comprehensive outsourcing evaluation process to determine which of these services should continue to be performed within the company and which would be better acquired through outsourcing.

This process led to the outsourcing of all of the infrastructure services, including: asset management, data center operations, energy management, space utilization, field leasing, design and construction, and project management. Also outsourced were all of the company's workplace services, including: food and retail services, ergonomics, mail and transportation, records management, parking and shuttles, facilities management, furniture management, employee relocations, safety and environmental, corporate security, aviation, and executive travel.

What was not outsourced were ABR Management Company's strategic services, including: real estate portfolio planning, relationship management, workspace management, performance management, financial analysis, sourcing analysis, supplier management, and IT planning.

Critical Success Factors

The success of this new operation was, in management's view, directly tied to achieving three critical success factors:

1. Alignment
2. Access
3. Accountability

Alignment was addressed through the creation of a senior management advisory board. This was important both to align ABR to the business and also to ensure effective communications and decision making around the changes that ABR would be going through, especially the planned, extensive use of outsourcing for many of its previously internally delivered services. The advisory board was made up of senior executives from each of Aetna's lines of business, the CFO, the CIO, as well as the company's human resources, legal, and communications/public relations groups. Not only did these executives provide alignment input to ABR, but they were equally instrumental in communicating the changes through their own organizations.

Access was addressed through the creation of a new position called a *client services manager.* Dedicated client services managers became responsible for working with ABR's internal customers to ensure their ability to access the most appropriate ABR services for their need in the most effective and productive way for that customer. Client services managers were created at the campus and location level and sometimes at the line-of-business level. They represented a single point of contact for all of ABR's services, whether provided internally or through an outsourced relationship. Sometimes they came from within ABR, but sometimes these individuals came from the client's business unit, giving them immediate knowledge and credibility in interfacing with customers and executives in that business location or unit. Customer councils were used to gain continual feedback on ABR's services, customer satisfaction, and suggestions for improvement.

Accountability was created through a new ABR Management Contract. It provides clarity and transparency around the services that ABR delivers. It answers such questions as: What does "good" look like? And what does it cost? How is ABR held accountable in a very structured, very visible way? The ABR Management Contract defined these parameters and formed the basis for the services being orchestrated for the client by the client services manager. It was an open-book approach. The last piece in terms of accountability was measuring customer satisfaction with ABR's services, using a well-defined, externally developed set of metrics and processes called ServQual.

Technology was used to support the client services managers to provide services to their clients. One use of technology was the creation of a central call center for all ABR customers. This provided not only an efficient way of interfacing with the client but of collecting data and tracking the services being delivered. This data could then be flowed into the tracking and reporting system on the performance of each of the service providers—both internal and external to Aetna. Aetna's intranet was reengineered as well and linked to its individual service providers, not just to access information on the services available but, over time, for the end customer to request and track those services.

These same three critical success factors were carried into the supplier community as ABR selected, crafted, and ran these relationships.

Alignment often looked at competence and culture. Access looked at the organization's willingness and ability to partner with Aetna as its customer. And accountability translated into the key performance indicators established for each supplier's services while focusing on a win-win approach designed to improve the performance of both organizations. Another key consideration was to select providers that the company felt its current employees would want to work for. On average, 91 or 92 percent of employees took positions with the service providers selected.

Results

Operating expenses at Aetna were reduced by 40 percent, or $70 million, annually. Over that same period, costs per employee for ABR's services were lowered from $7,000 to $4,000.

What's next? As Aetna's business has evolved, the company's overall financial measure has become its performance on a per-member, per-month basis. In turn, its shared services operations are now aligning its own and its suppliers' metrics on this same base—enabling it to ensure an even tighter link between its operating costs for real estate and administrative services, and its overall business performance. These costs can now be measured and reported on a per-member, per-month basis, as well. All outsourcing contracts signed during ABR's first wave of outsourcing were renewed and expanded at the time of their first renewal.

Aetna's stock has performed extremely well, having risen from lows in the $30-per-share range in early 2001 to end 2003 close to its 12-month high of almost $65 per share. Management attributes much of these results to the company's new collaborative approach to meeting its business needs.

Using Information Technology Outsourcing for Business Transformation: Campbell Soup Company

Background

Campbell Soup Company is a 133-year-old brand of iconic stature. It enjoys a nearly 70 percent market share in the soup business and overall sales in excess of $6 billion. Although best known for its soup brand, Campbell's owns many other well-known brands, including Pepperidge Farm,

Godiva Chocolatier, Swanson, Arnott's, and V8. The company operates in more than 22 countries and has more than 25,000 employees.[2]

Campbell's is at the center of a number of challenging industry trends, including: slow growth in the overall economy; lower demand in some of its traditional markets; changing consumer preferences for ready-to-eat products; growing power on the part of retailers (especially Wal-Mart, which has grown to represent 20 percent of the company's revenues); increasing competition; and ever-increasing pressure to innovate new products.

In 2001, the board brought in a new executive leadership team to spearhead a transformation program at the company intended to put it on a growth path, even in the face of these overall industry trends. IT outsourcing at Campbell's was undertaken as part of this publicly declared program to transform the company's operations.

Defining the New Look for IT at Campbell's

The key characteristics that defined the "new look" for information technology at Campbell's were: to become business focused, not technology focused; to establish a new operating framework that would link all IT decisions to the business's overall strategy; and to recraft its current outsourcing relationships to be simpler with greater flexibility.

Included was an item-by-item review of every activity within the IT operation at Campbell's. Part of the evaluation was a classic "core competency"–based review: Was the company prepared to invest internally to perform the activity at world class standards? or would its business needs be better served by acquiring that activity from its provider? Another dimension, however, was a maturity model consideration. The question here was: Do we have the current activity well enough defined to outsource it? If not, it was felt that additional internal work needed to be done before the marketplace could be properly engaged. The analysis was done first at the regional level—North America, Europe, Asia Pacific—and then the model was synthesized at the companywide level.

Transforming to the New

As a result of this review, the IT roles that remain within Campbell's are: IT leadership and governance; most of architecture development (though in some areas it is now a shared activity); business enhancement (which is most often embedded in the business units themselves); some technology enhancement capabilities; and, of course, vendor management.

Services outsourced were:

- Mainframe, SP, AS/400 systems—including production operations, production control, maintenance and upgrades, system management control, capacity planning, and disaster recovery planning and services
- Data networks—including monitoring, measuring, reporting, tuning, capacity planning, maintenance, level 3 problem resolution, and disaster recovery
- Voice networks—including contracting with providers for long distance services and ordering lines
- Web-hosting services—including business-to-consumer sites
- Help desk services—including 24/7 coverage, password resets, level 1 support, and end-to-end ticket management
- Selected application services
- Local area network and server services—including monitoring, measuring, reporting, tuning, capacity planning, maintenance and upgrades, software installation, distribution and testing, and level 3 problem resolution
- Deskside services—including hardware maintenance and failed parts replacement

The agreement itself put specific service-level requirements in place around these services, but it also addressed provisions for relationship management, innovation, and gainsharing.

Results

At Campbell's outsourcing has become a central part of the company's transformation program. Executives attribute approximately 30 to 40 percent of the overall improvements within the IT function to outsourcing and about the same percentage of the company's overall improved performance to its IT function. To put that in financial terms, Campbell's stock price improved from about $20 in late 2002 to $28 in early 2004.

Using BPO to Redefine Real Estate Management: Computer Sciences Corporation

Over a three-year period, Computer Sciences Corporation saved more than $100 million through its BPO approach to corporate real estate.[3]

Background

Computer Sciences Corporation (CSC) is headquartered in El Segundo, California, and is a global provider of outsourcing and business process outsourcing services in information technology and related areas. The company has 90,000 employees in its worldwide operations and generated over $11 billion in revenue in 2003.

For most large companies like CSC, the corporate real estate function is made up of six major sets of activities: strategic planning, portfolio and asset management, acquisition and disposition, design and construction, information management, and facilities management. In CSC's case, prior to BPO, many of the operational activities were already out-tasked—that is, contracted for on a site-by-site, project-by-project basis—to more than 2,500 separate suppliers for everything from security to cleaning, food services, construction, maintenance, and shipping and receiving.

The Process

CSC began the process of identifying the best opportunities for outsourcing within its real estate operations by evaluating each in terms of strategic activities versus tactical activities. As a professional services company, the decision was made to keep in-house the strategic and operational planning activities, such as real estate planning, occupancy planning, energy, environmental health and safety planning, and security planning. Tactical activities, from building operations and maintenance to real estate transaction services and office services, were outsourced through a single integrated contract with United Systems Integrators of Stamford, Connecticut.

Web-based interfaces, providing real-time access to all of the information about the company's real estate portfolio and the status and performance of the activities that support that portfolio, were introduced, as well.

In developing this approach, CSC first built an internal business case that provided comprehensive understanding of its current internal spending at the activity level, as well of the service levels being achieved. When it came to selecting the provider, the most important factor was how well and how quickly the executive teams were able to come to a common understanding of the goals being sought and the strategy for getting there. It was a question of looking at capabilities and culture first, and then crafting a solution that fit the needs.

The contract was then tied to these goals and performance outcomes. Quarterly business reviews of performance and a pricing model tied to achieving the expected service levels help ensure that the level of ownership and the level risk are in balance.

Results

CSC was able to reduce its occupancy costs as a percent of revenue by as much as 3 percent and to lower its occupancy cost per employee by more than $3,000. The company reduced its overall real estate costs by 25 percent in just two and one-half years.

CSC also credits its real estate outsourcing relationship for its ability to weather the dramatic downturn in the telecommunications industry—a major customer segment for its services—that took place in 2001. This gave the company the controls it needed to be able to quickly adjust the cost of its real estate portfolio to bring it in line with the rapidly changing business realities.

Using Global Outsourcing to Redefine Applications Development: Circuit City Stores

Circuit City is the second largest electronics retailer in the United States, with 600 stores. The company is in the top 200 of the Fortune 500, with about $10 billion in revenue and 40,000 employees.

As with most retailers in the United States, the fall holiday season makes or breaks their year. Their fourth quarter accounts for about 40 percent of their annual revenue. This places demand on the company's IT group of about 700 people. Not only do they need to ensure high system availability and performance during this period, but they are often expected to roll out new systems in support of peak-season demands.[4]

Vendor Management

A key initiative for the company in 2003 was to improve vendor management and accounting, which is key to supply-chain and merchandising effectiveness. The IT systems currently used were a homegrown collection of spreadsheets and related tools. Circuit City knew these would not be able to keep pace with the growing number of different products being sourced and the increasing complexity of the deals being struck with suppliers. The goals of the new vendor management system were to standardize, streamline, and integrate the cross-functional processes involved; create standard operating procedures for the company; and to achieve over $1 million a year in savings that the company's Six Sigma analysis suggested was there.

With no package software available that would serve these needs, the implementation alternatives came down to either an internal or an outsourced development effort. A review of the existing commitments for internal resources and the fluctuating nature of the ongoing demand for applications development people made outsourcing the best alternative.

Virtusa, a Westborough, Massachusetts–headquartered provider of software development services, with employees in the United States, India, and Sri Lanka, was selected for the project. The provider led the entire project, beginning with a team of employees from both companies working collaboratively to define and refine the project scope and deliverables, through to the architecture, design, development, testing, and rollout of the application. An additional goal was to ensure that at least 30 percent of the software would reuse pieces of code already developed by the company for similar applications.

Results

Phase I of the new system went live on December 26, 2003. The application development costs were estimated to be at least 30 percent less than if it had been done in-house, and the expected savings from improved vendor management was realized. Additional features and functions continue to be rolled out on a regular basis.

Long-term benefits from the reusability of the software are expected to pay even bigger dividends—for example, a vendor management system for the store's music products is now being implemented.

Using BPO to Redefine Human Resources Management: Bank of America

Bank of America is one of the world's largest financial institutions, serving consumers, small businesses, and large corporations with banking, investing, asset management, and other financial and risk-management products and services. The bank serves clients in 150 countries and operates 5,700 retail banking offices and 16,500 ATMs.

As is the case across the banking industry, much of the bank's growth has been through mergers and acquisitions. The most recent of which was Bank of America's merger with FleetBoston Financial Corporation that closed on April 1, 2004.

Background

Constant growth through mergers and acquisitions presents a unique challenge for a company's internal operations. With each transaction people, assets, processes, and systems are acquired. As they are acquired, it creates an ongoing need for investment in technology to integrate and upgrade these systems. It's an ongoing investment that few, if any, organizations can sustain, especially for what are essentially back-office systems.[5]

BPO is one way to address this need. By outsourcing the transaction pieces of human resources, the consolidating process expertise and the investments in the enabling technologies come from the provider. This also frees the internal human resources professionals to spend more time on partnering with the business units, for strategic focus on workforce planning, and for policy making. Outsourcing the transaction-based activities actually frees more resources to focus on these strategic activities.

The Deal

The deal with Exult covered accounts payables, payroll, benefits delivery, all of the bank's human resources third-party contracts, its HR call centers, and its HR technology. It was a $1.1 billion contract for ten years and included the transfer of more than 700 of the bank's associates to the provider. The deal also included guaranteed annual cost savings as well as a significant equity stake for the bank in Exult's company.

For the bank, the goal was to link its people to Exult's process expertise while at the same time bringing in new technology to support the bank's HR service delivery. It also provided the bank a platform for marketing its financial products and services to Exult's partners, and its current and future clients, creating new revenue streams for the bank and the opportunity for both bottom-line savings and top-line revenue growth.

The Results

One early example was bringing online a new personnel call center, using Exult's technology platforms and service delivery tools. This immediately improved the quality of support provided to the bank's associates because of the availability of integrated, real-time data. One of the next projects was the rollout of employee self-service, Web-enabled tools. Both organizations shared revenues as these capabilities were then marketed to new clients.

Top-line revenue growth was also achieved through the successful marketing of the bank's global cash management services to BP, another Exult client. Bank of America was also able to offer its consumer banking services to employees of Exult's other clients. (Note: Exult was acquired by Hewitt in June 2004.)

Using Manufacturing Services Outsourcing (MSO) to Redefine By-product Management: Avery Dennison

Avery Dennison was founded in 1935 and is a $4.2 billion manufacturer of self-adhesive base materials, office products, labels, tags, retail systems, and specialty chemicals. The company operates in 39 countries with more than 200 manufacturing facilities and sales offices worldwide.[6]

By-product Management and MSO

A by-product is anything that leaves a manufacturing plant that is not a product. By-product management is actually just one process that surrounds a manufacturing operation. Manufacturing services outsourcing is the manufacturing equivalent of BPO. It includes manufacturing facility services as well as chemical management, fluids management, safety management, environmental compliance management, temporary labor, parts cleaning services, power management, lighting management, fork truck management, bag house management, and scrap metal management. It also includes managing the purchasing and vendor relationships associated with each of these services. In total, these services can represent as much as 20 percent of total manufacturing costs.

Avery Dennison began looking at potentially outsourcing by-product management as part of its overall effort to understand and reduce the liabilities and costs associated with both its hazardous and nonhazardous waste. The goals were to move toward a consistent companywide program to: manage all waste and recyclable materials, not just hazardous; improve recordkeeping; reduce risk of future liability from waste disposal; and control and, where possible, reduce costs associated with waste disposal.

The company examined a number of alternative solutions before deciding on outsourcing. These included: increasing internal head count; hiring a consultant to manage the process; increasing the disposal fees paid by the company's plants to cover the costs within the current structure; and finding a way to pay for the program improvements through direct cost savings. Outsourcing by-product management to Indianapolis-based Heritage Inter@ctive Services allows the company to integrate its waste management program with one provider, achieve the objectives, and cover those costs through direct savings in the waste management fees.

Result

Avery Dennison has seen an improvement in the risk profile associated with its waste. Record retention has been improved because all waste information now flows through a central repository designed and managed by Heritage. This information is available in real time to the provider; Avery's corporate environmental, health, and safety group; and to the individual plants.

Administration costs have gone down, and awareness of total costs has gone up. Cost controls are in place and verifiable, and real savings are being seen in the first year of the program. The program is also gaining acceptance and is expanding across the company's network of plants as these results are realized and plant managers who may have been initially hesitant are won over.

Using BPO to Redefine Check Processing: iPSL

iPSL was formed in December 2000 as a joint venture of Unisys (51 percent), Barclays, and Lloyds TSB (24.5 percent, respectively). It represented the simultaneous outsourcing of the check-processing operations of these banks and the commercialization of their existing capabilities through equity shares in the new company. A year later, HSBC became a third major customer and 10 percent owner, acquiring its stake in the company from the first two banks.

It's a classic BPO scenario. Check processing is a transaction-based, high-volume activity. Information technology is key to improving the process, raising quality and driving down costs—especially though the use of imaging technology that allows an "image" of the check, as opposed to the check itself, to be moved through the system. Check-processing transactions are placeless in nature and can be done anywhere, yet need to be immediately accessible electronically to the bank and its customers. Volumes on an individual bank basis were declining in the United Kingdom as consumers moved away from checks toward debit and credit card transactions—making the business case for technology investment in check processing hard to justify. Yet billions of transactions would still need to be processed every day and done so with absolute accuracy—without becoming a financial drain on the banks' overall operations.

Results

By the end of 2003, iPSL had more than 70 percent of the UK market for check clearing, processing 1.7 billion checks in 2003, and generating revenues in excess of $200 million from its operations. Within its first year of operations, the initial banks had seen a return on their capital investments. iPSL now has 11 banks as clients, and the scale of the operation, combined with the process transformation, has driven costs per transaction down by more than 20 percent. In the future, iPSL's services may be expanded to include remittance processing and other common back-office transactions.[7,8,9]

Appendix

THE OUTSOURCING FRAMEWORK

The outsourcing framework is a starting point for listing and categorizing the activities that take place in an organization. Doing this plays a pivotal role in developing a cohesive approach to global outsourcing. By seeing activities across the organization under a common framework, it becomes much easier to evaluate each in terms of its relationship to others, to rate and rank its contribution to the organization's competitive advantages, and to maintain focus on how it is sourced. See Chapter 5 for additional considerations in making effective use of the framework.

1. Operational Services (Value Chain)
    - 1.1. Marketplace Research and Analysis
        - 1.1.1. Customer Needs Research and Analysis
        - 1.1.2. Customer Satisfaction Measurement
        - 1.1.3. External Business and Technology Research and Analysis
    - 1.2. Product Research, Development, Manufacture, and Delivery
        - 1.2.1. Product Research and Develop
        - 1.2.2. Product Prototype and Test
        - 1.2.3. Capital Goods and Technology Acquisition
        - 1.2.4. Materials and Supplies Acquisition

1.2.5. Inbound Logistics Management
1.2.6. Component Manufacturing
1.2.7. Product Assembly, Test, and Packaging
1.2.8. Product Warehousing, Distribution, and Delivery
1.2.9. Product Installation and Service

1.3. Service Research, Development, Staffing, and Delivery
1.3.1. Service Research and Development
1.3.2. Service Prototype and Test
1.3.3. Capital Goods and Technology Acquisition
1.3.4. Materials and Supplies Acquisition
1.3.5. Human Resources Acquisition and Development
1.3.6. Service Delivery to Customer

1.4. Marketing
1.4.1. Marketing Plan Development
1.4.2. Product and Service Advertising
1.4.3. Product and Service Promotion

1.5. Sales
1.5.1. Sales Plan Development
1.5.2. Field Sales
1.5.3. Call Center Sales (Teleservices)

1.6. Customer Relationship Management
1.6.1. Customer Order Processing
1.6.2. Customer Service, Inquiries, and Complaint Handling
1.6.3. Customer Relationship Management (CRM) System Development and Management

2. Management and Support Services

2.1. Human Resource Management
2.1.1. Human Resource Strategy Development
2.1.2. Recruit, Select, and Hire Employees
2.1.3. Develop and Train Employees
2.1.4. Employee Relocation
2.1.5. Outplacement Services
2.1.6. Base and Variable Compensation Plan Development and Management

- 2.1.7. Employee Satisfaction, Workplace Health, and Safety Management
- 2.1.8. Employee Benefits Management and Administration
- 2.1.9. Internal Communications and Labor Relations Management
- 2.1.10. Human Resource Information Systems (HRIS) Development and Management

2.2. Information and Communications Technology Management

- 2.2.1. Information and Communications Technology Strategy Development
- 2.2.2. Data Center Design and Management
- 2.2.3. Distributed System Design and Management
- 2.2.4. Desktop/Mobile System Design and Management
- 2.2.5. Data Network Design and Management
- 2.2.6. Communications Systems and Network Design and Management
- 2.2.7. Internet Services (including Web hosting)
- 2.2.8. Application Development and Maintenance
- 2.2.9. Enterprise Resource Planning (ERP) System Development and Maintenance
- 2.2.10. Data and Database Management and Maintenance
- 2.2.11. Help Desk Services
- 2.2.12. Systems Security and Controls Management

2.3. Document Management

- 2.3.1. Document Layout and Design
- 2.3.2. Document Imaging, Storage, and Distribution
- 2.3.3. Printing and Publishing
- 2.3.4. Centralized and Convenience Copy Services

2.4. Financial Management

- 2.4.1. Budget, Cash Flow, and Risk Management
- 2.4.2. Accounts Payables Processing
- 2.4.3. Payroll Processing
- 2.4.4. Invoicing, Accounts Receivables, Credits, and Collections Processing
- 2.4.5. Travel and Entertainment Expense Management and Processing

- 2.4.6. Internal and External Financial Accounting and Reporting
- 2.4.7. Internal Auditing
- 2.4.8. Tax Management and Processing
- 2.4.9. Financial Information Systems (FIS) Development and Maintenance

2.5. Real Estate and Capital Asset Management
- 2.5.1. Real Estate and Capital Asset Plan Development and Project Management
- 2.5.2. Real Estate and Capital Asset Transaction Management
- 2.5.3. Real Estate and Capital Asset Engineering and Maintenance
- 2.5.4. Energy Management

2.6. Facility Services
- 2.6.1. Food and Cafeteria Services
- 2.6.2. Mailroom Services
- 2.6.3. Shipping and Receiving
- 2.6.4. Security
- 2.6.5. Parking

2.7. Administrative Services
- 2.7.1. Secretarial/Clerical Services
- 2.7.2. Data Entry/Transcription Services
- 2.7.3. Records Management
- 2.7.4. Travel Services
- 2.7.5. Workplace Supplies Management

2.8. Corporate Services
- 2.8.1. Purchasing
- 2.8.2. External Communications and Public Relations Management
- 2.8.3. Legal Services

Notes

Chapter 1

1. Audience survey, The Outsourcing World Summits 2001–2004, produced by Michael F. Corbett & Associates, Ltd.

2. David Sibbet, "75 Years of Management Ideas and Practice 1922–1997," *Harvard Business Review,* supplement vol. 75, no. 5 (Sep/Oct 1997): 1, 10p, 1 diagram, 2c, 6bw.

3. James Brian Quinn, personal letter to the author, April 2, 2002.

4. Peter F. Drucker, comments at the Special Libraries Association Annual Conference 2002, Los Angeles, CA, June 10, 2002.

5. Peter F. Drucker, "Sell the Mailroom," *The Wall Street Journal,* July 25, 1989, A16.

6. C. Prahalad and G. Hamel, "The Core Competence of the Corporation," *Harvard Business Review,* March/April 1990: 79–91.

7. James Brian Quinn and Frederick G. Hilmer, "Strategic Outsourcing," *Sloan Management Review,* Summer 1994: 43–55.

8. Research materials developed by the author from multiple sources and published on Firmbuilder.com.

9. Ibid.

10. Survey of attendees at The 2004 Outsourcing World Summit, February 23–25, 2004, Lake Buena Vista, FL.

11. John B. Goodman, "Improving the Combat Edge through Outsourcing and Privatization," The Outsourcing Leadership Forum, Washington, D.C., April, 1995, 10.

12. Steven S. Brown, "Coors Brewing Company Outsourcing Case Study," The Outsourcing Research Council, Denver, CO, April 21, 1998.

13. "Exel Provides Network Solution for Coors," Exel plc press release, April 8, 2002, retrieved December 8, 2003, from http://www.exel.com.

14. H. Bernard Davis, "General Motors Corporation: Outsourcing Innovation," The 2001 Outsourcing World Summit, Palm Springs, CA, February 20, 2001, 12.

15. Michael F. Corbett, "How America's Leading Firms Use Outsourcing," Michael F. Corbett & Associates, Ltd., April 1999.

16. Michael F. Corbett, "An Inside Look at Outsourcing," *Fortune,* June 9, 2003, S2.

17. Corbett, "An Inside Look at Outsourcing," *Fortune,* June 9, 2003, S6.

18. Dr. Wendell Jones, e-mail to author, December 9, 2003.

19. James E. Ellis, "McDonnell Douglas: Unfasten the Seat Belts," *BusinessWeek,* February 14, 1994, 36.

20. James Brian Quinn, "Outsourcing Innovation: The New Engine of Growth," *Sloan Management Review,* Summer, 2000, 13–27.

21. Gregg Keiser, "Gartner Says Half of Outsourcing Projects Fail," http://www.crn.com, March 26, 2003, retrieved December 8, 2003.

22. "IT Outsourcing: Mindset Switch Needed to Improve Satisfaction with Supplier Relationships," PA Consulting Group, http://www.paconsutling.com, March 3, 2003, retrieved December 8, 2003.

23. Mark R. Ozanne, "The Barometer of Global Outsourcing," The Outsourcing Research Council, New York, NY, September 14, 2000, 8.

24. H. Bernard Davis, "General Motors Corporation: Outsourcing Innovation."

25. James Brian Quinn and Frederick G. Hilmer, "Strategic Outsourcing," 51.

Chapter 2

1. Michael Hammer, "The Process Enterprise: An Executive Perspective," Hammer and Company, 2001, retrieved from http://www.hammerandco.com December 12, 2003.

2. Michael F. Corbett, "ROI Outsourcing," *Fortune,* December 10, 2001, S8

3. Michael F. Corbett, "Outsourcing for Business Transformation," *Fortune,* June 7, 1999, S10.

4. Xerox Health Insurance Case Study, "HealthNow New York Inc.," Copyright 2003, retrieved from http://www.xerox.com on December 23, 2003.

5. HealthNow 2002 Annual Report, retrieved from http://www.healthnowny.com on December 23, 2003.

6. Michael F. Corbett, "E-sourcing the Corporation," *Fortune,* March 6, 2000, S8–S10.

7. Jay Hurst, "How BASF Uses E-sourcing," E-sourcing the Corporation, produced by Michael F. Corbett & Associates, Ltd., September 19–20, 2000, New York, NY.

8. Vipin Suri, "Shared Services: 'Internal Outsourcing' of Service Functions," The 2001 Australian Outsourcing Summit, August 14, 2001, Sydney, Australia.

9. 2003 Annual Report, retrieved from http://www.bhpbilliton.com December 24, 2003.

10. Fay Hansen, "Shared Services," *Business Finance,* March 1999, retrieved from http://www.bfmag.com on December 24, 2003.

11. Scott McReynolds and Brian O'Brien, "Shared Services: Earnings Pressures Boost Shared Services," *Financial Executives International,* January-February 2002, retrieved from http://www.fei.org on December 24, 2003.

12. "The Next Wave of Supply Chain Value," Cap Gemini Ernst & Young, retrieved from http://www.cgey.com on December 23, 2003.

13. Michael F. Corbett, "Harnessing the Power of Outsourcing's Next Wave," The 2003 Outsourcing World Summit, February 24, 2003, Palm Desert, CA, content based on previous research.

14. Morrison Management Specialists announcement retrieved from http://www.looksmart.com on December 24, 2003.

15. About Foodbuy, retrieved from http://www.foodbuy.com on December 24, 2003.

16. Michael F. Corbett, "Harnessing the Power of Outsourcing's Next Wave."

17. Michael F. Corbett, "Commercialization Through Outsourcing," An Outsourcing Insights Web Conference, June 4, 2002, material developed through earlier research.

18. Frederic Cantin, "How to Optimize Benefits of Supply Chain Outsourcing," The 2003 Outsourcing World Summit, February 25, 2003, Palm Springs, CA.

19. Michael F. Corbett, "Outsourcing 2000: Value-Driven Customer-Focused," *Fortune,* May 29, 2000, S36.

20. Noel Ward, "Beyond Textbooks," *Digital Asset Directions,* March 2002, retrieved December 21, 2003 from http://www.ondemandpublishing.com.

21. "Global Supply Chain Management," a publication of Bertelsmann Distribution, Berlin, June 12, 2001, retrieved December 21, 2003 from http://www.cww.tu-berlin.de the Web site of the Center for Change and Knowledge Management.

Chapter 3

1. Procter & Gamble 2003 Annual Report, 54.
2. William Metz, "Launch Plan for a Global IT Sourcing Program," The 2003 Outsourcing World Summit, Palm Springs, CA, February 26, 2003.
3. http://www.hoovers.com, retrieved December 8, 2003.
4. Aram Janigian, "Job Support for Linux Developers," http://www.linuxworld.com, October 8, 2002, retrieved December 8, 2003.
5. Pete Engardio et al., "The New Global Job Shift," *BusinessWeek,* February 3, 2003.
6. M.M. Sathyanarayan, *Offshore Development,* M.M. Sathyanarayan, 2003, jacket cover.
7. http://www.hoovers.com, retrieved December 8, 2003.
8. Khozem Merchant, "GE Champions India's World Class Services," *Financial Times,* June 3, 2003.
9. Pete Engardio et al., "The New Global Job Shift," graphic.
10. Steven Greenhouse, "I.B.M. Explores Shift of White-Collar Jobs Overseas," *New York Times,* July 22, 2003, retrieved from http://www.nytimes.com July 22, 2003.
11. Pete Engardio et al., "The New Global Job Shift."
12. Manjeet Kripalani and Pete Engardio, "The Rise of India," *BusinessWeek,* December 8, 2003, 66–78.
13. Nelson D. Schwartz, "Down and Out in White-Collar America," *Fortune,* June 23, 2003, 79–86.
14. Jagdish Dalal, "Off-shore Outsourcing," The Outsourcing Research Council, Raleigh, NC, October 23, 2002, 11, 13.
15. Shamus Rae, "Offshore Resourcing: Once Adventurous, Now Essential for Financial Services Firms," IBM Corporation, 2002, 12.
16. Andrew Wang, "Indian Workers See Biggest Salary Gains in Asia, U.S. Study Says," Associated Press, November 12, 2003, retrieved from http://www.yahoo.com December 8, 2003.

17. Patrick Thibodeau, "Group Touts Vermont as Outsourcing Alternative," *Computerworld,* May 5, 2003, 16.

18. George Gilbert and Rahul Sood, "Outsourcing's Offshore Myth," December 15, 2003, retrieved from http://www.cnetnews.com on December 17, 2003.

19. Diane Brady, "All the World's a Call Center," *BusinessWeek,* October 27, 2003, 43.

20. Bob Brewin, "User Complaints Push Dell to Return PC Support to U.S.," *Computerworld,* December 1, 2003, 6.

21. Yilu Zhao, "When Jobs Move Overseas (to South Carolina)," *New York Times,* October 26, 2003, BU 4.

22. Andrew D. Cvitanov, conversations with the author.

23. Khozem Merchant, "GE Champions India's World Class Services."

24. John Ribeiro, "India Moves Up the Outsourcing Ladder," *InfoWorld,* August 29, 2003, retrieved from http://www.Infoworld.com on December 9, 2003.

25. Gilbert and Sood, "Outsourcing's Offshore Myth."

26. Lisa Takeuchi Cullen, "Who's Hiring . . . And Where," *Time,* November 24, 2003.

27. Ian Ailles, "Transformation from a Finance Perspective," The 2003 European Outsourcing Summit, Brussels, Belgium, June 2, 2003.

Chapter 4

1. Mary Crawford, "Business Process Outsourcing at American Express," Business Process Outsourcing for Competitive Advantage, produced by Michael F. Corbett & Associates, Ltd., November 28, 2000, New York, NY.

2. Research by the author, multiple sources.

3. Conversations between Jagdish Dalal and the author January 2003.

4. Conversations between John Maher and the author, January 2003.

5. Survey of 500-plus attendees at The 2003 Outsourcing World Summit, February 24–26, 2003, Palm Desert, CA.

Chapter 5

1. Michael F. Corbett, "A Market-Driven Approach to Healthcare Information Technology," Eclipsys Technologies Corporation, March 2003.

2. Fred Brown, "BJC Health System Case Study," The 2001 Australian Outsourcing Summit, August 14, 2001, Sydney, Australia.

3. H. Bernard Davis, "General Motors Corporation: Outsourcing Innovation," The 2001 Outsourcing World Summit, Palm Springs, CA, February 20, 2001, 12.

Chapter 6

1. Extrapolation based on "The Global Outsourcing Market," Michael F. Corbett & Associates, Ltd., June 2002.

2. Michael F. Corbett, "Outsourcing's Next Wave," *Fortune,* June 10, 2002.

3. Jay Cousins and Tony Stewart, "What Is Business Process Design and Why Should I Care?" retrieved March 6, 2004 from http://www.rivcom.com.

4. Jag Dalal, "Offshore Outsourcing: Creating a Compelling Case," The 2003 India Outsourcing Summit, October 15, 2003, Bangalore, India.

5. Michael F. Corbett, "Best Practices in Managing Outsourcing at the Customer Interface," Michael F. Corbett & Associates, January 2001.

6. Ian Rushby, "Outsourcing at BP Amoco," The 2000 Outsourcing World Summit, February 22, 2000, Lake Buena Vista, FL.

Chapter 7

1. Roger Fisher and William Ury, *Getting to Yes* (New York: Penguin Books, 1983).

2. Audience response system, The 2004 Outsourcing World Summit, February 23, 2004, Lake Buena Vista, FL.

3. Michael Useem and Joseph Harder, "Leading Laterally in Company Outsourcing," *Sloan Management Review,* Winter 2000, 25–36.

4. Jean-Francois Poisson, "Managing Outsourcing as a Core Competency," The 2003 Outsourcing World Summit, February 24, 2003, Palm Desert, CA.

Chapter 9

1. Jack Keen, "Don't Ignore Intangibles," *CIO Magazine,* September 1, 2002, retrieved April 2, 2004, from http://www.cio.com.

2. Bill Hall and Kyle Andrews, "Proving the Value of Your Outsourcing Solution," The 2004 Outsourcing World Summit, February 25, 2004, Lake Buena Vista, FL.

3. Andrew Cuomo and Jonathan Cooper-Bagnall, "How to Get Best Value from IT Outsourcing," The 2002 Outsourcing World Summit, February 24, 2002, Lake Buena Vista, FL.

Chapter 10

1. Julian Millstein, "Creating and Managing Outsourcing Contracts for Flexibility and Change," The 2003 Outsourcing World Summit, February 26, 2003, Palm Desert, CA.

Chapter 11

1. Audience response system, The 2004 Outsourcing World Summit, February 23, 2004, Lake Buena Vista, FL.

2. Arthur Andersen and Clemson University Studies conducted in 1997 and 1998 and reported on http://www.arthurandersen.com in 2001.

3. Margaret Hurley and Christina Costa, "The Blurring Boundary of the Organization: Outsourcing Comes of Age," KPMG Consulting, 2001.

4. Michael F. Corbett, "Managing the People Impact of Outsourcing," Michael F. Corbett & Associates, Ltd., August 2002.

5. Peter F. Drucker, "Sell the Mailroom," *Wall Street Journal,* July 25, 1989, A16.

6. Rolfe Schroeder, "Outsourcing Employee Issues," The Outsourcing Research Council, November 7, 2001, Falls Church, VA.

7. Michael F. Corbett, "Managing the People Impact of Outsourcing."

Chapter 12

1. Audience response system, The 2004 Outsourcing World Summit, February 23, 2004, Lake Buena Vista, FL.

2. William Metz, "PMO as a Governance Tool," The 2004 Outsourcing World Summit, February 24, 2004, Lake Buena Vista, FL.

3. David Jarman, "Welcome to the Workplace," The 2004 Outsourcing World Summit, February 24, 2004, Lake Buena Vista, FL.

4. Jean-Francois Poisson, "The Outsourcing Business Plan," The 2002 Outsourcing World Summit, February 20, 2002, Lake Buena Vista, FL.

5. James Brian Quinn, Frederick Julien, and Michael Negrin, "Outsourcing Strategy: Managing Strategic Risk," published April 4, 2001, http://www.firmbuilder.com.

Chapter 13

1. "Employment Shifts in High Technology Industries 1988–96," retrieved from http://www.itaa.org, April 3, 2004.

2. Michael Useem and Joseph Harder, "Leading Laterally in Company Outsourcing," *Sloan Management Review,* Winter 2000, 25–36.

3. James Brian Quinn, "Outsourcing Innovation: The New Engine of Growth," *Sloan Management Review,* Summer 2000, 13–27.

4. John Hindle and Leslie Willcocks, "Knowledge in Outsourcing: The Missed Business Opportunity," The 2004 Outsourcing World Summit, February 23, 2004, Lake Buena Vista, FL.

5. David Britman, "The Role of Risk Management in Outsourcing," The 2004 Outsourcing World Summit, February 24, 2004, Lake Buena Vista, FL.

6. Rick Julien, "Outsourcing Contracts and Meeting Sarbanes-Oxley Requirements," The 2004 Outsourcing World Summit, February 24, 2004, Lake Buena Vista, FL.

Chapter 14

1. Michael P. Cassidy, "Transforming Shared Services: Outsourcing from the Customer-In," The 2003 Outsourcing World Summit, February 25, 2003, Lake Buena Vista, FL.

2. Terry Bilbo and Nicholas J. Westley, "Leveraging the Untapped Value in Corporate Real Estate," The 2004 Outsourcing World Summit, February 23, 2004, Lake Buena Vista, FL.

3. Mick Jennings, "Enabling Business Transformation with IT Outsourcing," The 2004 Outsourcing World Summit, February 23, 2004, Lake Buena Vista, FL.

4. Joe Cipolla and Jim Moran, "Changing the Fundamental Way in Which Mission-Critical Solutions Are Built," The 2004 Outsourcing World Summit, February 23, 2004, Lake Buena Vista, FL.

5. Mary Lou Cagle and Kevin Campbell, "Taking HR from a Cost Center to Revenue Generator at Bank of America," The 2002 Outsourcing World Summit, February 18, 2002, Lake Buena Vista, FL.

6. Kenneth Price and Roberta Macklin, "Outsourcing By-product Management," The 2004 Outsourcing World Summit, February 23, 2004, Lake Buena Vista, FL.

7. Janet Russell, "iPSL: A New Paradigm in Payment Processing," The 2002 Outsourcing World Summit, February 20, 2002, Lake Buena Vista, FL.

8. Ken Wang, "Unisys Outsourcing," presented to Michael F. Corbett, December 26, 2003, LaGrangeville, NY.

9. "Outsourcing Allows British Banks to 'Check Out' of Check Processing," Unisys Corporation, retrieved from http://www.firmbuilder.com December 28, 2003.

Index

A

B

H

I

J–K

L

M

N

O